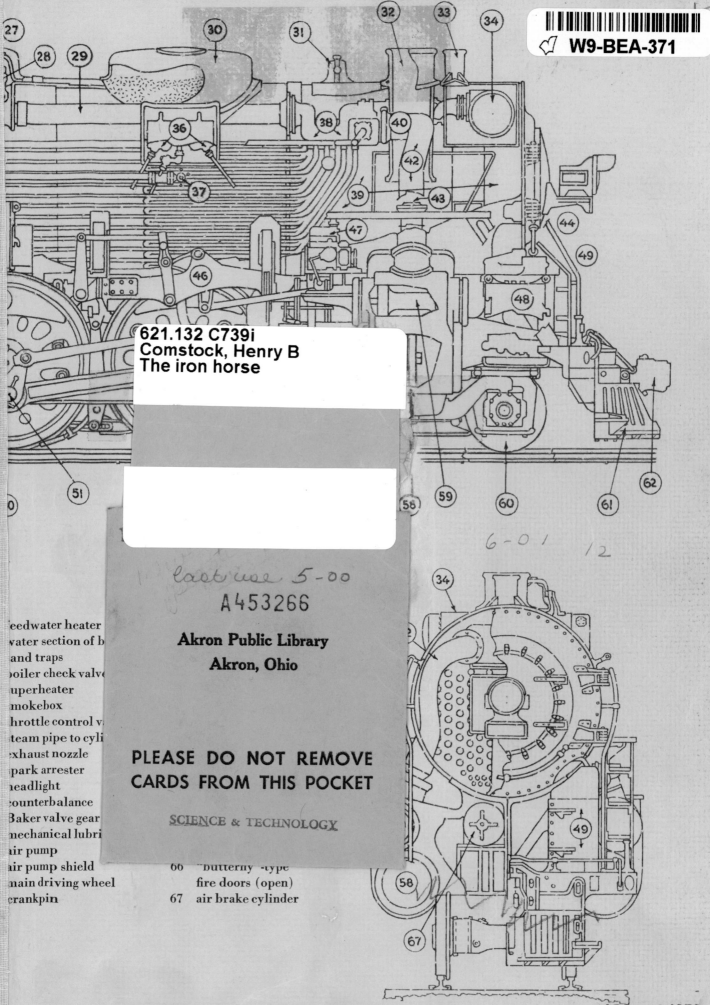

last use 5-00

feedwater heater
water section of b
and traps
boiler check valve
superheater
smokebox
throttle control v
steam pipe to cyli
exhaust nozzle
spark arrester
headlight
counterbalance
Baker valve gear
mechanical lubri
air pump
air pump shield
main driving wheel
crankpin

66   butterfly -type
      fire doors (open)
67   air brake cylinder

The Iron Horse

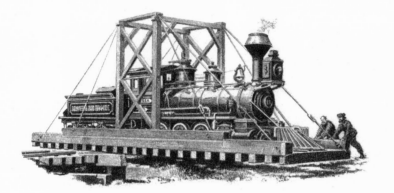

A Denver & Rio Grande "gallows turntable" at Monarch, Colorado, 1884. The central gantry provided cable-tensioned rigidity for the track-supporting bridge.

A Chesapeake & Ohio Class F-19 "Pacific."

Thomas Y. Crowell Company New York Established 1834

The Iron Horse

Henry B. Comstock   Illustrations by the Author

To our grandsons
Paul
Christopher
Mark
Stephen

Contents

1   STEAM BEFORE RAILS / *2*

2   OVERSEAS HERITAGE / *8*

3   FOALING THE AMERICAN FILLY / *16*

4   TOO MUCH ORIGINALITY / *26*

5   AN UNPROFITABLE BUSINESS / *32*

6   PRIDE IN "COMPANY" ENGINES / *40*

7   THE DEAN OF INDEPENDENT BUILDERS / *50*

8   PHILADELPHIA'S TRANSIENT DESIGNERS / *58*

9   THE TRIALS OF WHISTLER AND WINANS / *68*

10   MELODIES CAST AND WROUGHT IN METAL / *83*

11   HIGH-WHEELERS AND CABBAGE CUTTERS / *106*

12   THE MIGHTY MALLETS / *138*

13   YEARS OF GLORY / *152*

     GLOSSARY / *209*

     BIBLIOGRAPHY / *221*

     INDEX / *223*

The Iron Horse

1 Steam Before

Nearly two thousand years before the first steam locomotive wheezed over a tramway in Wales a mathematician and physicist living in Egypt wrote and illustrated a book called *Spiritalia seu Pneumatica*. That bilingual title made it clear to Greek and Roman scholars alike that the subject was air. More specifically the author, Hero of Alexandria, described and pictured those devices of the ancient world which either harnessed or opposed the atmosphere for man's service and entertainment.

Among the mechanisms was a clever toy called an *aeolipile* in deference to the Greek god of the winds. Its principal parts were a caldron, a tight-fitting lid topped by a pair of ornate columns, and a hollow metal ball pivoted between the fluted uprights. Vapor released from water boiling in the lower container rose through one of the columns, and having filled the sphere, was voided to the atmosphere through two small pipes. These were placed 180 de-

grees apart, on a plane at right angles to the ball's bearing points. Further, the pipes were elbow-shaped, with their exhaust ports pointed in the same equatorial direction. When steam jetted from them, the globe reacted by twirling the opposite way.

Fortunately, copies of Hero's *Spiritalia seu Pneumatica* proved more durable than the Roman Empire, and with the coming of the printing press, translations found their way into castles and monasteries throughout Europe. So intriguing was the account of the *aeolipile* that models of it became playthings of the nobility. Monks found equal pleasure in the pagan invention, which spared them the dull chore of turning roasting spits.

Then in the early 1600s, an Italian named Giovanni Branca produced a more effective engine. Its boiler was cast in the form of a bust of a West Indian. When water simmered in its bronze bosom, steam filled the head and escaped through a cheroot-like

Rails

Ancient Greek aeolipile was a reaction turbine.

tube protruding from the monstrosity's lips. The jet was directed at the vanes of a miniature mill wheel set on a vertical shaft.

Like the ball of the *aeolipile,* this wheel spun rapidly but with little force. To trade velocity for power, Branca used reduction gears similar to those in the clocks of his day. As their wooden teeth chattered, two cams on a spindle alternately raised and lowered a pair of pestles within mortar bowls.

Here was a new twist. The *aeolipile* had turned itself by the reaction of the steam passing out of its spouts. But in the Italian's machine, the thrust of the expanding gas was applied to a movable object by a stationary nozzle. Today we would call the first a "reaction turbine," and the second an "impulse turbine."

Branca believed that larger versions of his cigar-smoking Indian could be used to operate pumps. The notion had sales appeal, because a growing demand for ore and coal had brought with it the problem of removing water from deep pits and mines. However, a motor as wasteful as his was not the answer. It could have been if he had thought to inclose the nozzle and vaned wheel in a snug-fitting casing.

Instead, inventors turned their attention to what seemed a more practical way of harnessing steam. Men had long lifted water by moving pistons up and down in cylinders. Why not attach a second such pump to the first and alternately direct vapor in and out of it, using the steam piston to drive the water piston.

The first successful machine of this sort was a two-story-high monster installed in an English pumping station in 1705. A resourceful blacksmith, Thomas Newcomen, had contrived it from great quantities of oak, iron, and brick. To these he added the services of a youngster named Humphrey Potter. And here is what Humphrey did—four times each minute:

First, he opened a valve which sent steam at hardly

3

Giovanni Branca's impulse turbine.

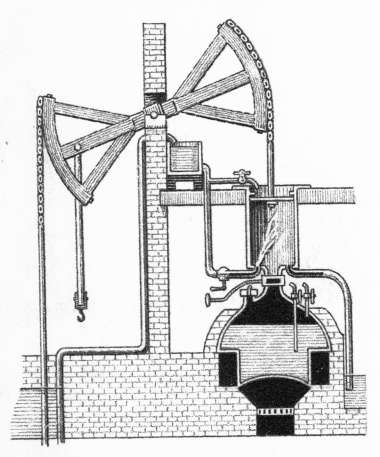

Thomas Newcomen's atmospheric engine.

more than atmospheric pressure into an upright cylinder. At the top of this chamber was a piston, which had been raised to that position by a counterbalanced lever, or walking beam. As soon as the cavity was full, Humphrey shut off the valve and opened another. This one directed cold water from a reservoir to the outer surface of the now hot cylinder.

As a result, the steam condensed, creating a vacuum. Down came the piston, driven by the normal pressure of the air above it. That lowered the attached end of the walking beam. At the same time the other extremity rose, hoisting water from the sump pit of a mine below.

Humphrey was a bright lad, and it occurred to him that he would have more time for ale breaks if he could connect cords to the walking beam in such a way that they would open and close the valves automatically. His efforts were so successful that he soon found himself without a job.

Curiously, a mechanical defect further improved Newcomen's "atmospheric engine." One day its piston shuttled up and down six times a minute instead of the previous four. Upon inspection it was found that a faulty valve was letting water from the cooling reservoir enter the cylinder, speeding condensation. It was a simple matter to produce the same effect by running a pipe directly into the cavity. The fame of the big engine spread, and eventually more than 150 of them were built, to work sump pumps in England and on the continent.

The next improvement in the use of steam power was made by one of those gifted men whose accomplishments are so great that it becomes fashionable to give them more credit than they deserve. This was James Watt who, according to several generations of schoolmasters, took one look at his mother's teakettle and cried: "Some day I shall invent the world's first steam engine."

The fact is that Watt was an established maker of mathematical instruments when, in 1763, the University of Glasgow sent him a model of a Newcomen mine pumper for repairs. While working at it he asked himself: What is the volume of steam as compared with water? How much water can be evaporated in a particular type of boiler with one pound of coal? Is there a relationship between the elasticity of steam and temperatures beyond the boiling point? With painstaking and often hazardous experiments he found the answers to these and other questions which had not yet occurred to his contemporaries.

To the hardware of the piston-type, or reciprocating, engine he contributed:

1. The first closed cylinder (those in Newcomen engines were open at the top to admit air for downward thrusts).

2. A double-acting engine—one in which steam was directed alternately into the two ends of the closed cylinder, eliminating unpowered return strokes.

3. The fly-ball governor, whose throttle-controlling levers were raised by centrifugal force to decelerate an engine running above a desired speed.

Less constructively, Watt insisted for years that the expansive force of steam could never be safely applied to a piston. While others labored on so-called "high-pressure engines," he concentrated upon improvements to the Newcomen machine. In the modified design which he finally marketed, steam was condensed, not in the cylinder, but in a more efficient chamber below it. From there he redirected the hot water to the boiler, where it was again evaporated. These fine Scottish tricks saved a great deal of fuel, and by 1775 the demand for Watt pumpers was such that a plant in Birmingham tooled up for their production.

In that factory an engineer named William Murdoch became Watt's assistant. This talented young man saw no reason to dedicate himself wholly to his master's immortality. Nor did he accept as gospel truth every opinion voiced by the now autocratic "father of the steam engine." Thus in 1784 he squandered days and weeks on drawings for a road vehicle to be propelled by a high-pressure engine.

Nothing could have irritated Watt more, because he had repeatedly stated that steam-powered carriages were impractical. In writing of his attitude three-quarters of a century later, the noted engineer-journalist Zerah Colburn concluded that "no one man did more in this way to retard the development of the locomotive."

Fortunately, Watt did not have the authority to sack his assistant. The worst he could do was to report the affair to the owner of the plant, who advised Murdoch to complete the project on his own time. The result was a miniature tricycle, with a centrally placed boiler heated by a spirit lamp. A cylinder no larger than a pill vial was immersed in the water section, and a piston passed motion to a hinged beam overhead. In turn, the beam raised and lowered a rod connected to a crank on the rear axle.

Legend has it that Murdoch felt it wise to test the toy under cover of night. He chose a lonely lane down which a vicar happened to be accompanying one of the prettier lambs in his flock following Sunday evening services. Escaping its builder, the tiny tricycle hissed out of the darkness, flapping its rocking arm like an angry demon and spuming sparks and smoke. Thereupon the cleric took off in the opposite direction, leaving Murdoch to comfort the young lady.

Whether or not the story is true, Watt's assistant never carried his transportation venture further. Instead, he went on to invent the coal-gas lamp. It was probably just as well, because a Frenchman named Nicholas Cugnot had put together two more impressive road engines in 1769 and 1771. The second, financed by the government of Louis XV, was designed to haul an artillery piece weighing more than nine tons. Necessarily it had a massive frame, supported at the rear by two stoutly spoked wheels. A third wheel with a cleated tire was placed in a fork up front. This "driver," together with a pair of up-

The first locomotive made in England was William Murdoch's steam tricycle of 1784.

5

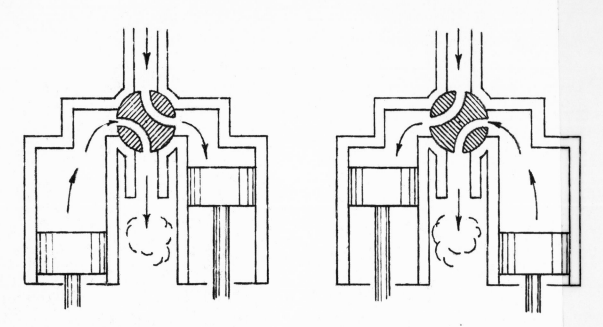

Steam was directed into the vertical cylinders of Cugnot's engine by a "four-way valve"—an oscillating disk with two curved channels, each of which served alternately as an intake and an exhaust passage.

Sponsored by France's war minister, the Duke of Choiseul, Nicholas Cugnot's cannon-hauling steam tractor clattered over the streets of Paris in 1769.

Sensitive to the public outcry against steam carriages in the 1830s, a London artist achieved immediate if not enduring fame with his prophetic painting of mechanized chaos in Regent's Park. Note the generous sprinkling of "compacts."

right cylinders above it and a kettle-like boiler ahead, turned as a single unit when a steering bar was swung to the right or left.

The boiler was of copper, with its lower third roofed over to form a firebox, fitted with grates and an ash pit. Two short chimneys carried off the smoke, and a pipe ran from the top of the water section to a valve between the cylinders. Rocked by a shaft attached to the wheel below, the valve applied steam first to one and then the other of two single-acting pistons. The motion of the driving rods was like that of a cyclist's legs, but instead of delivering smooth torque to the forward axle with half cranks, each downward thrust advanced a pair of ratchet wheels a quarter of a revolution.

It has been said that the machine caused more annoyance than amazement when it was turned loose on the streets of Paris. Snorting furiously, it hitched along at a top speed of two miles an hour. Worse, each ten minutes it balked, and would not move again until it had been fed a fresh supply of wood.

Under such circumstances, a spectacular accident seemed unlikely. But one morning, while attempting

a turn in the neighborhood now occupied by the Madeleine, an artilleryman cut the steering bar too hard. Over on its side flipped the big tricycle. Screaming steam and rocketing embers filled the air. The beast was promptly locked up in an arsenal, where it remained a forgotten prisoner for nearly thirty years. During that time an upheaval of a different sort produced more fearful sounds and pyrotechnics throughout France.

The Revolution over, and Napoleon not quite yet an emperor, arrangements were made to repair Cugnot's three-wheeler and run it in the presence of the great general. But on the day set for the demonstration, the Corsican took off for Egypt.

Meanwhile there were other attempts to apply steam to carriages. They continued sporadically for over a hundred years. Such was the condition of both city streets and country roads that the worst of the vehicles blew up and the best broke down. What was needed was a relatively smooth running surface, not so much to spare engine parts as to minimize shocks and skewing action upon vulnerable boilers. In 1804 the proper surface was found.

2 Overseas

A day's journey from Cardiff, in southern Wales, a tramway ran nine miles from a large ironworks to the bustling town of Merthyr Tydfil. It was by no means a pioneer venture, for as early as 1556 a German woodcut had shown miners shoving a cart along timber rails. Nevertheless, this Pen-y-Darran line was as good as most at the turn of the nineteenth century. Its trackwork consisted of parallel stringers bedded in the earth, with a topping of cast-iron bars, or "plates." Upturned flanges on their inner edges guided the wheels of wagons passing over them.

One of the officers of the foundry served by the tramway was a venturesome industrialist named Samuel Homfray. On an autumn day in 1803, he and several associates were watching a dray horse tug three heavy trucks along the main stem. They commented favorably upon the animal, a crossbreed of Belgian and Shire not long before brought down from Scotland. Then the small talk drifted to a more provoca-

tive subject—a steam carriage which had just been exhibited in London. It was the work of a Cornishman, a giant who might have bent bars in a circus had he not been blessed with brains to match his brawn. He was Richard Trevithick, well known in the mining trade and greatly respected both as an amateur wrestler and a designer and builder of dependable high-pressure pumping engines.

Homfray owned a substantial interest in the patent rights to those machines. For that reason, perhaps, he took a more serious view of the inventor's latest contraption than those of his companions. At any rate, he wagered a thousand guineas ($5,250) that ten tons of iron could be moved from one end of the Pen-y-Darran line to the other with force of steam alone. He found ready takers, and turned to Trevithick for help.

So it came about that in February, 1804, a strange machine was readied for the world's first locomotive

8

Heritage

A Leeds colliery manager, John Blenkinsop, patented the world's earliest cog railway system in 1811. One year later Matthew Murray completed a locomotive whose steam-powered spur gear engaged a tooth-flanked running rail applied to the company's track.

run. It weighed 11,000 pounds and had a horizontal boiler five feet long cradled between two pairs of 52-inch wheels. A single cylinder with an eight-inch bore was all but buried in the boiler's aftersection. The piston rod worked between guides so awkwardly placed that the lad who stoked the furnace ran the constant risk of decapitation. The stroke was four and one-half feet—far greater than that on any locomotive built in later years. To convert the shuttling action into smooth rotative force, a flywheel nine feet high flanked one side of the boiler. A yoke, a mainrod, and a crank formed the linkage. Then a train of spur gears advanced the motion to both sets of wheels.

Once it was crowbarred off dead center, the engine got its specified load underway and clanked the nine miles to Merthyr Tydfil in a little more than two hours. Samuel Homfray won his wager. But the locomotive was too heavy for the track, and left such a trail of broken plates that it was hastily retired.

Still, Trevithick had shown that wheels with smooth tires turning upon equally smooth track could haul substantial tonnage. He had also improved the performance of horizontal boilers. In those supplying steam to the stationary mine engines of that day, a straight duct carried hot gasses through the water section to a front-end chimney. But Trevithick gave the pipe a reverse turn at the head of the barrel and brought it back to a smokestack at the rear. The return flue greatly increased the evaporative surface, producing more steam, faster, with a given amount of fuel.

A second improvement was a tube which he directed from the chimney's exhaust port to the base of the stack. After each piston stroke, steam burst from the end of the tube with an exuberant chuff. Then, as these charges rushed up the larger pipe to freedom, they dragged along the gasses in the flue. "So vigorous is the action," wrote an eyewitness, "that the

9

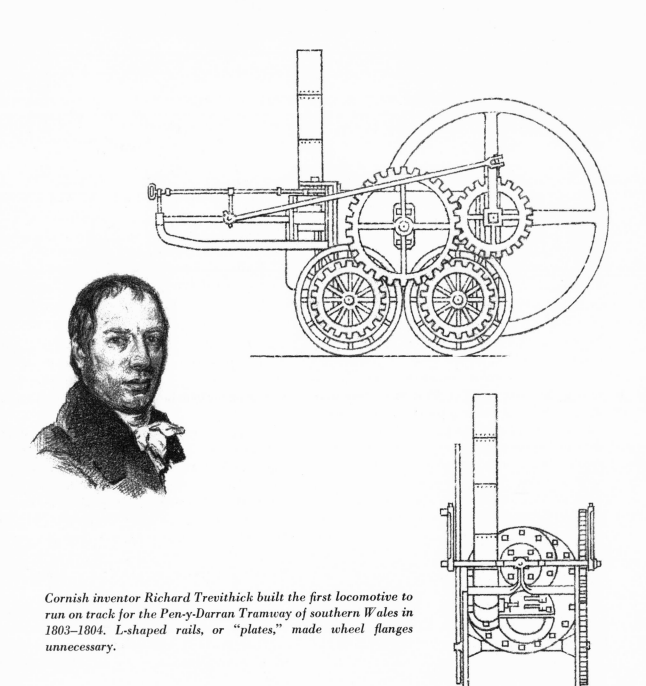

Cornish inventor Richard Trevithick built the first locomotive to run on track for the Pen-y-Darran Tramway of southern Wales in 1803–1804. L-shaped rails, or "plates," made wheel flanges unnecessary.

fire in the furnace pulses with incandescence, forcing the conclusion that the draft is much enhanced."

It seemed that a commercially successful engine was only a step away. But Trevithick's later locomotive-building efforts were uninspired and sporadic. He became involved in other projects, devising steam drills and dredges, marine engines, and a screw propeller. He attempted to drive a tunnel under the Thames, and had almost succeeded, when water broke through and his backers withdrew their support. Financially disastrous mining ventures in Peru and Costa Rica rounded out his mercurial career.

Meanwhile, men of single purpose labored to "reinvent" the locomotive, for the sound features of the Pen-y-Darran machine could not be appreciated until alternatives were tried.

Traction was given more than its share of attention. Admittedly, the Cornishman had erred by using too powerful a cylinder in relation to the weight upon the wheels. That mistake, often repeated by later designers, produced some slippage. But effect was confused with cause, and wonderful ingenuity was wasted at the wrong end of the engine. There were proposals to place sharp spikes on the tires, and to spurn the earth beside the track with sharp-clawed wheel extensions. In 1811, the proprietor of a colliery near Leeds patented a running rail with iron pins projecting from its outer surface. While the company's tramway was being equipped with this Blenkinsop "rack," a local mechanic named Matthew Murray built the first of a number of locomotives fitted with power-driven gear wheels which engaged the pins. Slipping was eliminated, but the installation proved costly. Too, the difficulty of maintaining alignment at rail joints discouraged fast running. To John Blenkinsop's credit, however, his cog system soon proved its worth on inclined railways throughout the world.

A man named William Brunton gained fame of another sort with an engine which literally walked along the track. This was accomplished by suspending two iron legs, hinged at their centers, behind a boiler riding on four wheels. Then, with a single cylinder, a spring, and numerous levers, the limbs were flexed in such a way that they delivered diagonal thrusts to a towpath between the rails.

When its feet were not stuck fast in sloughs, Brunton's *Mechanical Traveller* plodded along with vast

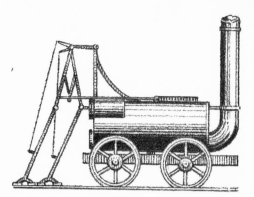

In tried-and-proven equine fashion, William Brunton's 1813 Mechanical Traveller *clopped along at a speed of 3 miles an hour, propelled by backward thrusts of its iron legs.*

dignity, sometimes clocking a mile in twenty minutes. Apparently its boiler grew tired of such pedestrian efforts, for one day it exploded with terrible force, showering the right-of-way with hot water and sheet iron.

Trevithick's return-flue and forced-draft arrangements were also ignored until William Hedley, the superintendent of a colliery near Newcastle-on-Tyne, re-introduced them in 1813. Hedley had been encouraged by his employer to produce an engine which would be more than a mechanical curiosity. He and the foreman of his blacksmith shop, Timothy Hackworth, did it by artfully combining the best features of all former designs. In their *Puffing Billy* they used:

1. An improved version of Trevithick's boiler, insulated, or "lagged," with a covering of wooden staves.

2. Two cylinders, eliminating the need for a flywheel. Here, Cugnot and Murray had pointed the way.

3. A driving arrangement involving rocking beams similar to the one on Murdoch's tricycle.

4. Smooth driving tires, with power applied to all four wheels through gearing. Again, a bow to Trevithick.

Puffing Billy did more than carry coals to Newcastle or, more accurately, to neighboring Wylam. It triggered such a rash of locomotive building that within sixteen years some fifty engines were tossing

A onetime blacksmith, Timothy Hackworth, supervised the construction of William Hedley's Puffing Billy *for the Wylam Railway in 1813. He later managed George Stephenson's Newcastle works, served as the Stockton & Darlington's chief of motive power, and became one of England's outstanding designers.*

smoke, cinders, and loose parts about the English countryside. Regrettably, the tramway owners were interested only in hauling heavy tonnage. So the accent was on long piston strokes, low wheels, and a multiplicity of gears.

Nevertheless, farsighted men envisioned another use for steam power—transporting great numbers of passengers at speeds beyond those of the swiftest mail coaches. That called for better trackwork and long stretches of it, rather than segments extending only from mines and mills to nearby waterways. Locomotives, too, would require such niceties as springs, to hold all wheels in constant contact with the rails. More basic was the problem of boilers. The return-flue type could satisfy the demands of engines leading wagons from the pits. But at high velocities, steam would be bled off faster than it could be made.

In 1828 the solution came from an unexpected

quarter. A London engineer, James Neville, held the belief, as popular then as it is today, that the best place for breakneck speeds was on the public roads. To produce a self-propelled carriage which would outrun a furiously driven horse, he developed a small but extremely efficient steam generator. No less than thirty-two copper tubes passed through its water section. Each was a miniature fire tube, imparting only a fraction of the fierce heat of escaping gasses to the liquid surrounding it. Yet the combined evaporating surfaces were far greater than that of one large duct folded back upon itself. Neville's carriage responded with enthusiasm, hissing along the highways at a spine-tingling speed of 25 miles an hour.

A Frenchman was the first to apply this multitubular arrangement to a locomotive boiler. He was Marc Seguin, chief engineer of the St. Etienne Railway, near Lyons. In 1828 he found himself in a situa-

William Church's 1835 omnibus broke down often enough to afford its 50 passengers a fine sampling of the wayside pubs between London and Birmingham.

tion of great awkwardness. Two engines he had just imported from a Newcastle-on-Tyne factory refused to travel at a pace satisfying to his countrymen. Seguin gutted the barrels and used, as his patent stated: "the principle of hot air circulating in separate tubes of small dimension." No single improvement could have advanced the cause of railroading more.

Across the Channel, Seguin's innovation was quickly adopted by George Stephenson, the operator of the Newcastle works. Stephenson had been the captain of the Killingsworth High Pit near Wylam when Hedley's *Puffing Billy* first rained embers on the rooftops of that coal town. Convinced that he could turn out a better machine, he had promptly disproved it by assembling an engine so burdened with refinements that it spent more time in the repair shop than on the road.

Thereafter, Stephenson concentrated on simplicity. He took a dim view of the noisy gears used to transmit power to more than one axle, unsuccessfully tried a chain drive, and finally settled for a simple arrangement of connecting rods and crank pins which would never be improved upon.

By 1823, Stephenson had set up a plant in Newcastle for the production of his "Killingsworth" locomotives. One year later he was appointed chief engineer of a new line being projected between Stockton and Darlington. In that capacity he supervised the laying of track, the design of the rolling stock, and the building of the road's first motive-power unit, *Locomotion No. 1.*

A newspaper account of the inaugural run in 1825 was surprisingly restrained. It read: "The engine started off, drawing six loaded wagons, a passenger carriage, and 21 trucks fitted with seats. Such was

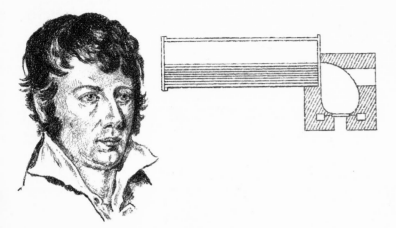

Marc Seguin, mechanical engineer of France's St. Etienne Railway, introduced the multitubular boiler and applied it to two Stephenson locomotives in 1828.

the velocity that in some parts the speed was 12 miles an hour. The number of passengers was counted to be 450, which, with coals and other things, would amount to nearly 30 tons. The engine and its load did the first journey of eight and three-quarter miles in five minutes over an hour."

Without a doubt a dozen other locomotives could have performed as well. But Stephenson's association with the first steam-operated public railway worked to his advantage. Within two years he was chosen to supervise a bolder project—the laying of a thirty-five-mile line between the textile city of Manchester and Liverpool, the nearest seaport.

Merchants in the area were willing to invest millions in the trackwork. But they were not impressed by the plodding performance of self-propelled engines. Searching for something better, the directors considered placing stationary power plants at intervals along the road. These would impart the energy of steam to ropes running rapidly over sheaves between the rails. Grips on the undersides of wagons and carriages would lock onto them, whisking the vehicles from one station to the next.

Stephenson and several other locomotive builders objected. At about this time, word of Marc Seguin's success with multitubular boilers gave them a bargaining point. The Liverpool & Manchester Railway responded by offering a prize of £500 for an engine

that would best meet its needs. Entries were to be put through forty road tests on the completed track at Rainhill in October, 1829. One stipulation was inflexible; each machine must have a safety valve placed beyond the driver's reach. That way there would be no temptation to hold the lever down for superior performance.

Three contenders showed up for the colorful events. The first, *Sanspareil,* was the work of Hedley's former blacksmith foreman, Timothy Hackworth. The second, *Novelty,* was offered by the team of John Braithwaite and the same John Ericsson who would later revolutionize naval architecture with his "cheesebox on a raft," the *Monitor.* George Stephenson and his son Robert entered a machine which they had named the *Rocket.*

Of the trio, a reporter for the Liverpool *Mercury* observed, the grand prize of public opinion was overwhelmingly awarded to the *Novelty.* Certainly it took the honors for fast running, attaining, without cars, a top speed of 40 miles an hour. Under comparable circumstances, the *Rocket's* best effort was 29½, and the *Sanspareil's* 17.

Novelty also showed the greatest fuel economy, burning hardly more than half a pound of coke for each ton of engine and train weight moved a mile. But it was plagued with breakdowns throughout the contest. So was Hackworth's heavier and more powerful *Sanspareil* which, alone, retained the old return-flue type of boiler. Only the *Rocket* rambled through all the tests without mishap.

There is no doubt that George and Robert Stephenson had counted upon this kind of dependability to impress the management. Never had the parts of a locomotive been better arranged for trouble-free operation. First, there was an easily stoked furnace at the rear of a horizontal boiler amply supplied with open flues. That put the blistering-hot stack up front, a nicety appreciated by the fireman. Second, the cylinders were inclined, eliminating much of the bobbing action set up by the vertical type then in general use. Third, the mainrods worked directly upon the driving wheels. With *Rocket* adjudged the winner, the Stephensons soon became the most important locomotive builders in England. In America, too, a great potential market beckoned, for here was a land as much made for railroads as tracks had been made for steam power.

Entered in the 1829 "Rainhill Tests" conducted by the Liverpool & Manchester Railway, George Stephenson's Rocket outclassed its competitors in reliability. With his equally gifted son, Robert, the inventor went on to expand a small shop at Newcastle-on-Tyne into the world's largest engine manufactory.

3   Foaling the

In 1804, the same year that Richard Trevithick's monster rumbled over the rails at Merthyr Tydfil, a two-ton curiosity named *Oruktor Amphibolis* snorted out of a millwright's shop in Philadelphia 3,000 miles away. Basically is was a dredging scow, ordered by the town fathers for channel and harbor clearing. To this the builder, Oliver Evans, had added a stationary engine of his own design—a long-barreled affair which nearly filled the hull. Then, with belting, he had linked a pulley on its flywheel shaft to a fan-shaped paddle wheel at the stern.

Philadelphians were already conditioned to steamboats, the late John Fitch having launched the first of three upon the Delaware River in 1787. But no one had anticipated the amphibious arrangement which Evans used to move the dredge a mile and a half across the city to the tributary Schuylkill. The parts were simple: a pair of axles set in bearing blocks attached to the bottom planking, four stout wheels,

and a second belt drive from the engine to apply turning power.

Throughout the dusty portage the forty-nine-year-old inventor played the dual role of captain and engineer. When there were corners to be turned he shouted to those who marched beside the chugging scow: "Give her nose a shove, boys." The absence of a steering mechanism made such maneuvers necessary. The throttle response was lively, for Evans had weighted the safety valve to pop at the awesome pressure of 150 pounds to the square inch, or three times what would be considered a prudent limit when the *Rocket, Novelty,* and *Sanspareil* were run at Rainhill a quarter of a century later.

It didn't matter that a poorly designed paddle wheel would soon put an end to the aquatic career of *Oruktor Amphibolis.* The important thing was the overland voyage. For the first time, a machine was propelling itself upon American soil.

16

In 1804 Oliver Evans drove his 2-ton Oruktor Amphibolis *halfway across Philadelphia to a launching site on the Schuylkill River.*

American Filly

Records show that seven years earlier Evans had been granted a patent by the neighboring State of Maryland for a more sophisticated steam wagon. However, the dredge on wheels was the closest he would ever come to giving reality to his dream. As in the case of John Fitch, who had been driven to suicide by ridicule and frustration, it was his misfortune to have invented a device before the world was quite ready for it.

A Hoboken, New Jersey, merchant, Colonel John Stevens, fared little better in 1812, when he published a brochure bearing the ponderous title *"Documents Tending to Prove the Superior Advantages of Rail-Ways and Steam Carriages over Canal Navigation."* Colonel Stevens had the advantage of counting among his personal friends some of the most influential men in the Hudson River Valley. He also was respected for his mechanical ability, having, as an avocation, built a pair of moderately successful steamboats.

Nevertheless, when Stevens's cronies read the *"Documents,"* they could only conclude that exposure to too much vapor had softened the good fellow's wits. How else could this passage be explained:

"I can see nothing to hinder a steam-engine from moving at a velocity of 100 miles an hour. In practice, it may not be advisable to exceed 20 or 30 miles an hour, but I should not be surprised at seeing carriages propelled at 40 or 50."

It was Stevens's further misfortune that the Secretary of the United States Treasury, Albert Gallatin, had recently proposed investing a growing federal surplus in canal-building projects. With such a pie to be cut, entrepreneurs were not likely to heed Stevens's warnings against waterways.

A second war with England accomplished for a time what his brochure could not. By drying up the national till, it put an end to all ditch-digging dreams until moneys could be raised on the state and local

17

levels. Meanwhile, Stevens nailed down two charters. One, dated 1815, was the first ever granted in the United States for a railway. It called for "as many tracks as deemed necessary" to be pushed across the midriff of New Jersey from New Brunswick to Trenton. The other, wheedled from the Pennsylvania State Legislature in 1823, gave him the authority to project a line between Philadelphia and the Susquehanna River a few miles south of Harrisburg.

Unable to raise funds for either project, Stevens laid out a 630-foot oval of strap-iron track on the grounds of his Hoboken villa. There, in 1825, he demonstrated a locomotive of his own making. By British standards it was a very primitive affair, hardly more than a toy—a single cylinder applying power, through spur gears, to the teeth of a rack rail spiked between the running rails.

If the machine had a virtue, it was the boiler. This was a type which the colonel had patented in 1803 and later applied to his steamboats. Like the ones Seguin would introduce to the St. Etienne Railway in 1828, it was filled with small pipes. But Stevens did not direct flames into them. Instead, he placed a small reservoir at either end of the bundle, filled the whole assembly with water, and applied heat to the *outer* surfaces of the honeycomb. Years later, sophisticated versions of that water-tube arrangement would prove superior to the fire-tube type for service in ships and stationary plants, because they permitted far higher operating pressures. But to the dying days of the steam locomotive, water-tube boilers could never be made rugged enough to withstand the fierce punishment of railroad service.

If Stevens had hoped to impress anyone with his midget engine he could hardly have chosen a worse time. Five hundred cannon, spaced within earshot of one another, were about to relay a roar of triumph from Buffalo to the Atlantic Ocean, announcing completion of the Erie Canal. Already New York City was reaping a rich harvest from sections of the Big Ditch opened the year before. As a result, competitive seaports saw their trade in jeopardy and clamored for similar waterways.

It occurred to no one that nature had dealt all the aces to the Erie: the tidal Hudson; the not-too-precipitous Mohawk; comparatively level land beyond; and enough streams veining the gentle Ontario Shelf to insure ample water without lengthy feeder canals.

On the other hand, an extension linking Boston with Troy, New York, would have to cross three mountain ranges. One—the Hoosac—would require 220 locks in 18 miles.

Comparable obstacles lay west of Philadelphia, Baltimore, Washington, and Richmond. Yet the last two cities were already engaged in excavating canals paralleling the Potomac and James rivers, respectively. Dissatisfied with the federally financed National Road, a miserably maintained turnpike, which gave her indifferent access to the Ohio Valley, Baltimore considered tying into the Potomac project. Finally, Philadelphia endorsed the Pennsylvania plan to thread a canal up the Susquehanna and the Juniata, then down the Connemaugh and the Allegheny into Pittsburgh. To reach the first of those rivers, a trench would have to be dug across 100 miles of undulating country offering few cooperative watercourses.

Or would it? Certain Philadelphians, including some with large investors in the wagon trade, formed a fellowship which they called the "Pennsylvania Society for the Promotion of Internal Improvements." One of their members, William Strickland, was sent to England to study the horse-powered tramways there. When he returned with his report, some wished he had stayed home, for he downplayed the fact that one beast could haul 15 tons on metal rails. Instead, he recommended using steam locomotives similar to those he had seen hauling twice that weight on the Stockton & Darlington Railway. All references to the engines were carefully deleted before his findings were passed along to the Pennsylvania Canals Commission. In that form the document served its purpose, and track laying was begun between Philadelphia and the Susquehanna River town of Columbia, 27 miles south of Harrisburg.

At about the same time, two American engineers, John B. Jervis and Horatio Allen, were unconsciously preparing themselves for the unfamiliar task of designing locomotives. Jervis had begun his career as an axman, leveling woodlands in advance of the scraper and shovel crews building the Erie Canal. Promotions came rapidly, and by 1824 he was in charge of one-seventh of the great artery's construction work. Then another project beckoned—the completion of a hybrid transportation system to carry coal from the anthracite fields of northeastern Penn-

The precursor of 180,000 full-scale steam locomotives built in the United States between 1831 and 1949 was a diminutive cog engine constructed by Colonel John Stevens and demonstrated at his Hoboken estate in 1825. It failed to impress transportation magnates investing millions in canals.

Imported by the Delaware & Hudson in 1829, the Stourbridge Lion was the first locomotive operated on a commercial railroad in America. Whether or not the 7-ton engine carried an embossed head of the king of beasts on its boiler front remains a subject for debate. The embellishment did not appear on this replica, displayed at Chicago's World's Columbian Exposition 64 years later.

sylvania to the Hudson Valley at Rondout, New York.

When Jervis replaced the former chief engineer of this Delaware & Hudson venture in 1827, he inherited a pressing problem. The canal head was at Honesdale, Pennsylvania, and the mines still lay 16 miles to the west, behind formidable Mt. Moosic. Since there was neither money nor water for a continuing flight of locks, he packed off to Boston to inspect a three-mile tramway which has often been called America's first railroad. It wasn't, but certainly the Granite Railway had no equal for length or quality. An enterprising Quincy quarryman was using it to haul blocks for the Bunker Hill Monument to barges waiting on the Neponset River.

Jervis took note of the broken stone ballast, the cross-stringers set eight feet apart, the pine rails topped with oak and, above them, a surfacing of strap iron. Here was the answer to troublesome Mt. Moosic. Back at Honesdale, he directed the laying of a similar line across the barrier. On its steepest parts his railroad became a series of inclined planes. Big stationary engines and chain cables were installed on the five planes intended for ascending traffic. Another three planes handled downgrade movements, which were gravity-operated. To hold the descending vehicles in check, Jervis invented what might be called the first railroad airbrake. This was a windmill-like device mounted on each car and connected by gears to its axles. With the canvas blades outstretched, atmospheric resistance limited the speed to four miles an hour.

The original plan was to use horses on other sections of the road. But Jervis wasn't missing any bets. He persuaded the management to send a resident engineer to England to inspect and purchase four locomotives. Since each would cost in the neighborhood of $5,000, this was a whopping responsibility for twenty-six-year-old Horatio Allen, the second of America's embryonic engine designers.

The British machines, named *America, Hudson, Delaware,* and *Stourbridge Lion,* reached New York in the summer of 1829. The first, a product of the Stephensons' Newcastle plant, was stowed aboard the Hudson River packet *Congress* on July 16, for the continuing voyage to Rondout. We can imagine the lonely little beast, firmly hobbled and trussed to the open deck, pondering with an empty stomach and muted stack its future beyond the forbidding west

shore—and all we can do is speculate, because company records never mention the *America* again.

The other engines, built by Foster, Rastrick & Co., of Stourbridge, reached Rondout without incident. There, two were stored in a shed. The third, *Stourbridge Lion,* was floated up the canal to Honesdale, arriving on August 5. Here, as Horatio Allen told it, is what happened three days later:

"He who addresses you was the only person on that locomotive. The circumstances which led to my being alone on the engine were these: The road had been built in the summer; the structure was of hemlock timber, the rails of large dimensions notched on caps placed far apart. The timber was cracked and warped from exposure to the sun. After 300 feet of straight line, the road crossed the Lackawaxen Creek on a trestle about 30 feet high, and with a curve of 350 to 400 feet radius. The impression was very general that this iron monster would break down the road, or that it would leave the track at the curve and plunge into the creek. My reply . . . was that it was too late to consider the probability of such circumstances . . . that I would take the first ride alone, and the time would come when I should look back to the incident with great interest.

"As I placed my hand upon the throttle valve handle I was undecided whether I should move slowly or with a fair degree of speed. But holding that the road would prove safe, and preferring, if we did go down, to go down handsomely, and without any evidence of timidity, I started with considerable velocity, passed the curves over the creek safely, and was soon out of hearing of the cheering of the vast assemblage present. At the end of two or three miles I reversed the valve, and returned without incident to the place of starting, having made the first locomotive trip in the western hemisphere."

Either Allen hadn't heard of Colonel Stevens' little engine or found forgetfulness convenient when he unburdened these reminiscences in 1851.

After extensive improvements to the track, the *Lion* was given a second try. But its seven tons of unsprung weight invited derailments, and it was soon stored in a shed at Honesdale, where it remained until 1849, when its boiler and cylinders were cannibalized for foundry service in Carbondale. Years later, the owners of the shop shipped the parts to the Smithsonian Institution in Washington, D.C., where

21

Given favorable winds, the Baltimore & Ohio's sailing car Aeolus made a number of successful voyages over a completed portion of the railroad in 1830.

In an early attempt to eliminate towpaths between its rails, the B&O built and tested a treadmill locomotive. The replica shown here was exhibited at the company's 1927 Centenary Pageant. It seems probable that a more elaborate harness confined the horse to a fixed position on the original machine.

the wholly restored locomotive may be seen today.

The *Hudson* and the *Delaware* had no such history. Neither ever turned a wheel, and they were finally reduced to rubble in a warehouse fire.

If the *Lion*'s performance had not helped the cause of the steam locomotive, it at least brought cheer to those gentlemen of consequence who, in the past, had supplied horses to the stage and canal-packet companies. Now they could wholeheartedly endorse proposals for iron highways.

True, the publicly financed Philadelphia & Columbia Railroad would not greatly increase their fortunes, because any farmer was guaranteed the right to drive his own team and wagon on its tracks. But two privately backed lines chartered in 1827 were expected to buy beasts of the highest quality, and in large numbers. One, the Baltimore & Ohio Railroad, planned to push two tracks over the Alleghenies. The other, the South Carolina Railroad, was to be driven westward from Charleston to the headwaters of Savannah River navigation near Augusta, Georgia.

Still, the horse traders had their bad moments. One came when a construction engineer proposed that a tank filled with water be mounted on wheels and placed at the summit of each B&O grade. There, by means of a rope passed through a sheave, it would serve as a counterbalance for ascending cars. Each time it reached the bottom of the slope—and they the top—the water would be dumped. The description and drawings were so handsomely prepared that it was some time before anyone thought to ask: "Where do you find an abundance of water at high elevations?"

A more tangible threat was a specimen of basket weaving shaped like a sloop, fitted with wheels, and having a mast to which was rigged a square of canvas. Under command of an expert sailing master, the wicker craft made a number of voyages on a newly opened stretch of track near Baltimore. One passenger was so impressed that he asked permission to send a model of this *Aeolus* back to his government. He was Baron Krudener, the Russian minister to Washington.

But again, circumstances favored the horse traders. One day when the wind was unusually brisk, the skipper failed to strike his mainsheet in time, and the land ship plowed into a mound of earth at rails' end, catapulting a dozen dignitaries over the bow.

A similar experience with sail cars induced the South Carolina Railroad to offer a prize of $500 for any vehicle, other than one propelled by steam, which would save the cost of laying and maintaining a towpath between the irons. The winner was a Charleston inventor, C. E. Detmold. Adopting the treadmill arrangement used to turn mill machinery, he placed a chain platform on a car, connected it to the wheels, and set it in motion by driving a horse upon it. In a Baltimore & Ohio version of the machine the treadmill was inclined, the theory being that an animal forced to trudge upgrade would generate greater power.

Unique rather than efficient, the contraptions were soon discarded, and the B&O had settled for conventional horsecars when a wealthy New Yorker, Peter Cooper, paid a visit to its directors. A number of his investments, he explained, would suffer if their railroad didn't prosper. Were they aware that one beast upon a canal could do the work of two upon a track? How then did they hope to compete with the Potomac waterway? The directors smiled wanly. Possibly their guest had a suggestion. Indeed he did: steam locomotives. In reply, he was told that, the great George Stephenson had already been consulted and had stated flatly that no locomotive of any worth could ever be run through curves of less than 900-foot radius. That ruled them out, because natural obstacles had forced the B&O to accept minimal radii of 400 feet, with sharper curves anticipated when the line reached the Potomac River.

It was then that Peter Cooper decided, as he reminisced in the columns of the Boston *Herald* of July 9, 1882, that "I believe I could knock together a locomotive which would get the trains around . . . so I came back to New York and got a little bit of an engine, about one horse-power [it had a 3½-inch cylinder and a 14-inch stroke] and carried it back to Baltimore. I got some boiler iron and made a boiler about as big as an ordinary washboiler and then how to connect the boiler with the engine I didn't know . . . I had an iron foundry and some manual skill in working it. But I couldn't find any iron pipes. The fact is that there were none for sale in this country. So I took two muskets and broke off the wood parts, and used the barrels for tubing to the boiler. I went to a coachmaker's shop and made this locomotive, which I called the *Tom Thumb* because it was so

Noted manufacturer and philanthropist Peter Cooper personally "knocked together" the historic Tom Thumb *"only to show...that it could be done." The one-ton midget turned in the Western Hemisphere's earliest passenger run on August 28, 1830, hauling a single coachload of officials from Baltimore to Ellicotts Mills and back.*

insignificant. I didn't intend it for actual service, but only to show the directors that it could be done."

As soon as there was harmony between its parts the one-ton engine was coupled to a wagonload of worthies for a 13-mile junket to the end of track at Ellicotts Mills. Cooper, who doubled as engineer and fireboy that August day in 1830, "cracked" the throttle cautiously. *Tom Thumb* responded without enthusiasm until a blower belted to its rear axle began to fan the fire. Then the boiler pressure rose, as did the spirits of the passengers. One mile was run in three minutes and twenty seconds.

Halfway to the Mills a water stop was made at Middle Depot, later called Relay Station. Thereafter the grades and curves grew uncooperative. Still the little engine stuttered and squealed along at only slightly diminished speed. Then came the ultimate test. Returning to Baltimore, a horse-drawn car was met where double track began. A race was inevitable. Again the blower proved a handicap at starting. But each turn of the wheels increased the power. At last a moment when, with its safety valve popping, the iron filly passed its flesh-and-blood competitor.

Twenty corporate voices were raised in loud huzzahs. The blower belt was applauding, too—so violently that with a final slap it slid from its drum and became entangled with the axle. While Cooper struggled first to free and then to re-engage it, the engine's quick breath slackened. Again the horse was out in front—this time for good.

But if the race was lost, a more important victory was won. For having sampled the headiness of steam, the B&O's directors announced a "Rainhill Contest" of their own for locomotive engines of American manufacture. There and elsewhere, native ingenuity would assert itself in remarkable ways.

4   Too Much

The nature of the B&O's contest was first made public in the Baltimore *American* of January 4, 1831. The company would pay $4,000 for the best engine offered for testing on its rails before June 1 of that year, and $3,500 for the runner-up. Entries were required to weigh no more than 3½ tons, yet be capable of drawing 15 tons at 15 miles an hour on level track. A four-wheeled undercarriage equipped with suitable springs was to support all of the machinery, the distance between the front and rear axle being held to four feet to prevent binding on curves. Locomotives having horizontal or vertical boilers were equally acceptable, but in the interest of passenger safety, operating pressures above 50 pounds to the square inch were not recommended. Further, the B&O reserved the right to put all barrels, cylinders, and connecting pipes through hydrostatic tests before the trials began, applying cold water to those parts at three times normal steam pressure. Entries

also were required to burn coal or coke and "consume their own smoke." The latter stipulation had public-relations value but of course it was physically impossible for any locomotive to consume its own smoke. In practice, this requirement was interpreted to mean that gasses and embers leaving the furnace had to be blended with the steam exhaust and voided through the same chimney. It was hoped that this would produce a reasonably clear emission, and since such an arrangement was essential for a well-drafted fire, engine builders were happy to comply. Finally, entrants were assured of the company's full cooperation. Throughout the tests, supplementary cars, or "tenders," stocked with fuel of the highest quality, would be furnished by the railroad without charge.

Five contenders responded to this and later notices placed in Philadelphia's *National Gazette* and New York City's *Commercial Advertiser*. Three of the entrants—Phineas Davis of York, Pennsylvania, and

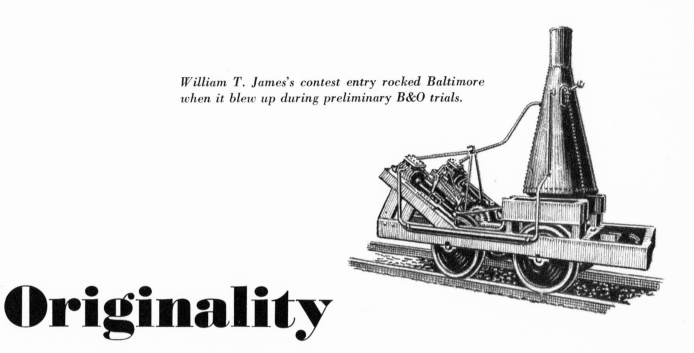

William T. James's contest entry rocked Baltimore when it blew up during preliminary B&O trials.

Originality

Stacey Costell and Ezekiel Childs of Philadelphia—were former watchmakers. A fourth, George W. Johnson, owned the Baltimore machine works in which Peter Cooper had assembled the *Tom Thumb*. The fifth, William T. James, was already chugging around the streets of New York in a steam carriage of his own design.

Late in February, Davis completed and submitted a little engine named the *York*. That gave him ample time to run it upon the line, note its shortcomings, and take steps to correct them.

First, the boiler proved troublesome. It was of the upright type, with a disproportionately large central furnace. Water was heated in a slim, encompassing jacket and a shallow drum suspended above the grates. Peering through the fire door, observers thought the drum resembled a solid dairy product, and the whole assembly was officially designated ·a "cheese" boiler. Thus began a railroad tradition—the

coining of a lingo baffling to laymen but understood wherever flanged wheels roll. Unfortunately, the "cheese" quickly filled with sludge and scale, sharply reducing the steam output. The solution, suggested by Mr. Cooper, was to lower the firebox roof, or "crown sheet," and run flues through a water section placed above it.

The driving mechanism also presented problems. In its original form, both sets of wheels were powered by vertical cylinders activating mainrods coupled to the centers of a pair of side rods. As a result, the pistons traveled varying distances when the axles bobbed upon their springs. Again, when the engine was worked at full steam on grades, each tug and thrust jacked up one side of its frame and pulled the other down, giving it the gait of an old man climbing a flight of stairs with his hands in his pockets. Davis finally resorted to a geared drive which, though far from ideal, eliminated those objections.

27

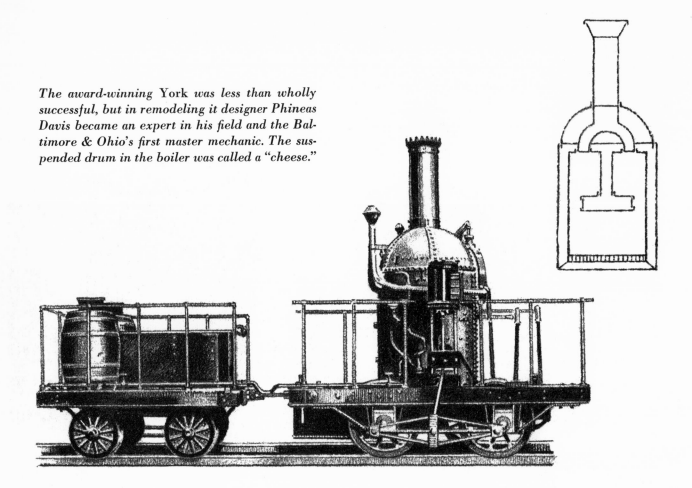

The award-winning York *was less than wholly successful, but in remodeling it designer Phineas Davis became an expert in his field and the Baltimore & Ohio's first master mechanic. The suspended drum in the boiler was called a "cheese."*

One of the Philadelphians, Costell, also was committed to gears. Uniquely, his engine's cylinders were mounted on pivotal bearings. By letting the cylinders rock to and fro, it was possible for the piston rods to work directly upon the cranks of a countershaft, eliminating wrist joints and mainrods. However, oscillating cylinders large and heavy enough for locomotive service were bound to vibrate violently at all but the lowest speeds. Available records indicate only that the machine was a failure, but it is safe to assume that the principal reasons were rapid bearing wear and leakage at the flexible steam connections.

The equally unconventional Childs engine was propelled by a turbine of sorts—a single cylinder rotating on a hollow shaft which did double duty as an admission and exhaust pipe. Based upon the per-

formance of a preliminary model, the builder predicted that his full-scale entry would develop 50 horsepower. Why it failed to do so neither the railroad nor the press ever took the trouble to explain. As further evidence of the indifferent coverage given the trials, authorities later disagreed as to what role, if any, the locomotive played in the contest.

Johnson displayed originality of another sort by providing his engine with two furnaces. If the object were to increase thermal efficiency, well-drafted flues would have served as well without compounding the duties of the fireboy. Still, that should not have disqualified the machine, and what did remains another mystery.

James, in turn, courted disaster by using a "Hazleton" boiler—an upright type named for the Pennsylvania coal town where it was developed for pumping

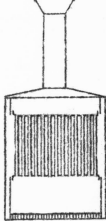

Overhead rocking beams suggested a nickname for the 7-ton Atlantic and 17 basically similar locomotives—"grasshoppers." While their multitubed vertical boilers were highly efficient, roadway clearances restricted their size.

CAM-ACTUATED
WATER PUMP

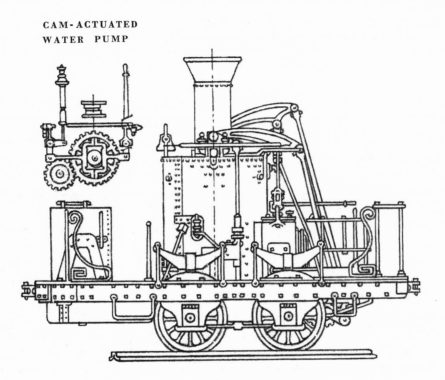

B&O "ATLANTIC"—SIDE ELEVATION

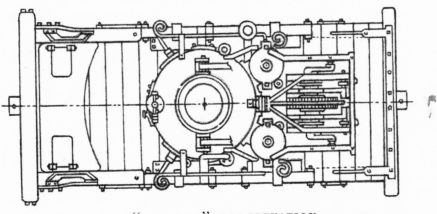

B&O "ATLANTIC"—TOP ELEVATION

and cable-hoisting plants. Shaped like a porter bottle, it applied the heat of a central fire to a water jacket whose inner wall bristled with hollow studs exposed to the flames. The design was adequate for stationary installations but vulnerable to rupture on a jouncing locomotive. This was dramatically demonstrated when the engine blew up during an experimental run. Down-staged by the explosion was a mechanical innovation, a lever which could be thrown, on upgrades, to disengage one set of gears and align the teeth of another, decreasing speed but increasing power. Prematurely, then, James set the pattern for today's manual automobile transmissions. The second noteworthy feature was a reversing mechanism superior to any previously used.

After weighing the somewhat dubious merits of the entries, the B&O awarded first prize to the *York*. Davis might well have pocketed the $4,000 and declined further responsibility for the engine. Instead, he continued to improve it, and under a banner headline the Baltimore *American* of July 13, 1831, reported that the perfected machine had just drawn five fully loaded coaches in handsome style from Ellicotts Mills to the road's home terminal on Pratt Street. Only then did the Pennsylvanian return to York. With him he carried an order for a much larger passenger hauler—a seven-ton brute capable of outpulling forty-two horses.

The following summer his *Atlantic* was ready for service and, considering the restrictions imposed by the B&O's curves and clearances, it was a remarkable locomotive. Packed with 282 fire tubes, its plump vertical boiler generated ample steam for two 10- by 20-inch cylinders. Power was transmitted to the rails by a roundabout route involving overhead walking beams and a pair of countershafts fitted with meshing gears which doubled the rotative speed applied to four 36-inch wheels. Thus the extremely compact engine performed as well as one equipped with six-foot drivers.

Financially disinterested spectators may not have been impressed by the fact that the *Atlantic* could wring enough energy from a ton of anthracite costing $8 to move a 50-ton payload 80 miles. But they were intrigued by the action of its walking beams and the long rods which turned a pair of cranks on one of the countershafts below. The motion was like that of a locust's hind legs, and in its 1832 annual report the railroad took notice of the similarity by announcing that other locomotives of the "grasshopper" type were being constructed by Davis and a machinist-partner named Gartner in the company's newly completed Mount Clare (Baltimore) shops. All told, these builders turned out 18 of the strange machines. While the "grasshoppers" had no permanent effect upon engine design, they served an immediate purpose, and proved so durable that sixty years later a few could still be found performing light switching chores in and about the plant which had produced them.

In 1833, a tragic accident left a young and fumbling craft without the steadying influence of the ever-practical and persistent Davis. The circumstances were described in the minutes of a Baltimore & Ohio board of directors meeting. An excerpt read:

"On September 27 he [Davis] having completed a new engine, availed himself of the occasion of trying it to take his numerous workmen on a visit to Washington. On his return the engine, striking the end of a rail, which the breaking of an iron chair had permitted to get out of alignment, was thrown from the structure, and, being on the tender, he was dashed forward against the engine and instantly killed."

There is a railroad saying that an engine is no better than its track, and here was early proof of it.

5　An Unprofitable

On a spring night in 1831, an unprecedented event took place on the South Carolina Railroad. The location was a lonely stretch of track supported by piles driven into the malarial marshlands west of Charleston. Late in the evening, a blanket of fog lifted somewhat from the surface of the swamp. Under the white canopy, a bright orange starburst moved steadily from one horizon to the other, accompanied by rhythmically repeated hissing sounds. For the first time on this continent, a locomotive was making its way through the darkness. Ahead of it clanked a "track illuminator"—a flatcar covered with a thick layer of sand on which rested an iron brazier filled with blazing pine knots. This was the original headlight.

A second flatcar followed. Then came the engine, resembling a huge speaking trumpet, placed mouthpiece upward, at the rear of an abbreviated wagon. Inside the frame, a pair of cylinders stroked cranks

on the second axle. The engineer stood on a small platform up front. Behind him, the fireboy stoked the furnace with his back to the wind.

Scorning the comfort of a trailing carriage, a third man shared the deck with the crew. He was the same Horatio Allen who had driven the *Stourbridge Lion* intrepidly across the Lackawaxen River bridge. His Delaware & Hudson apprenticeship had served him well, for now he was chief engineer of the South Carolina Railroad. In that capacity the young Yankee intended to prove that trains could be run around the clock. The incentive was great, because the line would soon have a terminal-to-terminal length of 136 miles. It was an awkward distance—impossible to span between dawn and dusk, and too short to justify a layover.

If the fire did more to blind the engineer than light the way, the rails at least held the cavalcade on course. Next day the press hailed the experiment,

Intended to do away with turnarounds at terminals, Horatio Allen's double-ended South Carolina *eliminated runs as well, for it spent most of its time in the repair shop.*

Business

and reviewed the brief but colorful career of the engine used for the test. Readers were reminded that the *Best Friend of Charleston* was the first successful commercial locomotive built in the Western Hemisphere. Two native sons had collaborated in the design. One was a prominent merchant, E. L. Miller; the other, the inventor of the road's former treadmill engine, C. E. Detmold. Actual construction had been undertaken, during the summer of 1830, by a New York City establishment principally engaged in manufacturing ship fittings—the West Point Foundry.

It was reported that the five-ton *Best Friend* had performed beyond all expectations, achieving speeds of up to 20 miles an hour. Its only fault was a tendency to emit loud crackling noises upon entering curves. This was corrected by replacing the wooden spokes of its driving wheels with spokes of wrought iron. Finally, the citizens of Charleston were asked to recall the excursion-train run made by the loco-

motive in December of the previous year. It had been a gala affair, with two hundred of the city's gentry accommodated in a string of elegant coaches, and a trio of artillerymen firing salutes from a cannon lashed to the deck of a flag-draped flatcar ahead.

Having accomplished so much, the *Best Friend* might have been spared its most spectacular claim to fame. It happened on a morning in June, 1831. Responding to a diet of pine slabs bubbling with pitch, the safety valve was screaming. Hoping to silence the din with an overdraft, the wood passer opened the fire door. That failing, he presumably tied down the valve lever. Some historians go further, maintaining that he sat upon it, but this seems unlikely, since it was placed in a region of searing heat where the boiler tapered to a smokestack.

In any case, there were several minutes of silence. Then came a blinding flash and a deafening roar. From a cauliflower of steam emerged the ruptured

33

Although primarily engaged in producing steamboat machinery, New York City's West Point Foundry turned out seven of the earliest engines manufactured in the United States. Delivered to the South Carolina Railroad late in 1830, its Best Friend of Charleston drew the first train of passenger cars in America, and the West Point left its shop some 6 months later. Both locomotives were of the inside-connected type.

WEST POINT

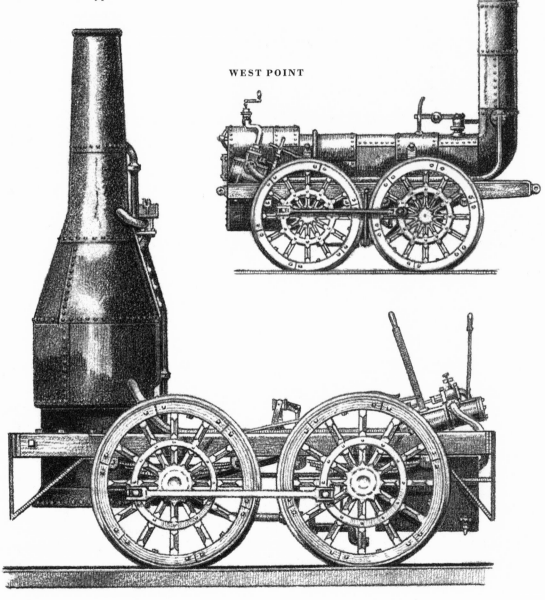

BEST FRIEND OF CHARLESTON

barrel and the fireboy, pinwheeling in opposite directions. The engineer and two trainmen were similarly airborne.

A mechanic named Julius Petsch took what was left of the locomotive and rearranged the parts so ingeniously that the South Carolina Railroad appointed him its "master of machinery." Petsch thus became the first American railroader to bear this title. At the same time the directors gave a new name to the machine he had rebuilt. Realizing the irony of calling a locomotive that had nearly blown itself to bits the *Best Friend of Charleston,* they rechristened it the *Phoenix* in memory of the mythical bird which rose unruffled from its own funeral pyre. In a further attempt to improve the company image, it was announced that a "barrier car" would be placed between the engine and coaches of all future passenger trains. "Loaded with six bales of cotton," an advertisement read, "it will protect travelers

when the locomotive explodes." Plainly, more eruptions were expected.

By now a second Miller creation, the *West Point,* was puffing up and down the line. Unlike its predecessor, it had a horizontal boiler. But the cylinders were still inside the frame, with the mainrods turning cranks between the wheels. On the other hand, Petsch had moved the driving mechanism of the *Phoenix* outside the wheels. Miller's arrangement produced less yaw and roll, for the closer cylinders were placed to a locomotive's centerline the smoother the action became. However, Petsch foresaw the difficulty of servicing inside connections and predicted that neglect would soon cancel out the *West Point's* superior performance.

As might have been expected, Horatio Allen had some thoughts on the matter, and he found time to develop plans for an engine unlike any seen before. Built at the West Point Foundry and shipped to

Charleston late in 1831, his *South Carolina* was, in effect, two locomotives joined back to back, with the boilers sharing a single furnace. Each boiler, in turn, consisted of two slender drums placed side by side like shotgun barrels. The whole assembly was mounted on a pair of four-wheeled trucks. Finally, the axles nearest the furnace were driven by a single cylinder apiece.

The twin-headed monster solved many problems. With power applied along a line midway between the wheels, the tendency of the engine to nose from side to side was eliminated. The independently cranked axles reduced slipping. Sharp curves were easily negotiated by the swiveling trucks. And when the locomotive pulled into a terminal there was no need to turn it around. On the other hand, the *South Carolina* rarely pulled into terminals. Its mechanical complexities led to one road failure after another, and it was soon dismantled.

Several months before the *South Carolina* reached Charleston, another West Point Foundry machine produced a reasonable facsimile of the last days of Pompeii while hauling a distinguished group of New Yorkers. The occasion was the opening of the 16-mile-long Mohawk & Hudson Rail Road. Ostensibly, the Albany-financed project had been undertaken to save travelers a tedious trip through the locks of the Erie Canal between the state capital and Schenectady. The real object, however, was to draw trade away from nearby Troy which, as the eastern terminus of the waterway, was prospering alarmingly. For that reason, the tracks bypassed the upstart city, crossing a high plateau to the south with the aid of inclined planes and hoisting stations at either end.

On the morning of the inaugural run, the governor, members of the legistature, and the mayors of Albany and Schenectady composed themselves with dignity within and atop three refurbished stagecoach bodies. These had been slung on leather straps between C-clamps bolted to railroad undercarriages. The bright yellow vehicles were chained together on a level stretch of track above the not-yet-completed Albany plane, near the site of the present State House. The hoisting station's principal features had already been explained to the assemblage, and everyone agreed that the road's chief engineer was building for the ages. He was Horatio Allen's former mentor, John B. Jervis.

The one-time Erie Canal axman received more praise when a locomotive which he had designed in collaboration with a West Point Foundry mechanic, Adam Hall, backed onto the cars. Few were aware of the problems already posed by the diminutive *DeWitt Clinton*. During preliminary trials the 3½-ton engine had rejected its intended diet of anthracite. The reason should have been clear; the exhausts from two 5½-by-16-inch cylinders became lost in an absurdly large smokestack and created little draft. Next, coke was tried. That worked so well the grates had melted. In a spirit of compromise, the present fuel was wood.

With everything in order, conductor John T. Clark blew a clarion blast on a tin horn. Thereupon the driver, David Matthew, opened the throttle. The engine puffed joyously and plunged ahead, setting the loosely coupled coaches in motion with all the finesse of a slingshot. Inertia being what it is, the inside passengers facing aft rose from their seats as one man and fell into the arms of those across the transverse aisles. Then came the inevitable counter-surge and a reverse migration. The spirited game of musical chairs continued until the pulsing of the cylinders leveled off.

Forewarned of each lunge by a stack eruption, the rooftop passengers fared better at first. But as speed increased, the white puffs were replaced by a banner of black smoke, studded with sparks, blazing embers, and incandescent blobs of pitch. At the peak of the updraft the galaxy hung motionless. Then each fragment streaked like a meteor toward some finely blocked beaver, handsomely tailored frock coat, or impeccably snug trouser leg. Even the umbrellas that some passengers had brought along were no protection against the sparks and embers.

Mercifully, there was a water tank ahead. Here a stop was made to soak down the smoldering garments and their owners. Seizing the opportunity, the train crew pilfered a number of fence rails and, cutting them to the length of the chains connecting the cars, lashed them in place beneath the links. That at least took care of the free slack for the remainder of the run.

Following its return to Albany, the *DeWitt Clinton* was shipped downriver for reworking at the West Point Foundry. At about the same time, a stable mate of twice its size and weight arrived from England.

36

Of historic interest itself, this full-scale reproduction of the DeWitt Clinton and three Mohawk & Hudson coaches was built at the New York Central's West Albany shops more than three-quarters of a century ago. It is now on permanent exhibition at the Henry Ford Museum in Dearborn, Michigan.

This was the *Robert Fulton,* soon renamed the *John Bull,* a "Samson" class locomotive developed by the Messrs. Stephenson. A British passion for fast locomotives had forced its builders to abandon the *Rocket's* wonderfully simple driving arrangement, for as operating speeds climbed, so did engines with outside mainrods—right over the railheads and into the green meadows beyond. To prevent such derailments, the *Bull's* cylinders were tucked closely together in the forward section, or "smokebox," of the locomotive's horizontal boiler. The purpose was to envelop them with hot gasses rushing toward the chimney, so that steam would not condense before it drove the pistons.

Jervis took a tolerant view of the awkward servicing location. But he could not ignore the havoc the seven-ton *Bull* played with his metal-surfaced wooden rails. Given the funds, he would have replaced them with English imports made completely of wrought iron. The latest of those sturdy forgings were called "fish bellies" because they swelled downward between the clamps, or "chairs," which anchored them to stone blocks. It seemed likely that they would never be improved upon. Yet they cost $58 a ton, and the few domestic foundries which could duplicate them quoted a figure half again as high. At either price, the Mohawk & Hudson might as well have considered a roadway of solid gold.

Caught in this predicament, the civil engineer went back to his drafting table to design what he hoped would be a less destructive engine. It was clear that the *Bull's* behavior was caused by a lack of flexibility. On rough track, one wheel after another rose from the rails and crashed down again. Axle springs were supposed to prevent such hammer blows, but their responses were too slow. The problem called for a basic solution.

Jervis knew that he had found it when, in 1832,

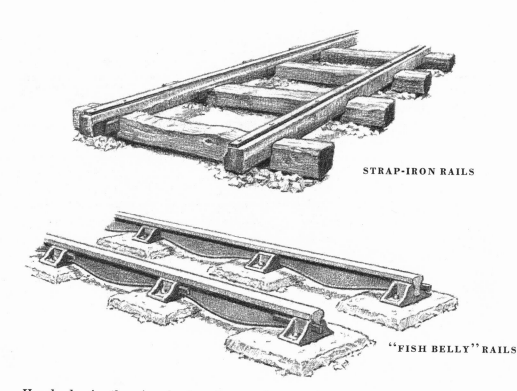

STRAP-IRON RAILS

"FISH BELLY" RAILS

Hundreds of miles of early American track were of strap-iron construction. Not infrequently the pressure of one set of wheels teetered a rail point upward, permitting the next pair to underride and peel it from the stringers below. When that happened it became a "snake," in railroad lingo, knifing its way through car floors and impaling hapless passengers. Widely used in England, "fish belly" rails were far superior, but few domestic roads could afford them.

John B. Jervis was responsible for the greatest single improvement made in locomotive performance during the 1830s. Incorporated in his Brother Jonathan, *a swiveling guiding truck pivoted at its center provided both a three-point suspension system and lateral stability when an engine entered curves.*

the West Point Foundry delivered a locomotive built from his plans. It was fired up for testing, and with David Matthew at the throttle, the amazing *Brother Jonathan* chugged westward out of Albany, nonchalantly adjusting itself to every dip and rise and dogleg curve. The secret of its smooth performance was a three-point suspension system. Two of the "points" were the driving wheels at the rear. The other was a center pin beneath the boiler front, upon which swiveled a two-axled guiding truck. In a burst of enthusiasm Matthew later wrote: "With this engine I have crossed the Mohawk & Hudson from plane to plane, fourteen miles in thirteen minutes, making one stop for water." Possibly his watch needed regulating, but why quibble?

Jervis applied the same wheel arrangement to the *Bull,* and his troubles with that machine were over. The immediate reward was small, for he was caught in the crossfire of an ugly managerial skirmish.

Those who won control of the Mohawk & Hudson demanded his resignation on the grounds of incompetence. The absurdity of the charge was demonstrated when he went on to enlarge the Erie Canal, construct the great Croton Aqueduct, and serve as an able president of the Chicago, Rock Island & Pacific Railway.

In later years, Jervis must have recalled, with amusement, an incident that occurred soon after his dismissal by the M&H. Appointed chief engineer of the newly chartered Saratoga & Schenectady Railroad, he prepared the plans for a passenger locomotive, fully expecting the West Point Foundry to undertake its construction. To his surprise, he was told that the firm was doing too well in the burgeoning riverboat equipment trade to devote further time, shop space, or effort to a business as unprofitable as engine building. In retrospect it was an unfortunate decision.

6 Pride in "Company"

In 1830, two years before Jervis rendered his plans for the *Brother Jonathan*, the New Jersey legislature approved a charter for a line to be projected across the state between Raritan Bay and the Delaware River community of Bordentown, New Jersey, 28 miles north of Philadelphia. This Camden & Amboy Railroad would, for the most part, follow the route proposed by Colonel John Stevens in 1815. Gone were the skepticism and ridicule of an earlier day. When stock in the new venture was offered in February of that year, the entire issue, amounting to $4,000,000, was snapped up in ten minutes.

Appropriately, two of the colonel's sons spearheaded the operation. One served as treasurer, and another doubled as president and chief engineer. Assuming dual responsibilities was nothing new for handsome Robert L. Stevens; at the age of twenty-one he had been both captain and stoker of his father's second steamboat on a 13-day voyage from

Hoboken around Cape May to Philadelphia. That fog-plagued run had made history as the first of such a craft upon the open sea.

Now, at forty-two, he embarked on another voyage. The vessel was the Black Ball liner *Hibernia*—its destination, Liverpool. Stevens's mission was to buy British rails and a locomotive. The former purchase troubled him. Not that he doubted the merits of the fish-belly type, or lacked the funds for a substantial order. Rather, he resented having to turn to foreign suppliers for first-rate track components. Since the American foundries could not manufacture sophisticated rails and chairs on a competitive basis, he decided to try his hand at developing something equally serviceable but less complex.

Given a four-week crossing, a jackknife, and a block of pine supplied by the ship's carpenter, Stevens produced a pattern for an all-metal rail shaped like an inverted "T." The only fasteners

40

Engines

Weighing up to 152 pounds to the yard, the steel "T" rails in mainline use today differ only in size and strength from those that Robert L. Stevens designed and helped a Welsh ironmaster roll in 1830. The first imported shipments were laid on granite stone ties hewn by the convicts at New York's Sing Sing Prison.

needed for a rail of this sort would be offset-headed spikes. Still, it was one thing to whittle sweet-smelling softwood, and quite another thing to find an English ironmaster willing to roll the unfamiliar form. The owner of every large shop he approached regarded the model with glassy eyes and shook his head. Stevens found out why when an old Welsh friend of his father undertook the commission with misgivings, and a pledge that he would be paid in full for any damage done his equipment. "The first rails came out twisted and crooked as snakes," wrote Stevens, "and we were about ready to give up before we contrived a way to work them straight while the iron was still hot."

Twenty-two packets laden with the 16-footers put into Philadelphia in 1831. From there, Delaware River sloops relayed the shipments to Bordentown. Another shallow-draft vessel arrived one August day, bearing an engine presumably similar to the Mohawk

& Hudson's *John Bull.* Instead, those who waited hours for a first glimpse of the machine, saw on the deck only a stackless boiler and half a dozen packing cases.

The Camden & Amboy's president had not availed himself of a Stephenson extra—company technicians sent along to assemble locomotives delivered in knocked-down form. It was just as well, for wherever those roving mechanics were employed, Anglo-American relations suffered. In contrast to American mechanics, who could not resist displaying their skills or offering advice, both good and bad, to anyone who cared to watch and listen, the British put on airs, refusing to answer questions and working behind locked doors to guard trade secrets. However, Stevens felt sure the shipwright's apprentice he had pirated from a Philadelphia yard could put the contents of the crates together. His confidence was based upon the young man's proven ability to make

41

Centered on the John Bull's *first tender was a whiskey barrel filled with innocuous water. A hose stitched from cowhide carried the supply forward to the boiler. Young master mechanic Isaac Dripps later replaced the locomotive's straight smokestack with one that diverted embers to its base.*

marine engines behave beyond their designers' expectations.

It was no simple task for twenty-two-year-old Isaac Dripps to identify the unlabeled parts. Nevertheless, the locomotive took shape and, with it, a fuel car of his own making. In designing a similar tender for the *DeWitt Clinton,* John Jervis had mounted a shallow metal tank on four wheels, placing two barrels above it for coal or wood. Years later, this "water bottom" arrangement would be re-examined and widely adopted. Dripps relied on a more primitive reservoir—a charred-oak whiskey cask, placed at the center of the tender. Then, needing a flexible joint in a pipe which carried water forward to the locomotive, he had a local shoemaker stitch together a leather sleeve.

Officially named the *Stevens,* the engine, like many of the others imported from England during the 1830s, was usually called the *John Bull,* due to the resemblance between the full-boilered little English locomotives of this period and the portly gentleman who personified the country of their

origin. The *Stevens* hauled its first passenger coaches over a short stretch of track on November 12, 1831. Lest anyone think Bordentown a provincial village, two illustrious guests turned out for the occasion: Joseph Bonaparte, eldest brother of Napoleon, who having failed as a king, first of Naples and then Spain, now managed the affairs of a Delaware Valley farm with greater skill, and Madam Murat, niece by marriage of the former emperor, a beautiful and gay young woman, whose presence is said to have inspired courage, if not confidence, among her fellow passengers.

Robert Stevens had, by this time, supervised the laying of a double row of stone blocks well across the state. Cavities were drilled in each cube, then stopped with maple dowels. Next, square iron plates with matching holes were placed above them. Finally came the rails, secured with spikes driven through the plates and into the plugs.

The pace of track laying had slowed painfully as the roadway approached South Amboy. There, the warden of New York's Sing Sing Prison had con-

Anachronisms crept onto the Camden & Amboy's John Bull when it was restored for a run under steam from New York to Chicago—62 years after a British packet delivered it to Philadelphia in 1831. The stack resembles neither the original chimney nor the flaring type applied later, and old drawings indicate that there were no counterbalances on the cranked rear wheels. Correctly, the side rods furnished by the Stephensons were omitted, for it is known that they were removed at an early date to reduce the locomotive's nosing.

tracted to supply the stonework. But his quarrymen showed no enthusiasm for the project, and their indifferent efforts finally forced the Camden & Amboy to resort to wooden crossties. Stevens regarded the use of wood as a stopgap measure, and fully intended to have the squared logs removed as soon as more granite footings arrived. He changed his mind when this section of track proved to be the best on the line. Its resilience made for remarkably smooth running, which in turn permitted higher operating speeds. In the end, it was the costly blocks which were replaced.

There still remained the problem of winter and spring maintenance. An inadequate bed of crushed rock caused the roadway to drain sluggishly, and the *John Bull* periodically called attention to frost-heaved rails by plowing into the offending ballast. Without waiting for more stone to be spread, Dripps hinged a pushcart-like assembly under the locomotive's chin. Its "handles" were stout oak beams attached to extensions of the forward axle. A coil spring on a yoke ahead transferred part of the engine's weight to a pair of small guiding wheels. The nonswiveling appendage left much to be desired, but it put an end to the derailments. Of particular interest was its pointed prow, which may have been the first "cow-catcher," though it could not have been as effective at catching cows as the sturdy crossbar affixed to the front of a Pennsylvania & Reading Railroad engine at about the same time. Bristling with harrow-like teeth, it impaled a bull with such force that it took the strength of another locomotive, pulling on a rope, to remove the carcass. Overseas, there was no need for that protective device, stiff penalties being levied on farmers who failed to keep their fences mended. In America, it was the other way around. As a Kentucky judge once admonished a cheering jury: "The railroads must learn that he who kills his neighbor's ox, his ass, or his shoat, shall pay back twentyfold."

Dripps further improved the *John Bull* by slipping a downward tapering sleeve over its straight chimney. A cover of wire netting caught embers bursting from the stack and diverted them to the base of the outer shell. This spark-arresting mechanism was far better than a screen which merely trapped solids in the exhaust column and let them bounce about until they clogged it. The flamboyant "balloon," sun-flower," and "cabbage head" designs of later years were no more than variations of Isaac Dripps's innovative "trumpet" type.

Still a third new feature of the *Stevens* was a fully inclosed fuel car standing as high as a passenger coach. A forward extension of the roof offered protection of a sort for the engine crew from the elements. Greater consideration was shown the head brakeman. He sat on top of the fuel car, facing aft, in a shelter whose upper section was formed of canvas stretched over hickory bows—reason enough to call the cubicle a "gig-top."

Despite the four-wheeled tender's impressive contour, the engine could travel no more than 15 miles without stopping for water. Not surprisingly, a photograph of the *John Bull* made in the 1850s shows it coupled to a much larger version of the same tender, now riding on two trucks. Again there was a gig-top, but the roof projection up front had given way to a trim little cab straddling the locomotive's firebox.

Discounting the ravages of time, the machine underwent no further changes until 1893. Then it was removed from an engine shed where it had stood idle for twenty-seven years, and rebuilt for display at the World's Columbian Exposition. The restoration was undertaken by the Pennsylvania Railroad, which had absorbed the C&A in 1871. Trailed by two quaint coaches—one reclaimed from a Middlesex County farm where it had long served as a chicken coop—the tiny engine puffed from Jersey City to the Chicago fairground in something less than a week. Like the *Stourbridge Lion*, it is now on permanent exhibition at the Smithsonian Institution.

In 1832, a shop was erected in Hoboken, New Jersey, for the purpose of manufacturing the Camden & Amboy's own motive power. The fact that the locomotives would have to be floated by barge 25 miles to the line's eastern terminal did not trouble Robert Stevens, because he intended to collaborate with Isaac Dripps in their design, and the plant was only a short carriage ride from his home.

The first three "company" engines were noteworthy principally for the service they rendered between work-train runs. During those periods, Dripps used them as traveling schools for neophyte enginemen, explaining and demonstrating the proper procedures for getting traffic over the road.

To overzealous fireboys he emphasized the im-

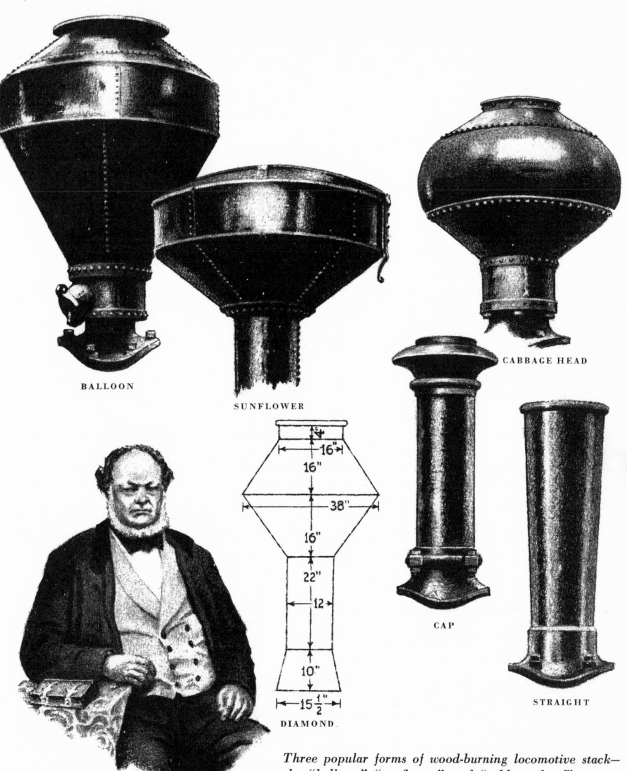

BALLOON

SUNFLOWER

CABBAGE HEAD

16"
16"
38"
16"
22"
12
10"
15 $\frac{1}{2}$"

DIAMOND

CAP

STRAIGHT

*Three popular forms of wood-burning locomotive stack—
the "balloon," "sunflower," and "cabbage head" types—
evolved from the more conservative C&A chimneys. The
"diamond" stack design, shown with its inventor, George S.
Griggs, was applied to practically all coal-burning engines
built between 1852 and the late 1870s. Thereafter, netting
arrested solids in the smokebox, permitting the use of
straight stacks, either with or without caps.*

portance of not overloading the grates with anthracite; the vast amount of air (approximately 250 cubic feet per pound of anthracite) required for rapid combustion could not penetrate a heavy bed of coal. Further, he discouraged them from spreading fresh fuel on a fire when a locomotive was working hard, since this lowered the furnace temperature at the worst possible time. In addition, the exhausts released by the straining cylinders created a fierce draft which drew nuggets the size of walnuts off a shovel and whisked them, unburned, through the flues and up the stack.

Similarly, water had to be admitted to the boiler judiciously. Since the pump used for injection was actuated by a half crank on one of the driving wheels, it ran whenever the engine did. Consequently, a shut-off cock was cut into the delivery pipe extend-

ing forward from the tender. It was the fireboy's responsibility to adjust it in ways that insured a conservative but adequate rate of feed. If the level in the boiler was too high, water sloshed through the throttle valve and entered the cylinders where, since it couldn't be compressed by the pistons, it blew out the heads. On the other hand, too low a level bared the vulnerable furnace crownsheet, causing it to buckle and let go. Then, because practically all of the fluid in the barrel was already heated to a temperature far above the atmospheric boiling point, the sudden release of the pressure which had kept it in a liquid state caused hundreds of gallons to vaporize in one horrendous sound. Tubular glass gauges had yet to be applied to locomotives, but spigots were placed at various heights above the crownsheet. If, upon being opened for checking, the bottom tap

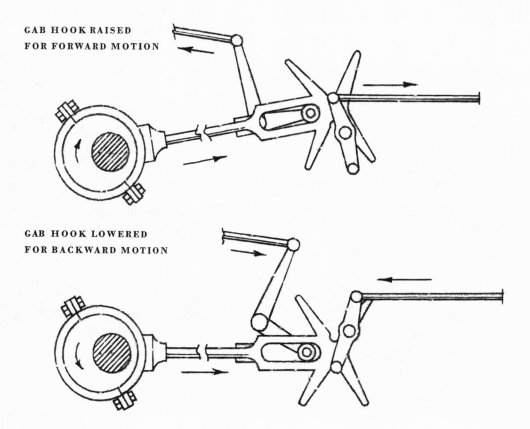

GAB HOOK RAISED
FOR FORWARD MOTION

GAB HOOK LOWERED
FOR BACKWARD MOTION

Basically similar to the Carmichael valve gear applied to steamboat engines, most early locomotive reversing mechanisms employed X-shaped "gab hooks" to impart motion to either the top or bottom ends of centrally pivoted rocker arms attached to the valve rods ahead. The assembly's prime movers were eccentrics mounted on the main axles.

46

Appropriately named the "Monster," the first of four 30-ton freight haulers placed in service on the Camden & Amboy shared with them the distinction of outweighing any other locomotives of that period. Their designer appeared bent upon incorporating all of the mechanical motions known to man.

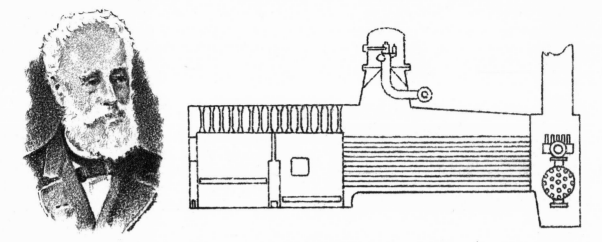

Innovative Isaac Dripps placed a dry boiler section ahead of the Monster's *firebox, and a blower equipped with a cluster of nozzles at the base of the stack. While both features were premature, the need for a combustion chamber, a multijet nozzle, and a stack blower arose a century later.*

spurted steam, it was time for the crew to signal for hand brakes and take unceremonious leave of the deck.

The driver's mechanical duties were limited to manipulating the throttle and a pair of reversing levers. Dripps and Stevens had adopted an arrangement then used by a number of British builders to work the pistons in the proper order for forward and backward running. Two circular plates with slightly off-center holes were mounted on a driving axle, and each of these "eccentrics" was girdled by a ring, or "collar," forged at one end of a long rod. On the opposite end was another forging shaped like a letter X, and this "gab hook" was given a push-pull action when the axle turned the eccentric. By throwing the reversing levers, the hooks could be raised or lowered to engage pins at either the top or bottom extremities of a pair of centrally pivoted rocker arms. In one position the hooks' shuttling motion caused the arms to teeter to and fro; in the other the sequence was changed to fro and to. Since the arms were linked to the valves which directed steam into and out of the cylinder ends, a corresponding change took place in the admission and exhaust pattern, and that reversed the locomotive. The entire mechanism

was called a "valve gear," and this particular design —the Carmichael type—had originally been developed for steamboat service by a firm in Dundee, Scotland.

Without doubt the Camden & Amboy's most impressive engine was a 30-ton freight hauler presumably built in 1834 and named the *Monster*. Apart from size, its most eye-arresting feature was a complex drive. Piston rods projecting forward from two 18-by-30-inch cylinders delivered tugs and thrusts to a pair of pendulum-like arms pivoted high on the smokebox front. As these "horse's necks" swung back and forth, their lower ends worked mainrods which stroked the third of four sets of 48-inch wheels. Connecting rods linked the first and second, and the third and fourth pairs, but power was transmitted from the third to the second through spur gears. That made it possible to position the two rods on each side of the machine, 180 degrees apart, and work them cooperatively, one pulling while the other pushed, and vice versa, thus neutralizing what would otherwise have been a collectively violent nosing action.

In designing the *Monster's* boiler, Dripps introduced an appendage that was of little value then but which proved indispensable a hundred years later.

This was a forward extension of the furnace, partially separated from the coal-burning section by a water-filled partition called a "bridge wall." Flames, gasses, and embers were forced to hurdle the obstruction and pass through the cavity before entering the flues. The object was to give the fuel particles escaping the grates additional time to be consumed. However, the small cavity contributed practically nothing to thermal efficiency and was soon converted into a supplementary furnace, fed coal through an opening on the right side of the engine. Inconveniently, stoking could only be done at terminals, way stations, or water stops. It remained for the huge boilers of a later day to make Dripps's "combustion chamber" theory work in practice.

Imperfect though the *Monster* was, it performed well enough for three similar machines to be ordered as late as 1853. Again Isaac Dripps supervised the construction, but the contract was handled by the Trenton Locomotive Works, which he and two partners founded that year. Nearly a decade earlier the Camden & Amboy's dwindling demand for new engines had made it impractical to maintain the specialized facilities and skilled labor force required to build them. Still, for a brief period the road's personnel had found satisfaction in championing the products of the Hoboken and Bordentown shops, maintaining that they were superior in every way to the offerings of independent manufacturers. "Company" locomotives would continue to be a source of pride for more than a century on the relatively few systems which "rolled their own."

7 The Dean of

In 1831 a Philadelphia machine-shop proprietor named Matthias W. Baldwin visited Bordentown to inspect the Camden & Amboy's newly arrived *Stevens*. He had just received an order for a locomotive and his customer, the Philadelphia, Germantown & Norristown Railroad, wanted one patterned along the lines of that Stephenson product.

A curious chain of events had led to Baldwin's commission. Like Davis, Costell, and Childs, he had been trained as a watchmaker, but in a city that still measured minutes and hours indifferently he found the trade unprofitable, and in 1825 he turned to manufacturing calico-printing cylinders and bookbinders' tools. Growing patronage soon led him to buy and install a cumbersome stationary engine to drive his lathes and pump the bellows of his forge. When it proved unsatisfactory he replaced it with a remarkable steam engine of his own design—an upright type mounted on a bed plate less than five feet

square. Contributing to its compact size was a cylinder whose outer face was grooved on opposite sides. An inverted yoke, with the piston rod gripping its center, slid up and down in the channels, eliminating the need for awkwardly projecting guide bars.

Almost at once, word of this little engine's reliable performance (seventy years later it still turned a shaft in a remote corner of the world's largest locomotive plant) brought Philadelphia's leading industrialists to Baldwin's Minor Street establishment to inspect it and order similar machines.

Another distinguished caller was Benjamin Franklin Peale, a son of Charles Willson Peale, the noted artist, scientist, and politician. Since his father's death this able promoter had managed a local museum bearing the family name. Always well attended, the institution became even more popular when he added to its fine-arts and natural-history exhibits a gallery devoted to mechanical wonders.

MATTHIAS W. BALDWIN

Matthias Baldwin founded the world's most productive locomotive works—a plant that produced more than 80,000 steam engines over a period of 118 years. A conservative designer, Baldwin predicated the success of his manufactory upon mechanical refinements, fine workmanship, and improved production methods.

Independent Builders

Peale's visit was prompted by an ambitious project. He intended to spike a circle of track to the floor and run a miniature locomotive upon it—one capable of hauling two cars seating eight adults at a time. He was certain that Philadelphians eager for rides would pack the hall for months to come, and equally convinced that Baldwin could build a successful locomotive. The challenge appealed to the shop proprietor, and with only vague published descriptions and drawings of England's Rainhill entries to guide him, he turned out a creditable steam midget which first clattered around the indoor loop on April 25, 1831.

True to Peale's prediction the attraction drew unprecedented crowds, a fact noted with particular interest by the directors of the newly chartered Philadelphia, Germantown & Norristown Railroad. They had not intended to use locomotives on the line they were pushing up the Schuylkill Valley, but

it now seemed likely that passengers would pay premium fares to be whisked across the countryside behind one. Further, an investment in an iron horse would indicate that they were men of vision meriting the confidence of potential investors. Certainly they kept a firm grip on the company's purse strings, for they offered Baldwin the penurious sum of $4,000 for a near-duplicate of a Stephenson machine. However, Baldwin was anxious to try his hand at a full-scale locomotive and accepted the assignment, though he must have known that imports not only commanded higher prices but were built by expert mechanics using metalworking tools superior to those in his or any other American shop. The boring machine had been introduced in England in 1775, the shaper in 1808, and the planer a decade later. Meanwhile, Baldwin and his fellow American mechanics of the early nineteenth century were hardly better off than James Watt, who thought he had a close fit

Out of this shop came the first of enough Baldwin steam locomotives to have formed a coupler-to-coupler power parade reaching from Philadelphia to St. Louis.

Similar to Stephenson's "Planet" class of engines, Baldwin's Old Ironsides *was built without benefit of the sophisticated power tools used by the English manufacturer.*

when, describing a stationary engine he built by hand in 1869, he wrote that the work was so well done he could not push a small coin between the piston and the cylinder at any place.

Examination of the Camden & Amboy's *Stevens* convinced Baldwin that a copy of that "Samson"-class engine would play hob with the PG&N's light trackwork. Instead he chose, as a prototype, a lighter Stephenson locomotive which applied the power of inside cylinders to a single driving axle. Construction problems led him to modify this "Planet"-class design. Among other frustrations he could find no foundry in the city capable of casting an iron wheel in one piece, and reluctantly resorted to built-up assemblies incorporating wooden spokes and felloes. The painstaking task of forming and fitting together a multitude of parts ended on November 23, 1832, when brass plates bearing the embossed name *Old Ironsides* were ceremoniously bolted to the boiler.

The five-ton locomotive underwent its first road test the same day, operating under a light head of steam from the company's depot on Ninth and Green streets to the township line and back again—a distance of six miles. A Philadelphia *Chronicle* reporter observed: "We rejoice in the success of the experiment, as it conclusively shows that Philadelphia, always famous for the skill of its mechanics, is enabled to produce steam engines for railroads combining so many superior features as to warrant the belief that her mechanics will hereafter supply nearly all of the public works of this description in the country."

The enthusiasm was premature, for on its first scheduled passenger assignment *Old Ironsides* ran aground when a driving wheel slipped inward on its axle. A call went out for a team of horses to return the train to the city and the engine to the Minor Street shop.

It was a simple matter to strengthen the wheel connections, but trouble of another sort plagued the machine during its first weeks of service. Upon opening the throttle wide, an intensified draft should have raised the furnace temperature. Instead, combustion was retarded. There, Baldwin had made the mistake of directing steam voided from both cylinders into a single duct shaped like an inverted T. As a result, heavy charges of vapor entering the two ends of the horizontal section lost their velocity when they collided at the base of the stem leading into the smoke-stack. The solution was to give each cylinder its own upward-curving exhaust pipe.

Thereafter, *Old Ironsides* ran as well as any other "Planet" engine—but not to the professed satisfaction of the PG&N's directors. Complaining of its failure to handle more than two coaches up a grade of 45 vertical feet to the mile, they refused to pay Baldwin the sum originally agreed upon, offering him instead a settlement of $3,500. He accepted it with the bitter pronouncement: "That is our last locomotive."

Within months he changed his mind to the extent of patenting a brass driving-wheel tire. His contention was that by varying the alloy's copper and zinc content a tread could be made sufficiently hard to withstand the punishment of high-speed passenger service, or soft enough to provide increased traction for heavy freight hauling.

He soon had a chance to test his theory. The prospering South Carolina Railroad needed a new engine, and when the West Point Foundry declined its order the company sent E. L. Miller north to evaluate the products of other builders. In Philadelphia the veteran designer liked the workmanship on *Old Ironsides* and persuaded Baldwin to sign his second commercial locomotive contract.

Miller recommended a hybrid machine combining the best features of the Mohawk & Hudson's *Brother Jonathan* and the same road's remodeled *John Bull*. While both of those engines had inside cylinders, swiveling guiding trucks, and single pairs of driving wheels, they differed in two important respects. One was the relative size of their boilers, and the other the placement of their cranked axles. By applying a very small firebox to the *Brother Jonathan*, John Jervis had provided enough clearance for the mainrods to straddle its flanks and stroke an axle placed behind it. On the other hand, the *John Bull's* capacious furnace blocked the passage of rods, and the axle was tucked under the barrel ahead. With a longer wheelbase, and no overhang at the rear, the *Brother Jonathan* rode smoothly at speeds above those considered safe for the tail-heavy *Bull*. Offsetting that advantage, the American engine's steaming capacity was limited, whereas the import's ample grate area and otherwise superior boiler insured rapid evaporation and abundant power. The Stephensons had borrowed the boiler design from another English locomotive builder, Edward Bury, of Liverpool. Offi-

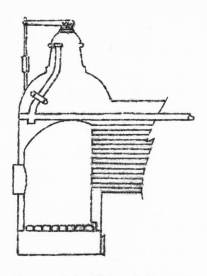

Invented by Edward Bury of Liverpool, the "haystack" type of firebox enjoyed international popularity for many years.

Baldwin gained more than half a foot in width for a Bury furnace by pressing the ends of half-cranked axles into off-center holes in the driving wheels. With that arrangement, the inner faces of the hubs became the webs of what were, in effect, full cranks.

cially the assembly bore his name, but railroaders on both sides of the Atlantic more often called it a "haystack" type because its most conspicuous feature —a very large steam-accumulating dome above the furnace—resembled the ricks favored by farmers at that time.

The challenge confronting Baldwin was to retain inside connections and still get a pair of mainrods around a Bury boiler's firebox to turn an axle at the rear. By placing his locomotive's cylinders as far apart as an engine's frames permitted, he could carry the rods past a slightly narrowed furnace. However these seemed no way to move the axle cranks corresponding distances outward, because those U-shaped members required thick side walls, or "webs," and the two adjacent to the driving wheels would take up all the space required for the crank pins.

Baldwin's solution to the problem was ingeniously simple. He forged an L-shaped half crank at each end of an axle and forced extensions of the pin sections into offset holes drilled through the wheel hubs. Thus the latter did double duty, serving as the outer webs of what, in effect, became widely separated full cranks.

Named the *E. L. Miller*, the South Carolina Railroad engine was completed on February 18, 1834. Apart from its brass tires, which wore down rapidly and were soon replaced with ones of iron, the machine proved so successful that the Pennsylvania Public Works Commission ordered a heavier Baldwin locomotive of the same type.

Three years earlier the state had opened to traffic portions of a single-track line being projected between the Schuylkill and Susquehanna rivers. This Philadelphia & Columbia Railroad was a unique transportation venture, since any resident of the commonwealth who owned a horse and a suitably flanged wagon or coach could, for a toll, play engineer, conductor, and dispatcher on its irons. Normal confusion turned to chaos when good Samaritans erected taverns wherever passing sidings were provided. There, potent cider brandy stiffened the determination of drivers, especially the teamsters hired by draying firms, to assert their rights on the rails ahead. Only one rule was inviolate. Any vehicle that passed a stubby mast placed halfway between two turnouts was authorized to proceed to the next siding, opposing traffic backing up the shorter distance. The

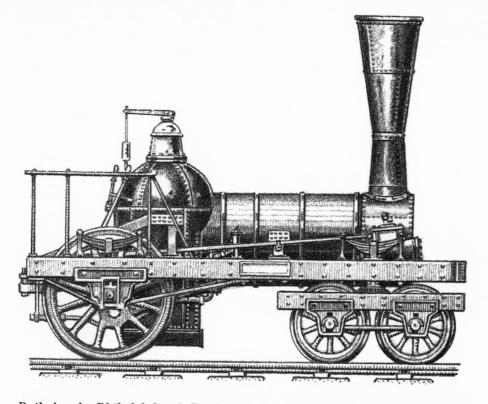

Built for the Philadelphia & Reading Railroad in 1837, Baldwin's Neversink *resembled his earlier* E. L. Miller *and* Lancaster. *During tests it handled as many as 52 coal "Jimmies" between terminals.*

prospect of having to yield as much as two miles of track encouraged teamsters and coachmen within contestable distance of a center post to rise from their seats and lay on the leather. Inevitably, head-on collisions were frequent and spectacular.

Trouble of another sort followed the commission's request, in 1832, to buy and test an English locomotive. Commercial draying firms objected, and they knew how to touch a whip to local senators and representatives. In turn, those guardians of the public trust showed a sudden concern for their rural constituents. Was a farmer bound for market on a facility paid for with his taxes to be crushed beneath the wheels of a monster which also fouled heaven's air and set the woodlands ablaze?

The farmers felt differently. The few who had risked life and limb on the line, as well as the many who had not, were weary of the carousing teamsters, and ready to let the locomotive come and drive them from the rails. Prominent Philadelphians, too, urged

the overseas purchase, pointing out that the growing number of steam trains serving Baltimore posed a threat to the Quaker City's inland trade. In the end the legislators knuckled under and approved the expenditure.

Following its arrival and assembly, the engine was transported by turnpike to Lancaster. The governor then declared a holiday, and thousands gathered at the county seat to watch the stranger thunder out of town. With some effort a preacher was found who was willing to risk perdition by offering a benediction. Presumably he made it long enough to turn celestial wrath to boredom, for when the throttle was opened the locomotive refused to budge. Draymen whistled and catcalled, but the crowd was generally sympathetic. Those nearest the engine seized every available handhold and tugged and shoved it into reluctant motion.

Despite the near-fiasco, the commission reasserted its faith in steam power by ordering five "Samsons"

Converted into a six-drivered locomotive in 1847, the Neversink *was destroyed by a boiler explosion the following year.*

from the Stephensons. Soon afterward, Baldwin received his Philadelphia & Columbia contract. With greater know-how and improved equipment, it took him less than four months to build a 17,000-pound locomotive named the *Lancaster*.

Among other innovations the engine introduced a new type of steam line joint. Previously, manufacturers had sealed those connections with canvas and red lead, a method which limited operating pressures to between 65 and 70 pounds to the square inch. The obvious way to prevent leakage was to set the safety valves to pop at 60 pounds and be content with moderately good performance. Baldwin was not. He provided all pipe ends with flanges, machined their faces flat and smooth, snugged them directly together, and had no trouble confining pressures of up to 120 pounds.

A second improved feature was a feedwater pump driven by one of the locomotive's piston rods. A hollow bar served both as a guide rod and the pump barrel, the plunger within it alternately drawing the liquid into a valve chamber at one end and ramming it on to the boiler. By releasing a single setscrew the chamber could be separated at the center, exposing every working part for cleaning or replacement.

The dependable and easily serviced *Lancaster* became a favorite of engine crews and mechanics alike.

The commission, too, took note of its economical operation and ordered ten more Baldwin locomotives before the close of 1836. In his annual report for that year, Master of Machinery A. Mehaffey commented on their trouble-free behavior and added with possible prejudice: "Two of the engines of English make have recently been sold, and it would have been a saving to the Commonwealth had they been given away for nothing the day they were placed upon the rails."

Baldwin found other customers for his six-wheelers, and from less than a dozen machinists and apprentices employed in 1834 his shop force burgeoned to three hundred. Production figures were impressive—five locomotives completed in 1834, fourteen in 1835, forty in 1836, and another forty during the opening months of 1837.

Then came the delayed reaction to former President Andrew Jackson's veto of a bill to recharter the Bank of the United States. Following the demise of that institution, which had helped regulate the nation's economy, there was a surge of easy credit, wildcat speculation, and inflation. Under these pressures the rivets in the national economy let go.

Business paralysis followed panic, and Baldwin, like other industrialists, was beset by creditors. Calling them together, he offered to surrender his new plant on Broad and Hamilton streets, his tools, his house, and lesser possessions. However, he pointed out that their total worth was no more than a quarter of what he owed. On the other hand, he confidently predicted that hard times would not long check the momentum of railroad building. In 1830 there had been 23 miles of line in the entire country; now there were nearly 2,000 either in use or under construction. Further, Pennsylvania led her sister states by a wide margin. According to a federal survey in 1836, Pennsylvania was in the process of adding 234 route miles to 392 already in operation, while that portion of Virginia which later became West Vir-

ginia ranked second, thanks to the ambitious Baltimore & Ohio, with 195 miles of track in service and 84 being built.

More locomotives obviously were needed for the lengthening lines, and Baldwin was sure that he could regain a profitable position in his trade once the nation's economy had recovered. Give him five years, he told his creditors, and he would pay back all his debts in full. They did, and he wiped the slate clean in 1842. Other trials were in store for Matthias W. Baldwin, but he was well on his way to becoming the dean of America's independent locomotive builders.

Philadelphia & Columbia coaches of the 1830s.

8 Philadelphia's

LONG AND NORRIS

Throughout his locomotive building career, Baldwin
never had to look beyond Philadelphia for competition. The greater part of it came from a firm originally
chartered as the American Steam Carriage Company
in 1828. The founder, Colonel Stephen H. Long, was
a graduate of the country's finest technical school—
the United States Military Academy at West Point.
Prior to, and during, the brief period he operated the
shop, Long was regularly employed as a construction
engineer by the Baltimore & Ohio and the Philadelphia & Columbia railroads. On both lines he left, as
evidence of his particular talent, handsome bridges
and viaducts fashioned of intricately spliced white
pine timbers. Although fragile in appearance, they
bore loads comparable to those supported by the far

58

more costly stone arches then in almost universal
use.

The colonel was less successful as a locomotive
designer. His first engine, completed in 1830, had a
boiler containing two flue-filled water sections arranged in tandem. Between them was a precursor of
the *Monster's* combustion chamber—a dry cavity in
which embers drawn from the rear honeycomb of
tubes were exposed to additional air and presumably
consumed. In actual practice, however, cinders accumulated there, blocking off the further flow of hot
gases. Following unsuccessful tests on the Newcastle
& Frenchtown Railroad, the four-ton engine was
dismantled.

Soon afterward, the colonel admitted to partnership his plant foreman, William Norris. That practical mechanic found no immediate profit in the
promotion, for Long was in the process of designing

Henry R. Campbell, a civil engineer employed by the Philadelphia, Germantown & Norristown Railroad, introduced the most popular nineteenth-century wheel arrangement with this 4-4-0 built in 1836. His failure to provide a weight-equalizing system made for poor roadability.

Transient Designers

an even worse locomotive. This time he placed two slender boilers side by side, with their forward ends sharing a single smokebox. At the rear they passed completely through a wide furnace. Those portions, enveloped by the fire, were provided with grooves which guided flames into a limited number of flues ahead. A large duct below the twin barrels carried additional gases to the smokestack. In still another attempt to create the strong draft needed to burn anthracite, the colonel made the chimney so tall it had to be tilted back on a hinge each time the engine approached a low bridge.

When the awkward machine went the way of its predecessor, William Norris assumed the role of chief designer and, with the assistance of a young mechanical genius named Joseph Harrison, he quickly gained a reputation for building more conventional—and more dependable—locomotives. In 1835 the firm pro-

duced the first of many six-wheelers resembling the Mohawk & Hudson's remodeled *John Bull*. Their fireboxes were necessarily placed behind the driving wheels, because Baldwin refused to grant rights to his newly patented half-crank arrangement. Making the most of the apparent handicap, Norris downplayed stability and stressed the traction gained by imposing all of the firebox weight upon the main axle.

In 1836 one of his sturdy freight haulers put an end to the widespread belief that locomotives could not climb heavy grades. The proving ground was an inclined plane on the Philadelphia & Columbia Railroad. Like the Mohawk & Hudson, the line had resorted to stationary engines and hemp cables to get traffic in and out of two river valleys. One installation was at Columbia, on the Susquehanna, and the other breasted a more formidable escarpment on the south side of Schuylkill, not far from the point where Philadelphia's Fairmount Park now crosses that stream. The latter, or Belmont Plane, raised and lowered cars 196 vertical feet in approximately half a mile. Since there was continuing trackage at both ends, a by-passing roadway was provided for teamsters and their horses.

Underrating the grip of smooth-tired wheels, the Public Works Commission gave little thought to building a similar bypass for locomotives, and less to the possibility of laying rails on a somewhat easier gradient and letting the new machines work trains up and down the hill. Instead, certain engines were assigned to the 12 miles of track below the incline, and others to the 70 miles extending westward from the summit.

Nevertheless, the ease with which a Norris six-wheeler hauled 135 tons of merchandise across the upland section of the road in the spring of 1836 led Master of Machinery Mehaffey to conduct a bold experiment. A larger locomotive of the same type—the *George Washington*—was delivered to the Philadelphia & Columbia on July 9, and the following day he had it fired up for a try at the Belmont Plane itself. The time was well chosen, that being a Sabbath, when all commercial traffic was barred from the line.

A reporter for New York City's *Railroad Journal* wrote of the event:

The weight of the George Washington is 14930 lbs. The load attached weighed 19200 lbs including the weight of 24 persons who were on the tender and Burthen Car. The Engine started immediately at the base without a running start, and dragged the said load of 19200 lbs the distance of 2800 feet in the space of two minutes and one second, or at the rate of 15½ miles per hour, pressure on the boiler a fraction under 60 lbs to the square inch. The Engine then descended the plane with the same load at various speeds, frequently stopping to test the security; the valves being reversed or set for going ahead; and when it was desired to stop altogether, the steam was let out very slowly, which brought her to a dead stand for a second or two, when she would immediately start up the grade. In this way, starting and stopping at pleasure, the time occupied in descending the 2800 feet was from 12 to 15 minutes, thus testing the perfect safety of her performance on the plane. She again ascended the plane with the same load and took her place on the road the same morning ready for service.

The report invites comment. First, there is the reference to steam braking—reversing the valve gear for deceleration. Awesome tonnages and mounting boiler pressures eventually put an end to the policy, but for many years enginemen resorted to it when emergencies warranted the risk of blowing out the cylinder heads. Again, it is interesting to note the uninhibited use of the pronouns "she" and "her." Clearly, at an early date, the sex of locomotives was authoritatively determined. Still one could wish the editors of the *Railroad Journal* had made an exception in the case of an engine named for the father of his country.

While the *George Washington* could not haul profitable payloads up the seven-percent Belmont slope, its performance demonstrated the practicality of two-, three-, and even four-percent grades. With that discovery engineers projecting rights-of-way through rugged country discarded the notion that inclined planes were as inescapable as locks on a canal. It took meandering routes to avoid them, but uninterruped flows of traffic justified the additional trackage.

The ability of Norris engines to handle heavy loads without slipping attracted other buyers—and the attention of Matthias Baldwin. Aware that four locomotives out of five were purchased for freight service, he had already taken one step to increase the pulling power of his own six-wheelers. Again he was indebted to E. L. Miller. In 1834 the Charlestonian had devised and patented a "traction increaser." It resembled a huge pair of scissors pointed downward and pivoted at the front of a tender. Normally, the crossed levers were spread wide apart, making no contact with the engine ahead. But when a train approached a grade the crew tugged up on the handles until they engaged two latches. In that position the partially closed blades bore down on extensions of the locomotive's underframe assembly, or "engine bed," transferring some of the fuel car's weight to the driving wheels.

Primitive though it was, the mechanism worked well enough for Baldwin to use it extensively, paying Miller a royalty of $100 a unit. However, any competitive edge it gave him was lost when Norris obtained rights to another levering device that served the same purpose and operated automatically. The

Dramatic proof that locomotives could climb heavy grades was provided by William Norris's George Washington, which blasted up the Philadelphia & Columbia's 7-percent Belmont Plane, northwest of the Quaker City, on July 10, 1836. Previously it had been thought that in mountainous country railroad cable hoists were as unavoidable as lift locks on a canal.

inventor was a Philadelphian named George Escol Sellers. In his arrangement the locomotive's main axle served as the fulcrum for a massive beam attached to the front of the tender and extending forward the length of the engine bed. Normally the beam was slightly elevated at the rear, but in response to the increased resistance of the trailing cars at starting or on grades it assumed a horizontal position and applied an upward thrust to the front of the locomotive, shifting much of the weight normally carried by the guiding truck to the traction wheels.

Baldwin's next move was to build heavier engines of three standardized designs, ranging from 20,000 to 26,000 pounds. Still shrugging off stability, his rival countered by switching from inside connections to more easily serviced outside cylinders and mainrods. Thus the sparring continued, with Norris holding an incontestable advantage. He was one of a large family of able engineers and business administrators who shared his enthusiasm for the screechings and clangings of the locomotive works, its fiery effusions, and the acrid smell of incandescent iron. Each of the Norrises contributed in his own way to the company's growth.

That orderly process was interrupted by the Panic of 1837. Then, in 1838, a windfall came when the post brought a letter from England, signed by a Captain Moorson, chief operating officer of the Birmingham & Gloucester Railway. It seemed that the line's locating engineer had bungled, elevating a stretch of track 286 feet in a distance of two miles. Aware of the *George Washington's* hill-climbing performance, the captain offered the sum of £1,500 for a locomotive capable of working 100 gross tons to the summit of this troublesome Lickey Incline at a speed of 14 miles per hour. Norris responded by building a 22,000 pound six-wheeler called the *England.* Delivered the following spring, it proved so satisfactory that the Birmingham & Gloucester sent back an order for sixteen more.

The purchase attracted attention throughout continental Europe. There, only the French were producing locomotives in large numbers, and the French machines were too individualistic to be mediocre—only excellent or very bad. Other countries tended to patronize British shops, but it now occurred to them that American engines might do better on tracks laid either in haste or over difficult terrain. Vexed by shipping delays, foreign customers urged American manufacturers to set up overseas plants. William Norris obliged, traveling by packet and stagecoach to Vienna, where he operated the Austrian empire's only locomotive-building works until the Revolution of 1848.

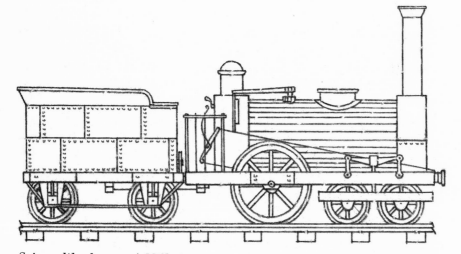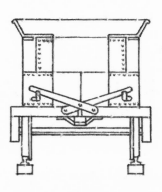

Scissorslike levers of Miller's traction increaser transferred part of the tender's weight to the engine's driving wheels when the handles were latched in raised positions.

After the Sellers brothers moved to Cincinnati, Ohio, George designed an eight-wheeler with auxiliary cylinders which drove a pair of rollers engaging the two sides of a central rail, to increase traction on hills. Although five successful engines of this type were constructed in the 1850s, Sellers collected only a fraction of the sum he personally invested in the venture.

CHARLES SELLERS

GEORGE ESCOL SELLERS

In Great Britain, both the Stephensons and Timothy Hackworth had already produced engines with six coupled driving wheels which could have lumbered up the Lickey Incline with heavier trains than the *England*. And Hackworth, in an early attempt to provide more pulling power, had even gone further, replacing *Puffing Billy's* four driving wheels with eight. However, the big British engines were stiff-legged brutes, better suited to colliery service than mainline running. They needed guiding trucks up front as much as the Norris and Baldwin products needed more traction wheels in the rear. The designer who first proposed combining the two features was the same Philadelphian who had invented the automatic traction increaser.

GEORGE ESCOL SELLERS

During the 1830s and early 1840s, this country's largest locomotive repair shops served the Philadelphia & Columbia Railroad at Parkesburg, forty-four miles west of the Quaker City. In peak years the complex boasted a plant manager, a foreman, thirteen machin-

ists, three blacksmiths, one coppersmith, three file makers, one pattern maker, three carpenters, one stationary engineer, four assistants, and a watchman. The monthly payroll for the 32 employees came to $1,087.88, or an average of slightly less than $34 apiece.

To the foreman, John Brandt, fell the responsibility of correcting the early mistakes of both British and domestic engine designers. Making the most of an 1834 inspection tour by members of the Public Works Commission, he suggested to the chairman, James Cameron, that better locomotives might be built by a Cardington, Pennsylvania, concern named Coleman Sellers & Sons. Cameron promised to look into the matter, and the next time business took him to Philadelphia, he coached to the nearby foundry and machine works. The father had recently died, leaving his two sons, Charles and George, to operate the establishment. The commissioner found them knowledgeable, and the plant's equipment second to none. Among other power tools, he was shown what was then the only iron planer in the state, and a lathe large enough to turn cylinders three yards long and nearly five feet in diameter. Both were used in the

63

manufacture of rolls and housings for metal, flour, and paper mills.

The prospect of designing and constructing a locomotive appealed to the younger brother, George, and he prepared a number of preliminary sketches. He had reason to regret it when Cameron and Brandt failed to see eye to eye on any of the original features he proposed, one disapproving of whatever the other was willing to accept. Ironically, they could only agree that the locomotive must have inside connections and driving wheels positioned behind the furnace—which was out of the question because Baldwin's half cranks were already protected by a patent application. Sellers finally submitted two designs, guaranteeing both against injurious oscillations. In one he adhered to the basic pattern of the Philadelphia & Columbia's recently acquired *Lancaster,* but moved the cylinders and mainrods outside the frames. In the other, those parts were set close together and drove a cranked main axle ahead of the firebox. Then, to improve stability, a second driving axle was placed behind the furnace. Outside connecting rods provided the power linkage.

There it was—the first proposed eight-wheeler, or in the Whyte classification system adopted in the twentieth century, a 4-4-0, the figures denoting an engine with four guiding wheels, four driving wheels, and no trailing wheels. Usually the eight-wheeler was simply referred to as the "American type," which was entirely fitting, for prior to 1900 American manufacturers turned out 25,000 of these machines, or three to one of any other kind.

Commissioner Cameron favored the innovative wheel arrangement, but Brandt objected to its complexity, and after much debate Sellers received an order for two 4-2-0s. Completed in 1835 and 1836, his *America* and *Sampson* introduced the traction increasers later adopted by Norris. Of greatest importance, they were the earliest engines to incorporate the following features:

1. Wedge-shaped weights bolted between the spokes of each driving wheel directly opposite the crank pins. Never before had counterbalances been used to reduce the nosing and hammering caused by flaying mainrods.

2. Engine beds formed of iron bars rather than cumbersome hardwood.

3. Guiding trucks with leaf springs beneath their swiveling cross members, or "bolsters," rather than on the locomotive's side frames above. The earlier setup had called for outside bearings to transmit weight to the truck sides, and when the two springs bottomed simultaneously there were four points of engine suspension instead of the desired three. That could not happen with the new design.

Sellers's 4-4-0 never got beyond the drafting board stage, but in 1836 an American-type locomotive was built by the neighboring firm of James Brooks & Company and placed in service by the Philadelphia, Germantown & Norristown Railroad. The patentee was Henry R. Campbell, a civil engineer employed by the line. His machine fell short of expectations because its independently sprung axles failed to equalize the weight applied to the rails.

Given the opportunity, it seems likely that George Escol Sellers would have turned his attention to this matter of load distribution. As it was, the Panic of 1837 closed the doors of the family plant in Cardington forever, and in 1841 he and Charles moved on to Cincinnati, Ohio, where they later established a rolling mill and wire-drawing works.

Presumably Campbell was too occupied with other matters to refine his primitive 4-4-0, and neither Norris nor Baldwin saw in the design an immediate threat to their six-wheelers. The latter was particularly critical of multiple-drivered engines, contending that the wheels would slip to varying degrees on curves, abrading the tires to unequal diameters. The two established builders reckoned without the competition.

EASTWICK AND HARRISON

Between 1830 and 1836 a short but amply financed line was pushed into the anthracite fields below Hazelton, Pennsylvania. The purpose of this Beaver Meadow Railroad was to replace a network of wagon trails linking back-country mines with the Lehigh Coal & Navigation Company's loading basin at Mauch Chunk (now Jim Thorpe). Already, more than a thousand canal boats shuttled between that terminal and Philadelphia, bearing 200,000 tons of fuel to market annually.

Anticipating heavy and enduring traffic, the Beaver Meadow's owners insisted upon the best available

Returned to its builder for remodeling in 1837, the Beaver Meadow's Hercules was vastly improved by Joseph Harrison.

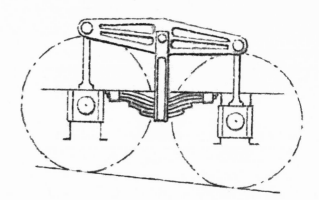

Harrison's principal contribution to the Hercules—*and the industry—was an equalizing system which kept all wheels in firm contact with the rails.*

trackwork. With optimism, too, they scorned the use of inclined planes where their contemporaries would still have thought such structures unavoidable. Thus, in a region of precipitous ravines, the roadway was elevated as much as 96 feet to the mile. It followed that no flatland locomotive could work a string of four-wheeled hopper cars, or "Jimmies," over the sharply tilted rails.

In 1835 the directors took their motive power problem to Philadelphia's Garrett & Eastwick, manufacturers of stationary steam motors. The junior partner, Andrew Eastwick, was a venturesome engineer who welcomed a chance to free his company's products from monotonously slapping factory belts, and within months he put together a creditable coal hauler.

Named for the Beaver Meadow's president, the *Samuel D. Ingham* proved so satisfactory that in the summer of 1836 the road awarded the firm a second contract. By then Eastwick had read descriptions of Campbell's forthcoming 4-4-0. He liked and adopted the basic design, but anticipated the shortcomings of the springing arrangement. His own plans called for the driving wheels to be mounted on what he called a "vibrating frame"—a separate carriage attached to the bottom of the engine bed with a transverse center bearing. This would permit the trucklike unit to rock forward and backward, accommodating itself to track irregularities.

As the inventor should have foreseen, his completed *Hercules* behaved in the desired manner only when the rails rose and fell in unison. More often, one running surface dipped where the other humped, and at such times the machine rode no better than Campbell's eight-wheeler.

Nevertheless, Eastwick had taken a step in the right direction. His next was to hire as his shop foreman Norris's former designing assistant. The entire industry benefited when, in the process of remodeling the *Hercules*, that brilliant young man introduced the most monumental locomotive improvement since the guiding truck. This was a wheel-equalizing system so sound that it is still used on practically every locomotive in the world, whether steam, electric, diesel, or gas turbine.

What Harrison did was to replace the teeter-tottering undercarriage with two spring-cushioned rocking beams, pivoted at their centers above the *Hercules'* side frames. From their ends, pins bore down on axle bearings, or "driving boxes," which were free to move vertically between flanking guide bars. Less awkward than Eastwick's vibrating frame, the assembly permitted the same seesawing action. In addition, the beams, or "equalizers," could tilt independently of one another, holding all four traction wheels in balanced contact with the most uneven rails.

Regrettably, no combination of equalizers and

66

springs could dampen the shock waves of the Panic of 1837. The two ensuing years were lean ones for the reincorporated firm of Eastwick & Harrison. Then, in the fall of 1839, an order came from the Philadelphia & Reading Railroad. A third of a century later, this greatest of anthracite carriers would absorb the Philadelphia, Germantown & Norristown and thereafter boast that *Old Ironsides* was its first locomotive. But at the moment, the up-and-coming line would not have paid the price of scrap metal for that little engine. Stone coal was moving again, and traffic demanded a workhorse of more than ordinary power. Between them, Eastwick and Harrison produced a chunky eight-wheeler named the *Gowan & Marx*. It tipped the beam at 11 tons, as against 15 for the *Hercules*. Still, by placing the firebox above, rather than ahead of the rear drivers, the weight used for traction was substantially increased. Further, a pair of 12⅛ by 18-inch cylinders stroked wheels only 3½ feet in diameter. Add a working pressure of 130 pounds to the square inch, and the Reading had every reason to expect sensational performance.

No one was disappointed. On February 20, 1840, the *Gowan & Marx* trundled 101 loaded Jimmies nearly 60 miles to tidewater at an average speed of 9.8 miles an hour. Granted, there was only one short stretch of ascending track. It remained remarkable that less than a decade earlier contracts had required engines to pull no more than three times their own weight, and here was a 22,000-pounder drawing 412 tons—a ratio approaching forty to one.

As it hammered down the Schuylkill Valley, the locomotive forged a strange future for its builders. Five thousand miles away, word of the exploit reached Nicholas I, Czar of Russia. Having rusted his hands with the blood of Persia, Turkey, and Poland, Nikolai Pavlovich was called the "Iron Czar" —and liked it. Now it occurred to him that he could improve the epithet by riding between St. Petersburg and Moscow behind huge iron horses. Accordingly, he dispatched a team of army engineers to Reading, where they watched the *Gowan & Marx* wring the work of 8,000 serfs from three tons of red-ash anthracite and 3,000 gallons of water.

Not long afterward, Eastwick and Harrison were invited to establish an engine works in Aleksandrovsk. They did, closing their Philadelphia plant in 1842. Among the two hundred locomotives the expatriates constructed for the St. Petersburg & Moscow Railway were the first of a new wheel arrangement— the 2-6-0. This Mogul type later found favor in the United States. So did its autocratic name. Journalists and fiction writers pounced upon it, and thereafter persisted in calling any engine of immense proportions a "mighty Mogul." Literature's gain was accuracy's loss, for 2-6-0s were soon eclipsed in power.

9 The Trials of

Prospering in well-established trades, New England's industrialists were in no great hurry to build locomotives. Add to that the region's distrust of any product manufactured south of Connecticut, and British suppliers enjoyed a brief monopoly there.

The most popular imports were the Stephensons' "Planets," and with them came the Newcastle mechanics who made such a mystery of uncrating and assembling the parts. Electing to stay on as engineers, these taciturn fellows became equally adept at turning the simplest throw of a lever or twist of a valve into a theatrical production. Their footplate performances and tasteful attire—they wore calf-hugging breeches, flowered waistcoats, and plug hats—won them the confidence of their employers and the admiration of the public.

Possibly the most accomplished dandy was a William Robinson, who drove the Boston & Lowell Railroad's first locomotive—it was another of those *John*

Bulls—throughout the late spring of 1835. Unlike the promoted mechanics, he had crossed the Atlantic for the express purpose of demonstrating the finer points of engine handling. He was at his best on those judiciously rare occasions when he flayed his arms for an unscheduled stop. As soon as the guards aboard the coaches mastered momentum the passengers could be counted upon to race forward to the green-and-black machine, where the engineer thoughtfully awaited their arrival before removing his topper, kid gloves, and vest. Then, spanner in hand, he dropped to the ground and disappeared between the driving wheels. Minutes later he crawled back out, holding up for all to see a heavy bolt worn so nearly through that it would have let go in another mile. No one knew exactly what its purpose was, or how the perceptive engineer had anticipated its failure. Only one thing was certain; Robinson had averted a frightful accident. To his further credit he

GEORGE WASHINGTON WHISTLER

An internationally recognized authority on the construction, operation, and management of railroads, George Washington Whistler was a second-generation soldier and engineer. His father, John Whistler, had served on the side of the Crown in the Revolutionary War, returned to America at the close of hostilities, and in 1803 supervised the construction of Fort Dearborn, near the mouth of the Chicago River. Born at Fort Wayne in 1800, his son was frontier-bred, attended the U.S. Military Academy at West Point, and was a member of the elite Corps of Engineers.

Whistler and Winans

carried a well-stocked tool chest, from which he produced an identical bolt in sound condition. It was amazing how quickly he got it in place and brought his train safely into Boston or Lowell.

Of course, neither bolt served any mechanical purpose. The worn bolt was tied beneath the engine with twine before the run began, and Robinson lashed the other to the undercarriage while he was presumably snugging it tight with his wrench. This king-bolt trick was as old as Europe's public coach trade. Overseas an accomplice planted among the passengers burst into grateful tears and offered his hat for contributions for the driver. Robinson's reward was more valuable than money—columns of praise in Boston's *Advertiser* and *Transcript*.

At that time, the superintendent of the B&L's locomotive and car shops in Lowell was Major George Washington Whistler, a soldier engineer with an impressive railroading background. Like Colonel Long,

he had attended West Point and been sent by the Army to assist the Baltimore & Ohio in the laying of its roadway. With him went William Gibbs McNeill, another Academy graduate whose sister he later married. In 1828 the young officers spent several months abroad, studying British railway practices and the characteristics of English engines. Upon their return they made good use of their abilities and experience—Captain McNeill becoming chief engineer of the Boston & Providence Railroad, and the major projecting the route for a connecting line which never got farther west than Stonington, Connecticut, but whose coaches bore the hopeful legend: "New York, Providence & Boston."

His surveys completed, Whistler moved on to Lowell in 1834. By then the B&L's *John Bull* had been standing idle for a year, awaiting the completion of track and the arrival of William Robinson. At the management's request, he filled in the time by

69

building two basically similar engines, thereby establishing New England's earliest locomotive manufactory. Prior to Whistler's venture into locomotive building, only one engine had been built in New England, the Boston & Worcester's *Yankee*. However, its manufacturer, the Mill Dam Factory, was not established for that purpose and it never produced another locomotive.

Late in June, 1835, the first of Whistler's homemade machines was ready for the rails, presenting the directors with a christening problem. They wanted to honor the road's president, but his surname happened to be Jackson, and a locomotive by that name would be a source of political irritation around Whiggish Boston. After giving the matter much thought they settled for his first name, and the little engine became the *Patrick*.

A more difficult situation confronted William Robinson when Whistler transferred the *Bull's* passenger assignments to the *Patrick* and its sister locomotive, the *Lowell*. The transplanted dandy considered this an affront to his motherland, but vanity compelled him to drive whichever Yankee machine was coupled to the coaches. Everyone agreed that he did it at great personal risk, for the 2-2-0s broke down with alarming frequency. Steam lines ruptured, water pumps clogged, and castings cracked. In desperation Whistler finally arranged for a trusted mechanic to stand a night's watch in the engine house. The following morning the truth came out. Robinson had paid the shed a predawn visit and painstakingly prepared one of the locomotives for another road failure. Not content with running him off the property, the major saw him aboard the next Liverpool-bound packet.

Work was begun on two more engines, the *Boston* and the *Merrimac,* before Whistler returned to Stonington to direct the construction of the New York, Providence & Boston's roadway. He had not been there long when the promoters of the most ambitious transportation venture yet franchised in New England sought his services as chief engineer. Their project, the Western Railroad, would accomplish what the advocates of a trans-Massachusetts canal had dreamed of doing ten years before—tap off a substantial part of New York City's lucrative inland trade at Albany. Agreements had already been reached for connections with the completed Boston & Worcester Railroad to the east and the recently chartered Albany & West Stockbridge Railroad at the New York State line. To link the two, the Western's irons must be thrust across the unaccommodating Berkshire Hills. Whistler undertook the task, and immediately found himself at odds with many of the directors who, on the one hand, favored holding construction costs to a minimum and, on the other, recommended a roundabout route serving every village willing to subscribe to the company's stock. His diplomatic success in winning support for the most direct alignment possible was matched by the engineering success with which he held the Western's maximum grade to a stiff but acceptable 87 feet to the mile.

The high point of his association with the road came three days after Christmas, 1841, when, at a banquet celebrating the safe passage of the first through train from Boston to Albany, toasts were drunk to his indomitable spirit and continued good health. Thereafter the directors who had previously opposed him did their best to undermine both. They pointed out that any number of bright young men would jump at a chance to assume his traffic supervising duties at a lower salary, and raised repeated objections to his having purchased a number of engines from an out-of-state builder—Ross Winans of Baltimore. The major ended the controversy by announcing that he was going to Russia at the Iron Czar's request, to lay out a route for the St. Petersburg & Moscow Railway.

Whistler remained abroad until 1849, when a cholera epidemic cut short his useful career. By then one of his sons, James Abbott McNeill Whistler, had attended the Imperial Art Institute, where he showed the beginnings of his great talent as a painter and etcher. Taking note of the senior Whistler's less familiar talent, Angus Sinclair wrote in 1907: "It is a curious comment on how the literary world discriminates between the man of utility and the man of art that encyclopedias have extended biographies of the son, the artist, while not one word is said about the father who originated methods and forms of railroad business which became the inheritance of the whole world and are used today."

Asked by the Czar to recommend an American qualified to set up a car shop in Aleksandrovsk, Whistler urged him to call on the man whose locomotives had caused such a rumpus on the Western Railroad. The Czar did, and Ross Winans not only constructed the plant but supervised the construction of a number of luxurious coaches before turning the property over to two of his sons, who managed it capably for twenty-two years.

Having no taste for life abroad, Winans resumed operations in Baltimore. He had first gone there in 1828 to sell horses bred on his Vernon, New Jersey, farm to the B&O. Like all others at that time, the company's cars were equipped with wheels that turned freely on rigid axles, and a ride in one of them convinced him that the arrangement was poorly suited to rail-borne vehicles. Lateral thrusts on curves were checked so abruptly by the unyielding rails that the hub holes quickly wore out of round, causing the encircling metal to drag against the axle offsets, or shoulders. Winans had a better idea—to press-fit the wheels firmly on their axles, and with the latter's projecting ends placed in outside bearings, or "journal boxes," let the assemblies rotate as one.

To prove the superiority of what he dubbed his "friction wheel" design (a misnomer since it reduced friction instead of increasing it), Winans conducted a striking demonstration in Baltimore's newly completed Exchange Building. A continuous stairwell passed through the structure, and he arranged with the management to lay a miniature track along an upper-story corridor. Then, placing a 100-pound car equipped with his undercarriage on the rails as far as possible from the open shaft, he attached a stout cord to it and ran the line over a pulley wheel at the edge of the well. Finally, he tied a half-pound weight to the cord's free-hanging end and invited one of the many B&O directors present to seat himself in the conveyance. The volunteer was ninety-one-year-old Charles Carroll, the only surviving signer of the Declaration of Independence. When Winans released the eight-ounce bob it descended to the foyer, drawing the car and its distinguished passenger smoothly along the track. The experiment was later repeated with what proved to be the maximum load the little weight could move—460 pounds! A contract was drawn up, and thereafter all of the B&O's coaches and freight wagons rolled on Winans's friction wheels.

This test was the first conducted in America in which a precise relationship was established between pulling effort and resistance on dry and level rails. Had it been possible to replace the car with an engine, whatever weight the machine could have hoisted up the well without slipping would have been its rated "tractive force." In days to come that important locomotive characteristic would be predetermined by a formula involving five factors: operating boiler pressure less 15 percent (this being the accepted loss between the boiler and the cylinders), piston area, length of stroke, driving-wheel diameter, and weight upon drivers. Meanwhile, trial and error had to do.

Winans next developed a swiveling truck incorporating his unitized wheels and axles. With two of these beneath it a coach more than twice as long as those then in service could negotiate the B&O's sharp curves. The first car constructed from his plans, the *Columbia,* was not as finely appointed as the ones he later designed for the Czar, but it introduced a number of lasting features. Among them were open platforms at the ends, a central corridor, and a coal stove that served its purpose as indifferently as the cuspidors flanking the aisle.

Like other inventors, Winans found it easier to obtain patents than to fight infringement on them. He was robbed of his friction wheels in England, just as the Stephensons and Edward Bury were denied the royalties they should have received from American imitators. He made out better when a New York court adjudged the Schenectady & Troy Railroad guilty of copying his coaches too faithfully. Still, no helpful precedent was set, for soon every line in the land was doing the same thing, and he had neither the funds nor desire to spend the rest of his life in litigation.

Winans turned his attention to locomotive improvements at an early date. His first opportunity came when the Baltimore & Susquehanna Railroad enlisted his aid in 1832. A "Samson" engine was damaging its rails, and with or without knowledge of John B. Jervis's new guiding truck he applied one like it to the import. Not long afterward he collaborated with Phineas Davis in designing a modified B&O "grasshopper" called the *Traveller.* Its most noteworthy feature was a combination of levers which gave an engineer the option of transmitting power to either one or two pairs of wheels. The latter hookup provided maximum pulling force while starting and on grades. At other times accumulated momentum reduced the need for traction, and the friction and bucking produced by the crude gears of that period were materially reduced by disengaging the forward axle.

Following the accidental death of Davis in 1833, Winans and the Baltimore & Ohio's superintendent of machinery, George Gillingham, operated the company's Mount Clare shops on a semi-independent basis. The understanding was that they would receive a flat $5,000 for each locomotive they built for the B&O and could accept orders from any other line during slack periods. The arrangement proved mutually unsatisfactory, the railroad demanding ever larger engines, and a new chief executive, Louis McLean, objecting to the builders' continued use of vertical boilers. Winans and Gillingham contended, rightly but nearsightedly, that the "pickle bottle" design developed by Davis was more efficient and safe than any horizontal type. They were still defending their stand when the Panic of 1837 gave McLean a good excuse to reclaim the plant and put his own mechanics to work overhauling idled cars and locomotives.

Among the last Winans engines turned out at Mount Clare were eight retaining upright barrels but employing horizontal cylinders. Their behavior was wonderful to watch, because their main and side rods stroked in opposite directions. Intermediate gears produced the strange action, which suggested that while the pistons made every effort to move the the machines one way, the wheels perversely drove them the other. Appropriately they were nicknamed "Crabs."

Winans spent the depression years drafting plans for locomotives powerful enough to challenge the mountains west of Cumberland, Maryland, and in his patent application of 1842 he incorporated all of his thoughts and claims in a single sentence long enough to confound the best of lawyers. It began:

"I claim as my invention, the construction and use of a locomotive engine, having six or eight driving wheels, the axles of which are placed parallel to each other, and which are to preserve that parallelism during the whole action of the engine, whether running upon straight or curved roads; the said axles having sufficient end play to allow the wheels, when the whole of them are provided with flanges, to adapt themselves to the curvature of the road; or instead of this end play of the axles, the constructing of two pairs of wheels where eight are used, without flanges. . . ."

In the more direct language of his trade he was proposing either lateral-play axles or "blind" tires to prevent binding on winding rails. There were more sophisticated ways of doing it, but his had the virtue of simplicity, and builder after builder adopted them. This time his patent could be legally contested, since neither arrangement involved an innovative mechanism. One was sorely needed when sliding axles were used—some sort of spring-loaded device which would return the shafts to their central positions on straightaways. Nearly a century passed before manufacturers gave the matter much thought. Meanwhile, flangeless tires were preferable, and served their purpose well.

Although Winans anticipated orders from the B&O, his first customer was an old acquaintance, Major Whistler. Their friendship dated back to the days when the army engineer was overseeing the laying of track out of Baltimore. More recently, Whistler had bought two of his "Crabs," built on speculation and stored at Mount Clare prior to their delivery to the Western Railroad in 1840. Unquestionably they were more powerful than the mediocre copies of Stephenson machines previously bought by the line, but the major's detractors belabored the fact that when their stacks were shortened to get them through the road's covered bridges some steaming capacity was lost. It could not have been much, for on May 6, 1842, the Springfield *Gazette* reported that one of them had just charged up the Westfield River gorge east of town with sixty-eight freight cars. Contributing to the train's gross weight of 356 tons were 1,330 swine, 40 cattle, 40 bales of wool, 350 barrels of flour, and 40,000 pounds of shingles.

Even more remarkable performance could be expected of the engines now proposed by Winans—locomotives similar in their mechanical action to the "Crabs," but employing eight 33-inch-diameter driving wheels. Risking the directors' further displeasures, Whistler ordered three of them, and for want of shop facilities Winans turned their construction over to the newly reorganized firm of Baldwin & Whitney.

By then the nation's economy was gathering mo-

William Norris's brother Septimus employed Winans's flangeless driving tire arrangement when he built the first 10-wheeler for the Philadelphia & Reading in 1874. Contrary to predictions, the Chesapeake did not jump the rails.

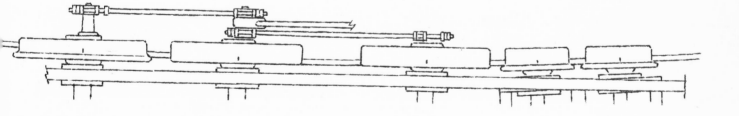

Disapproving of both "blind" driving wheel tires and lateral-play axles, Matthias Baldwin designed a "flexible beam" truck to provide flexibility for his multi-coupled locomotives. Ball-and-socket joints at the centers of the side frames permitted them to angle in every direction, and cylindrical bearings held the axles parallel when the wheels shifted out of alignment on curves.

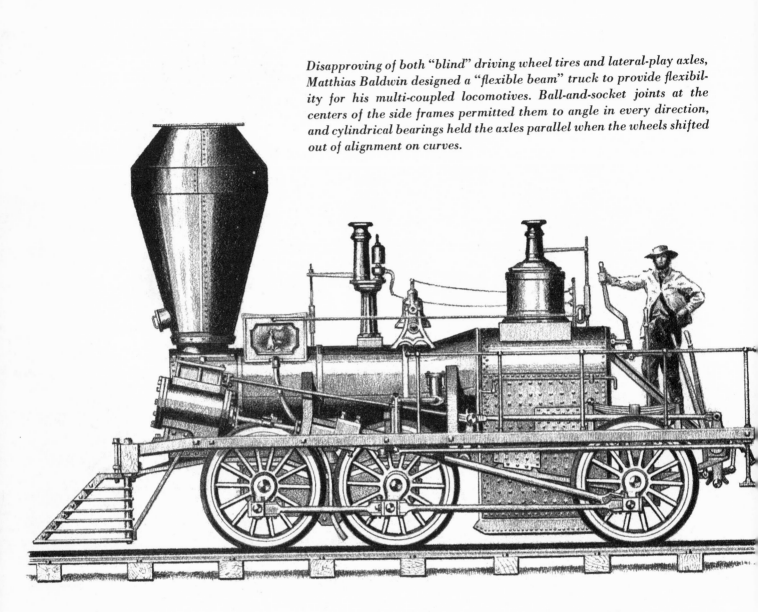

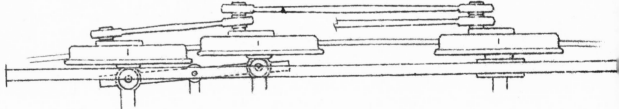

Shortly before Ross Winans opened his own Baltimore shops in 1844, he prepared the plans for three Western Railroad of Massachusetts "Mud Diggers," and turned the construction over to Baldwin & Whitney.

mentum for another boom, and with substantial loans from British investors the Baltimore & Ohio could not only continue its thrust toward Wheeling, Virginia, but add to its motive power roster. The road had already sampled the products of independent manufacturers, purchasing nine Norris 4-2-0s and five Eastwick & Harrison 4-4-0s. The latter builders' final offering, a slim-barreled passenger engine named *Mercury*, was clocked upon occasions at 60 miles an hour. Contributing to its roadability were long leaf springs which bridged the journal boxes on either side of the guiding truck. Like the equalizing beams above the driving wheel bearings, they tilted forward and backward on rough track, providing comparable stability up front. In two locomotives then—this swift machine and the freight-hauling *Gowan & Marx*—Joseph Harrison and Andrew Eastwick focused attention upon the remarkable potential of the "American" type as a dual-service machine.

Nevertheless, the design was poorly suited to the B&O's steep Allegheny grades, and between 1844 and 1847 Winans built 0-8-0s for the line in a new

plant of his own a stone's throw from the Mount Clare shops. If he resented having to use horizontal boilers with Bury furnaces at the road's insistence, he at least found satisfaction in improving the fireboxes by adding boxlike extensions at the rear to provide an unprecedented 17 square feet of grate area for slow-burning anthracite. Of more lasting importance, he introduced cast-iron drivers with "chilled" rims. His patented process called for that part of the mold which formed the wheel peripheries to be made of the same metal, rather than of sand. Where molten iron contacted the confining ring it solidified almost at once, producing treads and flanges of extremely hard and wear-resisting crystalline texture.

Although the locomotives bore such impressive names as *Gladiator*, *Hercules*, *Buffaloe*, and *Elephant*, enginemen chose to call them "Mud Diggers." Admittedly their hammering action caused clay to well up between the ties in wet weather, but in other respects they proved so satisfactory that a few remained in service until 1865.

Throughout the intervening years Winans all but

75

Against Isaac Dripps's advice, Robert Stevens saddled the Camden & Amboy with a fleet of ungainly "Crampton"-type locomotives between 1847 and 1852. Their slim boilers were inadequate, and the six-wheeled guiding trucks carried a great deal of weight which might better have been used for traction.

ignored the work of his contemporaries. Possibly that was because the only impractical engine he ever built resulted from his one attempt to fall in line with a briefly popular designing trend. The fad began in England, where such noted motive power authorities as T. R. Crampton, J. E. McConnell, and F. Trevithick (a son of the Cornish pioneer) convinced themselves and their customers that high express-train speeds called for single pairs of drivers seven to eight feet in diameter. It was true that on dry and nearly level track their machines could run as fast as men cared to travel, but the slender boilers and fireboxes squeezed between their towering wheels had neither the steaming capacity for sustained performances nor the weight to provide traction for heavy trains.

On a trip abroad in 1845, Camden & Amboy president Robert Stevens fancied he saw, in the "Cramptons," engines which could be operated at the 100-mile-an-hour velocities prophesied by his father. Back in the States he continued to hear glowing reports of the speedsters, and in 1847 he instructed Isaac Dripps to design a C&A version of the type. For unexplained reasons, two years elapsed before the reincorporated Philadelphia firm of Messrs. Norris Brothers delivered this *John Stevens*. Its most conspicuous feature was the saucer-like appearance of its eight-foot drivers, produced by filling the gaps between the spokes with wood insets. The object was to avoid picking up bits of ballast and paddling them far and wide. Of greater interest to locomotive his-

Defying classification by Whyte's system, the Utica & Schenectady's Lightning *was built by the Schenectady Locomotive Engine Manufactory from the drawings of Edward S. Norris in 1849. Discouraging sales led the designer and his brother, Septimus Norris, to relinquish control of the firm, which went on to become the principal plant of the American Locomotive Company.*

torians, the *Stevens* was the first engine ever equipped with a six-wheeled guiding truck and, with the exception of others of its class, the last until 1939. Unfortunately the swiveling assembly carried more than its share of the boiler's weight, aggravating the already serious problem of poor traction. Dripps opposed further efforts to improve the design, but he was overruled, and by 1851 the C&A owned a fleet of modified although hardly better 6-2-0s.

Ross Winans should have profited from the New Jersey road's experience. However, he may well have been misled by enthusiastic accounts of another high-wheeler of related origin. In 1848 a group of Schenectady, New York, businessmen raised $40,000 to construct a local engine manufactory. Knowing no-

thing about the trade, they urged the Messrs. Norris to equip and manage the plant with the option of buying and operating it later as a branch of their Philadelphia establishment. Indicating the prolific nature of the Norris family, one brother was named Septimus, and he and another, Edward, undertook the assignment, leaving a third, Richard, in charge of the home enterprise. Septimus had already worked on the *John Stevens*, and as chief designer of the Schenectady shops he drafted plans for a locomotive incorporating his own ideas of what an American "Crampton" should be. Unlike those built for the C&A, his *Lightning* defied classification by the customary digit-and-hyphen system, because two small wheels known as "bearers" were placed between its conventional guiding truck and a pair of seven-foot drivers. Again there was too little weight for traction, or what motive-power men preferred to call "adhesion." The engine made some remarkably fast runs on the Utica & Schenectady Railroad in 1850, including one of 16 miles and 88 feet in 13 minutes and 21 seconds.* However, it was replaced within a year by otherwise more capable machines. At about the same time the disheartened Norrises returned to Philadelphia, little imagining that the Schenectady plant would go on to become the country's second largest engine producer—the American Locomotive Company.

Unfazed by the failure of the domestic "Cramptons," Winans patterned his own high-wheeler more nearly along the lines of the British designer McConnell's "Bloomers." These were 2-2-2s, and they owed their class designation to the fact that inside mainrods and frames left their driving wheels as exposed as the legs of the feminists parading about London in the briefs just introduced by Amelia Bloomer. The engines had a similar way of disrupting the orderly pattern of English life, for their long rigid wheelbases tended to spread the rails on curves, preparing the way for derailments. Winans saw no reason for a smaller locomotive; on the contrary, his *Carroll of Carrollton,* built for the B&O in 1852, measured an impressive 30 feet between end beams. To provide flexibility, he applied blind tires to the machine's eight-foot drivers and pivoted a four-wheeled truck

* 105.58 Mph.

ahead of them and another beneath the firebox. Then, to make the best possible use of the 4-2-4s' considerable weight, he placed auxiliary cylinders on either side of the boiler, with vertical piston rods extending to the main-axle bearings below. When steam was admitted to these "vapor jacks," they raised the entire superstructure several inches, transferring much of the load normally carried by the guiding and trailing trucks to the traction wheels for maximum adhesion.

While the design overcame the principal objections to its predecessors, the *Carroll of Carrollton* must have been very hard on the rails, for its 96-inch drivers had no counterbalances and were stroked by outside mainrods. It was never used in regular service and soon went the way of a great many other noble experiments.

Winans had better luck with a new line of freight engines. Like the "Mud Diggers," they were 0-8-0s, brought up to date by abandoning gears. The first of more than two hundred of the odd machines left his shops in 1848. A stanchion-supported roof running the full length of the boiler gave it a top-heavy look, accentuated by placing a large steam dome, not above the firebox, but far ahead of it, the theory being that the boiling water below was less turbulent there, and not as likely to enter the throttle valve and flood the cylinders. The engineer's controls, too, were in front of the furnace. The whole effect suggested a dromedary with a rider on its back, and the ungainly

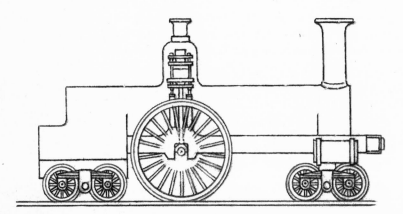

Winans's Carroll of Carrollton *was the first domestic locomotive to be equipped with a four-wheeled trailing truck. The 1852 monstrosity used upright steam jacks to apply more weight to its driving wheels at starting and on grades.*

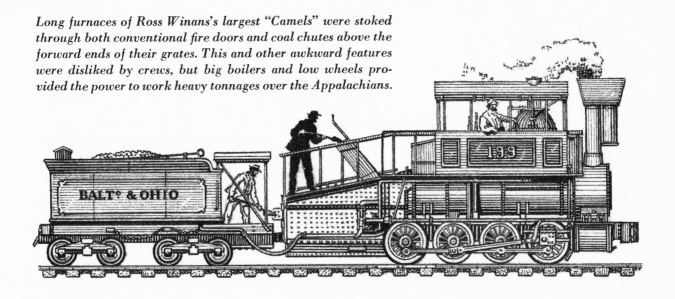

Long furnaces of Ross Winans's largest "Camels" were stoked through both conventional fire doors and coal chutes above the forward ends of their grates. This and other awkward features were disliked by crews, but big boilers and low wheels provided the power to work heavy tonnages over the Appalachians.

locomotive and others of its class were fittingly called "Camels."

Winans found customers in the B&O, the Philadelphia & Reading, the Delaware, Lackawanna & Western, the New York & Erie, and a fast-growing successor to the Philadelphia & Columbia—the Pennsylvania Railroad. To meet varying demands he offered furnaces of three sizes, all placed between and behind the fourth pair of drivers. The largest were so long that a fireman could not possibly stoke the front end from his usual station on the tender, so an auxiliary deck was provided on a higher level from which coal could be shoveled down a chute to the forward section of the grates. Crews complained of that awkward feature, and of the difficulty of working cooperatively while separated by twelve or more feet of clattering machinery. Yet it is doubtful whether any other locomotives of the 1850s could have matched the "Camels'" performance on the Baltimore & Ohio's famous "17-Mile Grade" west of Piedmont, Virginia—a heartbreaker with a vertical rise of nearly 2,000 feet.

One hundred and nineteen of the engines were operating on the B&O when, in 1857, a recently appointed master of machinery, Henry Tyson, decided

that more flexible motive power was needed. He favored 4-6-0s, a popular wheel arrangement first applied to a 20-ton Philadelphia & Reading anthracite hauler named the *Chesapeake* by Septimus Norris a decade earlier. Tyson's predecessor, Samuel Hayes, had already designed a 30-ton version of the type, and the new official liked the machines built from his plans well enough to prepare a set of drawings for five even heavier ten-wheelers.

Winans took it as a personal affront when he was given the specifications and asked to submit a bid. He not only declined but wrote and published a thirty-four-page pamphlet in which he extolled his "Camels," raised numerous real and fancied objections to the Hayes locomotives, and contended that any further investment in 4-6-0s would be ruinous to traffic and a betrayal of the stockholders' trust. The B&O's response was a fifty-eight-page document, citing so many shortcomings of the "Camels" that anyone unfamiliar with their generally reliable record would have thought the management dimwitted for having bought them in such numbers. The treatise was allegedly composed by President Chauncy Brooks and the directorate, but Winans surmised that Tyson had prepared it, and said as much in a

No amount of ornamentation could conceal the basic ugliness of Samuel Hayes's towering 10-wheelers. Nevertheless they were capable passenger locomotives, requiring help from Winans's "Camels" only on the B&O's famed "17-Mile Grade."

second pamphlet addressed to his superiors. The somewhat plaintive introduction read:

"My heretofore prosperous business, in the prosecution of which so many hundreds of persons have been supported, has been so prostrated as to render it not sufficiently encouraging to pursue it further—unless I can counteract the ill effect of Mr. Tyson's abuse of your names and influence, and by a proceeding to which you are parties, establish the injustice to which I have been subjected, and vindicate the reputation of those machines, as to whose particular properties I have the authority of the very founder of your board for saying, you owe the largest measure of your prosperity."

Unmoved, the top brass supported its master of machinery, and as Winans had anticipated, he was forced to close his establishment. But that was not the end of the matter. In 1861 a Confederate force led by Stonewall Jackson destroyed forty-two locomotives at the B&O's Martinsburg division point, and hauled another fourteen partially dismantled en-

gines, mostly over gravel-surfaced turnpikes, to the Rebel-controlled Virginia Central Railroad at Staunton. Hard-pressed for replacements, Tyson recalled that three unsold "Camels" were gathering dust in Winans's vacated plant and tried to buy them. The bankrupted builder's refusal was emphatic. "I would not sell them to *you*, he said, "for one hundred thousand dollars apiece."

In 1863 a new Baltimore & Ohio chief of motive power had better success, although he was forced to purchase, along with the "Camels," an experimental 4-8-0 which had also been stored in the shops. This premature "Mastodon" engine was all but forgotten when the Lehigh Valley Railroad reintroduced the wheel arrangement in 1882. Meanwhile Ross Winans, who had alienated most of his friends and associates by expressing sympathy for the Secessionist cause, died a recluse in his once hospitable Baltimore home. It was a bitter ending for Winans, a mechanical genius who had devoted his entire life to the betterment of transportation.

Dressed in their Sunday best, the B&O's shop and enginehouse force at Martinsburg, Virginia, turned out for the wet-plate photograph interpreted here not long before Stonewall Jackson's troops raided the terminal, destroying 42 locomotives and commandeering 14 more for use in the South.

10 Melodies Cast and

Halfway through the nineteenth century steam locomotives reached a stage in their mechanical development which discouraged radical departures from the beaten path. Under similar circumstances vehicle manufacturers before and since have switched designing emphasis from functionalism to styling, but never more abruptly than the engine builders of the mid-Victorian era. Dated color lithographs indicate that within the span of three years—1849-1851—relatively austere "kettles" gave way to machines resplendent with rainbow hues, burnished metal, and ornate woodwork. Deploring the trend, the later-day railroad journalist Angus Sinclair wrote: "The vagaries that move the red man and his squaw to paint their faces with red lead is not more inconsistent with a sense of harmony than were the untutored tendencies of the trade to burden its products with glittering brass." More charitably it can be said that the flamboyant decor applied to five very important

locomotive accessories was completely in keeping with their colorful and anecdote-embellished histories.

THE OIL HEADLIGHT

Horatio Allen's bonfire-on-a-flatcar experiment of 1831 did not encourage repetition, and with increasing engine speeds the longest terminal-to-terminal runs in the country could soon be scheduled between the hours of dawn and dusk. From the standpoint of safety there was every reason to avoid night operation, and for nearly a decade only trains delayed by breakdowns, derailments, or bad weather crawled over the irons after dark. Under such conditions hand lanterns were hung up front, not so much to light the way as to serve as warning beacons.

Then, in August, 1841, the following item appeared

A moonlit castle embellishes the sides of a formidable box headlight preserved by the California-Nevada Railroad Historical Society. The lamps were too cumbersome to be carried about by manufacturers' representatives, so half-scale models were often used as sales demonstrators.

Wrought in Metal

in a copy of the Boston *Advertiser:* "The Boston and Worcester Railroad are preparing a very bright headlight with reflectors to be placed on a locomotive, which is to be run on that road at night. The transportation of freight at night is a very natural gain in point of time, and diminishes the chance of collisions, while the slow rate of travel enables a locomotive to draw heavy loads without injury to the road."

This is believed to have been the first time a locomotive headlight was mentioned in print. Of more significance, the report indicates that at least one line had already encountered a problem which was to plague the industry for more than a century— that of getting slow freight over the rails without delaying fast passenger trains.

The new form of lantern quickly became an essential engine fixture, and a profitable item for specialty manufacturers. Generally the lamps were sold directly to the railroads, and to judge from the adver-

tisements of the day competition was too intense to be ignored. A typical example read: "Roads using our Headlights have paid less money by a third for more efficient service than has been paid by roads using Cheap John Headlights—E. L. Hall, Philadelphia."

The truth is that all of the products left much to be desired. The whale oil sloshing about in their reservoirs fed flat or tubular wicks irregularly, causing flames to leap and dance. No thought was given to concentrating the light with lenses, the distance it was thrown depending wholly upon tin-plated reflectors. In attempts to extend the field of vision, these parabolic bowls were made increasingly large until two-foot diameters became common. Nevertheless, speeding trains frequently ran ahead of the illuminated track in terms of their ability to stop, and like earlier hand lamps they functioned best as warning signals.

83

Cincinnati, which for many years built more steamboats annually than Boston, New York, and Baltimore combined, boasted four locomotive manufactories between 1845 and 1867. The largest—Niles & Company, and Moore & Richardson (originally Anthony Harkness & Son)—jointly produced some 200 engines. The unattractive relationship between the cylinders and guiding truck of the latter's Nathaniel Wright *had a purpose—to place more weight on the drivers.*

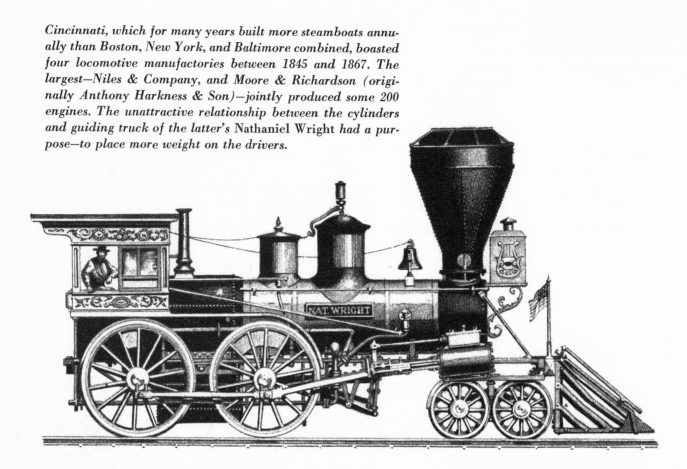

To the embarrassment of some engineers, nature provided a reasonable facsimile of an oncoming headlight. Among those throttle artists was a New York & Erie Railroad runner named Joshua Martin. Barreling over the crooked Delaware Division one night in the late 1850s, he whipped his eight-wheeler out of a long curve and found himself face to face with the brightest locomotive lantern he had ever seen. Shrieking for brakes, he tugged back on the reversing lever and managed to avoid a head-on collision with the moon.

The size and prominent positions of early box headlights inspired remarkable decorative effects. The brackets supporting them were filigreed stampings or castings, and not infrequently the outspread wings of brass eagles shielded chimneys from the wind. On the flanks of the lantern housings, artists depicted every subject imaginable—a noble stag, a crouching tiger, Grecian ladies plucking lyres, an ancient castle, and a homesteader breaking sod with his plow, to mention a few. Oddly, in view of the continuing practice of naming engines for celebrities, portraits were rare. Only Commodore Vanderbilt and a longtime president of the New York Central, Dean Richmond, seem to have been honored in this fashion. The former's likeness appeared on two locomotives, one owned by the Hudson River Railroad, and the other a Rensselaer & Saratoga machine.

The periodic inconvenience and cost of recommissioning artists to restore weatherbeaten masterpieces encouraged the adoption of scrolls, which could be applied with stencils in any railroad paint shop. The

The term "lantern" was still applied to locomotive headlights when this advertisement appeared in 1852 trade publications and newspapers.

Paintings of a young woman carrying a parasol graced the headlight of a Norris eight-wheeler built in the late 1840s. The treatment suggests that a contributor to another Philadelphia enterprise, Godey's Lady's Book, *was the artist.*

Swiveling lamp and reflector assemblies permitted Post & Company headlights to be serviced from the side. A small red rondel lowered from an overhead pocket indicated that a locomotive was backing up, while a green rondel advised opposing traffic that the engine displaying it was followed by another assigned to a separate section of what, on the timetables, appeared to be a single train.

Acetylene, stored under pressure in small reservoirs, was the illuminant for Bradley & McAlister headlights. The gas produced a bright beam, but it was considered unsafe to generate it on an engine, and the inconvenience of replacing exhausted tanks discouraged the widespread use of such lamps.

borders and cartouches became less elaborate as the pendulum of progress swung back toward functionalism in the middle 1880s. By then an Indianapolis inventor named Leonides Wolley had patented an electric headlight powered by a steam generator. Perversely, it worked only when an engine was standing still. Nevertheless the novel lantern drew attention to a new source of illumination far superior to an oil flame.

THE SAND DOME

A vague but generally accepted story credits the origin of the locomotive sander to an unidentified Philadelphia & Reading engineer. His inspiration, if it can be called that, was a plague of grasshoppers

that descended upon eastern Pennsylvania in 1836. The insects blotted out the sun, ravished crops, and greased the rails of the lines in the region with their crushed bodies. Track gangs sent out with brooms could make no headway against the continuing swarms, and traffic all but came to a standstill as locomotive driving wheels spun helplessly at starting and on upgrades. It was then that the unknown runner thought to place two bins on the sturdy crossbar, or "pilot beam," at the front of his engine. Dismounting whenever he approached a troublesome stretch of track, he opened petcocks which let the contents dribble onto the oily residue. In effect, each granule adhering to a rail or tire became a minuscule cog engaging others to produce traction.

Apparently the primitive appliances went the way of the locusts, for there is no record of anything like

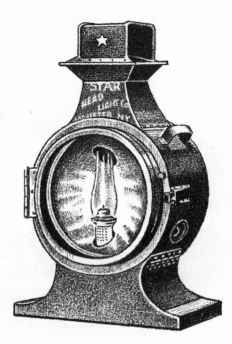

Relatively austere, Pennsylvania Railroad headlights were of a standard design throughout the system for more than 30 years. Standing 44 inches high, and weighing nearly 60 pounds without brackets, they displayed illuminated numbers and were painted a bright red accented with gold striping.

Round oil headlights were comparatively rare. Produced by a firm in Rochester, New York, the model shown here was intended to be placed above an engine's smokebox, a position that became popular when those boiler sections were extended to house spark deflectors more effective than wire screening on stacks.

it being proposed again until 1841. In that year a New York City stovemaker named Jordan L. Mott looked out of his shop window one day, saw a New York & Harlem Railroad engine slipping its wheels, and worked up a patent drawing for a pair of funnel-shaped sand reservoirs to be centered directly above the drivers of a six-wheeler. Those positions made it possible for crews to open or close the feed valves without leaving the deck.

Mott was still dickering for a customer when, in 1842, the Baldwin Works found a better location for a single box-shaped bin—straddling a boiler top. There, radiated heat from below evaporated any moisture in the stored sand, insuring its free passage through pipes on either side leading down to the rails. By drawing back the handle of a long rod, an engineer could uncover the two passages simulta-

neously. First applied to a Georgia Railroad 0-6-0, the device proved so satisfactory that it soon became a standard feature on the company's products. For unexplained reasons other builders lagged at least five years behind, and it was not until the early 1850s that sanders of one type or another were considered indispensable. Their forms ranged from a curious design resembling a giant acorn seated upright in its cup to cupola-like octahedrons and squat cylinders with rounded tops.

Whatever their shapes, these "sand domes" were as eye-filling as the headlights of the same period. Brass moldings girdled them, and those which did not carry paintings on their flanks displayed locomotive numbers rendered with so many flourishes that few could be identified at first glance. On the other hand, the varied contours of their burnished caps—

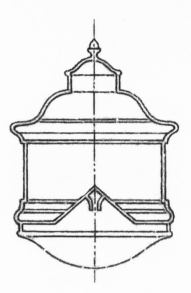

Jordan L. Mott made a fortune as the manufacturer of the first anthracite-burning kitchen stove, but never found a market for his 1841 locomotive sander—a pair of funnel-shaped bins that dribbled grit on the driving tires when the wheels slipped.

Cylindrical domes differed only in the distinctive contours of their brass caps. Conical bases directed sand outward and into delivery pipes on either side.

shallow, hemispheric, beaded, fluted, or otherwise distinctive—left no doubt about what firm had built a particular engine, because each shop developed and adhered to its own pattern. The big brass covers lost their advertising value only once. That was during the Civil War, when the salvaged parts of wrecked and reconstructed locomotives were indiscriminately interchanged.

With a return to austerity during the 1880s, not only the embellishments but occasionally the domes themselves disappeared. In those instances bins were placed behind sheet-metal aprons on both sides of an engine below the running boards. Anything gained in appearance, however, was offset by the inconvenience of having to service two reservoirs instead of one, and the arrangement never became popular.

THE BELL

A profile drawing of an 0-6-0 built by Timothy Hackworth for the Stockton & Darlington Railway in 1827 shows a bell no larger than a teacup dangling from a gooseneck stand on the boiler top. Since the rendering bears no date it is impossible to say whether the melodious accessory was included in the original design or placed on the locomotive at a later date. Either way, it failed to set a precedent in England. There, engines were given more penetrating voices in 1835—those of steam whistles. In densely populated areas where the screechings of the "quills" might have led to equally loud public protests, rights of way were so well protected with fencing and gates

Rectangular sand boxes were a characteristic of Baldwin engines built between 1842 and 1860. In this 1850 freight hauler, the builder combined his flexible-beam truck with four rigidly aligned drivers and used "blind" tires as well.

that there was little need to use them, or to retain bells, as American railroads did, in the dual interests of urban safety and tranquillity.

An undated engraving of Matthias Baldwin's *E. L. Miller* has often been cited as evidence that the engine bell made its American debut on that machine in 1834. If so, one wonders why Eastwick and Harrison, who were certainly aware of their competitor's efforts, provided the *Hercules* with a conspiciously inferior form of hanger three years later. Less controversially, Baldwin established a pattern for the industry by providing the *Miller's* bell with a deep-throated yoke shaped like an inverted letter U. That placed the axis upon which it swung low enough for a light tug on a pull rope to send it sweeping through its arc.

Other builders soon found ways to produce distinctive bells. First, there was the matter of tone, which could be varied by using particular blends of metals and differing contours. The standard bronze formula—one part tin to four of copper—was changed to suit the acoustical tastes of either the manufacturer or customer. Occasionally silver dollars were tossed into a molten mix, either for luck, or in the belief that they improved the alloy's resonance.

Once a casting hardened and cooled in a sand mold, it was turned to final form on a lathe. Pausing now and then to strike it with a hammer, the machinist feathered off just enough material to raise the pitch to that of a master bell or tuning fork. Thus it was said that anyone with tutored ears could identify the maker or owner of an engine clanging its way through the darkest night. Among the experts was L. R. Andrews, who put his knowledge to rhyme in a poem of epic length published by the Railway & Locomotive Historical Society many years ago. In a stanza picked at random he paid tribute to the offerings of Aretas Blood, the general manager and principal owner of New Hampshire's Manchester Locomotive Works.

But the Blood bell's tone is all its own,
    Sonorous, mellow and clear;
Its rhythmic ring and measured swing
    Is music I love to hear.

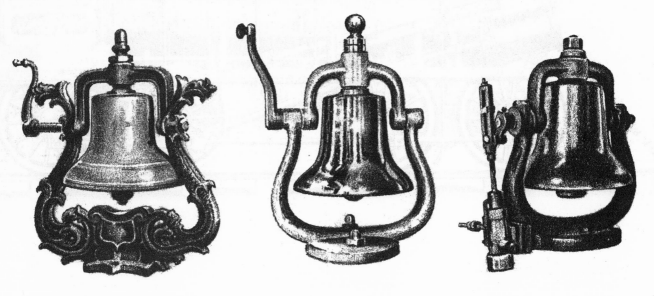

Large McKay & Aldus bell of the 1880s measured 17 inches across the mouth. Locomotive manufacturer Nathaniel McKay was the son of Donald McKay, one of New England's renowned clipper ship builders.

Like its competitors, the American Locomotive Company maintained a small bell foundry, and used a special blend of tin and copper for the castings. The 1900 model shown was applied to a B&O "Pacific."

Later-day automatic bell ringers were actuated by compressed air or vacuum systems. As early as 1870 the Great Western of Canada placed prongs on an axle which rocked levers attached to a bell rope.

A little six-wheeler on a 5-mile-long railroad, the Rogers-built Hackensack was as copiously decorated as any locomotive of its day. It first scurried across New Jersey's tidal meadowlands between Hackensack and Bergen Junction in 1864.

In traditional fashion a steam-locomotive bell was cast in a mold consisting of three "flasks," in which hard-packed sand retained impressions of the inner and outer contours of a wooden pattern. During pouring, a "sprue" hole vented air which would otherwise have been trapped by the molten metal. The hardened bell was removed 6 hours later and buffed to remove tool-dulling particles of sand, before it was placed on a lathe and turned to final form.

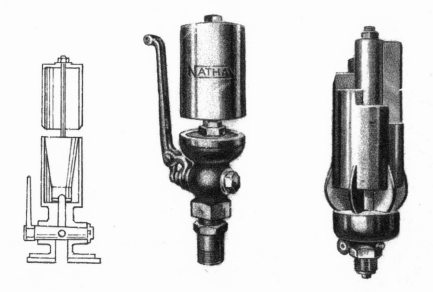

The "measured swing" was a characteristic determined by the designer rather than the rope puller, for it was difficult to hurry the beatings of a clapper if a bell pivoted on a low axis, and equally hard to retard them when the trunnions were placed nearly on a level with its top. Andrews took further note of the identifying cadences in a critical appraisal of a Taunton, Massachusetts, builder's products.

> Oh! the Mason bell is balanced well,
>> But its voice is not for me;
> As to and frow it sways so slow,
>> Like a bell-buoy on the sea.

Still, the mournful tolling of the most phlegmatic engine bells could not adequately express the national mood when Lincoln's funeral train rolled west in 1865. The clappers of those on locomotives assigned to the roundabout run were wrapped in cloth to damp the clanging of iron on bronze. It was further stipulated that the bells must be rung continuously—a full-time task for special crewmen.

Whatever their tonal qualities, the swinging auxiliaries were framed by increasingly ornate hangers throughout the 1850s. Some rocked between neoclassic columns, and others appeared all but hopelessly entangled in cast-iron foliage. The most popular motifs for the nuts which anchored them to their yokes were the acorn and the pineapple, but occasionaly a small federal eagle clung with brass talons to an oscillating perch.

THE WHISTLE

It is impossible to say when engine drivers first thought to raise the weighted arms of safety valves and use the shriek of escaping steam as a warning signal. However, it happened often enough to encourage a manufacturer of industrial equipment in Manchester, England, to put out a line of locomotive horns in 1832. These Sharp, Roberts & Company steam trumpets were more melodious than penetrating and found little favor. Three years later the firm sent a mechanic named Thomas Turner down to South Wales to install some shafting for an iron foundry. At this Dowlais plant, working days began and ended with the ear-splitting blasts of a homemade shop whistle. The mechanism consisted of two cylindrical cups placed mouth to mouth with a slight gap between them. An inverted cone directed steam to the brass lip of the cylinder above, causing the metal to vibrate and project sound waves in the manner of an organ pipe. Turner obtained permission from the inventor, William Stephens, to take a cutaway model back to his employers, who applied

93

Abundant water power at the falls of the Passaic River brought budding industrialists to Paterson, New Jersey—among them patternmaker Thomas Rogers. Switching to locomotive building, he was the first to apply a steam whistle to an American engine and to counterbalance driving wheels by filling pockets in their spokes with lead. An early champion of outside cylinders, the Stephenson-type valve gear, and wagon-top boilers, he was largely responsible for making Paterson known throughout the world as "The City of Iron Horses."

the principle to a small locomotive whistle. Tested on the Liverpool & Manchester Railway, it produced such strident notes with so little steam that others were soon applied to engines throughout Britain.

The earliest American locomotive to carry a "cup whistle" was a 4-2-0 constructed by Thomas Rogers, of Paterson, New Jersey, in 1837. The circumstances are of particular interest, because the builder and his machine paved the way for the bustling mill town to become the country's largest engine-building center.

Originally a carpenter, Rogers manufactured wooden looms until the growing popularity of iron machinery forced him to turn to patternmaking, foundry work, and machining. To finance a spacious plant and the best available power tools, he admitted two New York City inventors to partnership in 1832. As a sideline "Rogers, Ketchum & Grosvenor" solicited railroad orders, offering such specialities as structural bridge members, car wheels, axles, and springs. Assembling locomotives imported from England was not on the list, but the company welcomed

the opportunity to put one together for the Paterson & Hudson River Rail Road in 1835.

Rogers spent the next seventeen months designing and building the whistle-equipped six-wheeler. The New Jersey Railroad & Transportation Company had tentatively agreed to buy the engine, but J. H. James, president of a newly chartered line in western Ohio, dropped by at the Paterson plant one day and purchased the 4-2-0 on the spot. After embossed plates bearing the name *Sandusky* were cast and fastened to its sides it was shipped to that inland port for service on the Lake Erie & Mad River Railroad. The sale was quickly followed by others, and when Thomas Rogers died in 1856 his firm ranked with Baldwin's as a top producer of finely engineered motive power. Less to his credit, he was notoriously unappreciative of his underlings' contributions to the business, and a number of them left the plant to establish and staff other shops in Paterson. Through mergers, two of these companies—Danworth-Cooke and the Grant Locomotive Works—became formid-

94

The steam locomotive's most eloquent voice was first heard in America in October, 1837, when Thomas Rogers applied a cup whistle to his earliest engine, the Sandusky. *Its piping is said to have been a factor in the 4-2-0's prompt sale to the Mad River & Lake Erie Railroad.*

able competitors for Rogers, and by 1900 over 10,000 of the 60,000 engines built in the United States were products of "The City of Iron Horses."

Like the *Sandusky's*, all whistles applied to domestic locomotives during the next two decades were small and shrill. Some notion of their pitch is indicated by the experience of a hunter named John Quick, who during the late 1840s, stalked game around his cabin the wilderness west of Port Jervis, New York. One day he heard the unmistakable cry of a panther, and staked his traps throughout the area. They remained unsprung for a week while the unseen cat periodically screamed derisively. With exhausted patience and a loaded rifle, Quick finally set off over the mountains to track down and shoot the beast. He changed his mind after topping a rise overlooking the Delaware Valley. Far below him a little construction engine, the *Piermont*, was whistling its way up the newly laid rails of the New York & Erie with a flatcar load of ties.

As whistles grew larger, engineers found that they could vary their tones by controlling the amount of steam admitted to the cups, and they developed distinctive audio "signatures" to announce their comings and goings. Dissatisfied with the sobbings, hootings, and trillings of single quills, the more influential among them induced shop foremen to place two, three, four, and sometimes five in clusters fed by a single valve. The original purpose was to produce melodious chords, but with each cup responding to the admission of steam at a different intensity it became possible to play tunes upon them.

The story is told of a Louisville & Nashville runner, "Dutch" Eiford, who mastered this form of musicianship. One night a new preacher in Stearns, Kentucky, was midway through a sermon when Dutch drifted into the valley rendering a gospel hymn with great sensitivity. The parson stopped, and waited with upraised hand until the last note faded into the Cumberland hills, then cried, "Brothers and sisters, a devout man has just passed our way!" Sad to say, Dutch forgot himself a few Sundays later and clat-

CASEY JONES

Immortalized in song, John Luther (Casey) Jones was known to admirers from Canton, Mississippi, to Memphis, Tennessee, as the ballast scorcher who announced his whirlwind comings and goings with the plaintive cry of a whippoorwill, rendered on the big chime whistle of the 10-wheeler Number 382.

SIM WEBB

"Jump, Sim! Unload." Those were Casey's last words as he whipped Train Number 1, the Illinois Central's crack Cannonball Express, out of a cut at Vaughn, Mississippi, and plowed through a freight train that had failed to clear the main. Fireman Sim Webb survived the 1900 collision.

tered through town piping a bawdy air. The reverend sent a blistering note to the division superintendent, who reminded Eiford that steam was meant for pulling cars rather than entertaining the citizens of Stearns.

The corrosive effect of mineral-laden vapor eventually led to the abandonment of brass whistles. Thereafter they were made of iron, or steel, detracting from their visual appeal. Nevertheless they remained the most eloquent of the steam locomotive's many voices.

THE CAB

In 1843 a Boston & Providence employee, Joseph Davenport, proposed erecting a shelter above the deck of one of the company's locomotives. The suggestion was roundly opposed by several officials, who contended that full exposure to the elements kept enginemen alert. Fortunately they were overruled and the line joined others then in the process of providing "houses" for the comfort of their crews. Tarpaulins roped to stanchions soon gave way to wooden structures with glazed windows, similar in contour to those used for a century after.

Among early cab recipients was a dashing young engineer named Joseph Widrow Meginnes. He had already earned a reputation for fast running when, at the age of twenty-three, he left the Philadelphia & Reading to become one of the New York & Erie's first five locomotive drivers. Given a choice of engines, he picked a Norris-built six-wheeler, the *Orange,* and immediately endeared himself to the management and the public, for he not only made miles and minutes synonymous but did it in grand style. Edward Herold Mott, in *Between the Ocean and the Lakes* (1899), reported that Meginnes' sister, Mrs. Mary B. Freeman, recalled him as "having more the appearance of a man of letters than that of a locomotive engineer. He was dainty in his dress, and never appeared anywhere with oil or grime on his hands or face. His instincts were so fine that when, on a trip over the New Jersey Railroad, he saw for the first time a locomotive with cab, he became so dissatisfied with his engine that he made a demand upon the company for a cab to it. Time passing, and none having been provided, he called upon General Superin-

---

LOCOMOTIVE WHISTLE SIGNALS

(o indicates short blast; — indicates long blast)

o	Apply brakes. Stop.
— —	Release brakes. Proceed.
— ooo	Flagman protect rear of train.
— — — —	Flagman may return from west or south.
— — — — —	Flagman may return from east or north.
oo	Answer to — oo or any signal not otherwise provided for.
ooo	When standing, back. Answer to signal to back. When running, answer to signal to stop at next passenger station.
oooo	Call for signals.
— oo	(Single track) To call attention of engine and train crews of trains of the same class, inferior trains and yard engines, and of trains at train order meeting points, to signals displayed for a following section. If not answered by a train, the train displaying the signals must stop and ascertain the cause. (Two or more tracks) To call attention of engine and train crews of trains of the same class, inferior trains moving in the same direction, and yard engines to signals displayed for a following section.
— — o —	Approaching public crossings at grade. To be prolonged or repeated until the crossing is reached.
————	Approaching station, junctions, railroad crossings at grade, etc., as may be required.
— — o	Approaching meeting or waiting points.
o —	Inspect train line for leak or for brakes sticking.
o o o o o o o	Succession of short blasts. Alarm for persons or livestock on the track.

97

tendent H. C. Semour and informed him that unless one was furnished forthwith he would leave the road. It was supplied without delay, and that was the beginning of cabbed engines on the New York & Erie Railroad. This was in 1848."

By the flamboyant fifties, cab-building called for skilled cabinetmakers rather than carpenters. Birch, maple, and walnut were among the hardwoods used for exterior paneling and moldings; they were finished with as many as twelve coats of hand-rubbed varnish. Front and side window frames lent themselves to a variety of architectural styles ranging from Moorish to liberally mullioned Gothic.

Although conventional cabs were as wide as any part of an engine, crewmen could stand erect only in the area between the rear pair of driving wheels. The raised "floors" of the sections projecting over the tires formed benchlike seats, encouraging frequent inspections of the running parts below, for when crank pins failed the freed ends of the side rods were likely to flay up through the planking.

Again, a typical cab straddled the rear of the firebox, or "boiler backhead." That furnace wall, like those on the sides, was formed of two iron sheets held several inches apart by numerous studs, or "staybolts." Water filled the space between the outer and inner plates and did double duty, contributing to the steam supply and preventing the metal directly exposed to the flames from melting. Above a round or

oval fire door at deck level was a shallow "warming shelf," where tallow in a long-spouted tin or copper can was kept in a fluid state. This was the lubricant for the sliding valves which directed steam into and out of the cylinders. If an engine traveled any great distance without stopping, the fireman made his way forward along the jouncing runningboards and, while the engineer closed the throttle briefly, replenished the supply in two brass cups which fed the valve chambers from above. The procedure won him a lasting nickname—"Tallowpot."

Protected from the weather, a number of new fittings were mounted on the backhead in the late 1850s. They included a glass column which showed the height of the water in the boiler, and a circular steam gauge called in crew jargon the "clock." As in the past, pumps continued to ram water into the barrel, but the best of them worked only when a locomotive was in motion. Thus, if a machine was delayed at a terminal, way station, or siding, it became necessary to uncouple its train and run it slowly up and down the track to keep the furnace crownsheet covered.

Without originally intending to do so, a Frenchman named Henri Giffard found a way to eliminate this inconvenience. In 1852 he built a cigar-shaped balloon nearly 150 feet long, driven by a propeller connected to a three-horsepower steam motor. To avoid using a heavy pump, he invented a simple

Crude cabs were applied to a number of Baltimore & Ohio "grasshoppers," including the Andrew Jackson, *when they were demoted to yard service in 1850.*

When the New York & Erie's most popular engineer threatened to resign unless a cab was applied to his engine, the management hastily complied. Joe Meginnes was otherwise famous for a hair-raising run he made from Goshen to Piermont, New York, in 1842, with a copy of Governor Seward's annual address to the Albany legislature. Delivered to him by courier at Goshen, he relayed it to a waiting steamboat, where printers set it in type en route to New York City, enabling the Sun *to scoop the rival* Herald, *whose copy came by stagecoach.*

device which served the same purpose without mechanically activated parts. Steam from the boiler was piped into the nozzle of an atomizer, where it picked up water from a reservoir below. In the blending process the vapor condensed, and all the liquid rushed on through a tapered passageway. There it gained enough additional momentum to push aside a valve and enter the barrel, despite the pressure from within.

Giffard's dirigible was a failure, but around 1858 he sold his patent rights to the "injector" to the same English factory which had introduced the cup whistle. Reorganized as Sharp, Stewart & Company, the Manchester firm permitted Philadelphia's William Sellers & Company to produce the appliance on a royalty basis. The steam pump, as it was first called, supplemented rather than replaced the mechanical type on locomotives, because in its original form it worked poorly at pressures above 100 pounds to the square inch. However, the fact that it could be op-

erated when an engine was standing still justified its universal adoption. Moreover, the water it delivered to the boiler was preheated in the atomizing process, insuring fairly constant temperatures within the barrel, regardless of the rate of feed. In addition, injectors never clogged with ice in winter, whereas reciprocating pumps often did.

One other cab appurtenance deserves mention—a gong attached to the underside of the roof, which clanged when the conductor of a passenger train pulled on a bell rope extending through the coaches. According to Edward Herold Mott, author of *Between the Ocean and the Lakes,* a New York & Erie "train captain" improvised the communication system several years before Joseph Meginnes demanded a crew shelter. Weighing more than 300 pounds, this Henry (Poppy) Ayres found it difficult to clamber over the woodpile in the tender whenever he had to advise a pompous engineer named Hamel that an unscheduled stop was necessary to discharge or pick

99

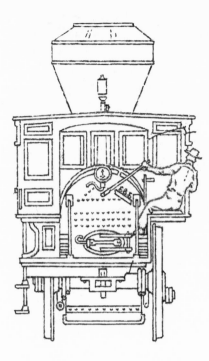

Early cabs of walnut, birch, and maple were as carefully crafted as fine furniture, but windows were designed to be seen, rather than seen through.

Seats for engine crews overhung the drivers.

up passengers. Finally he strung a long cord to the locomotive, tied it to a stick which slapped against a guard rail in response to a tug, and handed the runner a list of code signals. Hamel said nothing, but deliberately cut the rope, not once, but each time it was re-rigged and the captain back on the cars. The normally genial Ayres soon ran out of patience, collared the crewman, and, as Mott told it, established for all time the superior authority of conductors.

It might be added that the gong was not always a dependable source of instructions. A bell-rope story of uncertain origin illustrates the point. It concerns an engineer who was hammering over the rails with a wide-open throttle when, in acknowledgment of a harsh clang, he slammed the lever shut. At the same time the tallowpot leaped to the hand-brake wheel at the front of the tender. A moment later the gong sounded twice—the signal to resume speed. Then came three close-spaced clangs—an order to back up. Thoroughly confused, the runner let his locomotive drift to a stop. As the wheels came to rest the con-

ductor swung onto the deck, less than courteously curious to know what was holding up his train. The crew could only point to the gong, which continued to jangle inanely. It finally occurred to the three to shove open the door of an express car directly behind the engine. There the baggage man dozed on a tilted chair, oblivious to the antics of a chimpanzee which had broken out of its shipping cage and was swinging on the bell rope.

While builders and suppliers lavished decorative attention upon individual parts, they ignored the first principle of good design, which was to achieve an overall effect of unity. The exception was William Mason of Taunton, Massachusetts, a man of remarkable mechanical ability and foresight, notwithstanding the fact that his engine bells rocked too slowly to suit the poet Andrews. Like Thomas Rogers, he had begun by manufacturing textile machinery, but there the similarity ended, for he remained in that business throughout his life to finance locomotive building as

James Millholland, who at the age of 18 helped Peter Cooper build the Tom Thumb, *later became the Philadelphia & Reading's master of machinery and designed a number of engines with rounded cabs sheathed in metal. He placed the sand boxes of his 1859* Hiawatha *behind aprons below the running-boards.*

The New York & Erie's Number 102 was one of five inside-connected eight-wheelers built for the road by Rogers in 1851. Ten years later officials knuckled under when Erie enginemen protested a switch from wood to 48 percent less expensive coal as locomotive fuel, and full conversion did not take place until 1872.

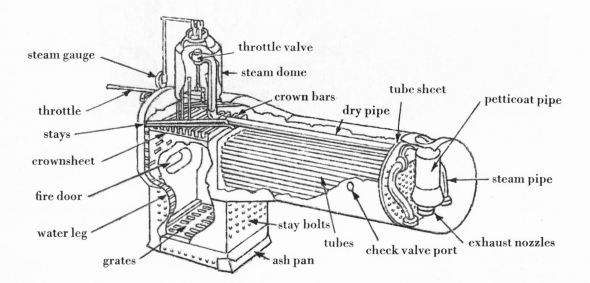

The General's boiler was of the "wagon-top" type, in which a conical section provided additional space for steam above the firebox roof, or "crownsheet."

WILLIAM MASON

A successful Taunton, Massachusetts, textile-machinery manufacturer, William Mason poured his profits into locomotive building and found it a costly hobby. While he failed in his efforts to promote unconventional designs, his more traditional engines were handsomely proportioned and free from the garish ornamentation relied upon by his contemporaries to attract sales. His work provided needed proof that artistry and functionalism could be combined to the benefit of both.

a hobby. As he once observed: "I tell my friends that I got up engines for fun, but it was the most expensive fun I ever had. I made just enough from my cotton machinery to make up my losses on locomotives."

Much of Mason's satisfaction must have come from giving the steam engine's many parts complementary contours and proportions. His good taste was displayed even in the running gear. Of his efforts he said: "I made the driving wheels with hollow spokes and rims. I also got up a set of truck wheels. Before that the ordinary truck wheels looked like cheeses. I wanted my truck wheels to have some relation in appearance to the drivers; therefore I never put a plate [disk] wheel under any truck I ever built. I also put the counterbalance into the rim of the driving wheels."

Mason might have added that he was the first builder to spread the two pairs of wheels on a guiding truck far enough apart for the cylinders to be centered attractively between them. Together with Rogers he was an early advocate of what came to be called "wagon-top" boilers—a type in which the portion above the firebox was elevated, not abruptly, but with a conical section ahead of it. In one of his few concessions to decoration, he covered the wooden lagging on the barrels of his engines with "wrapper sheets" of Russia iron, a metal brought to a rich shade of blue by a heat-induced oxidizing process.

Again, Mason achieved harmony by using complementary sand and steam dome profiles. Finally, he believed that cab windows were meant to be seen through, rather than seen, and provided them with plentiful glazing. All in all, he merited the praise of a contemporary designer, Matthias N. Forney, who wrote in *The Railway Gazette:* "It might be said of his locomotives that they were 'melodies cast and wrought in metal.'"

The most famous Rogers engine was the Western & Atlantic's General—seized by Federal spies commanded by James J. Andrews on April 12, 1862, and driven 86 track-sabotaging miles from Big Shanty to Ringgold, Georgia, before a pursuing Confederate force led by Captain William A. Fuller overtook the abandoned eight-wheeler and apprehended the raiders. The exploded drawing is based upon blueprints of the locomotive as it was restored by the Louisville & Nashville Railroad for a centennial run over the same route.

11 High-Wheelers

The most expensive part of William Mason's "fun" resulted from his unsuccessful attempts to promote two new forms of locomotive power: a double-ended engine and an 0-4-0 that combined engine and tender in a single unit.

The double-ended engine was the outgrowth of Mason's interest, dating from 1871, in the work of Robert Fairlie, the locomotive superintendent of Ireland's Londonderry & Coleraine Railway. Fairlie was a voluble champion of narrow-gauge lines, and his widely circulated treatises on the subject fired the imaginations of would-be railroad promoters throughout the world. He contended that the 4-foot, 8½-inch gauge most generally used in Europe and the northern United States was seldom justified on the basis of traffic. On firmer ground, he enumerated the savings which could be effected by holding the distance between the rails to one meter or less. With equipment scaled down in size, costs would be mate-

rially reduced. Moreover, narrower road beds would be cheaper to construct, especially when the terrain demanded rock cuts. Reassuringly, he always pointed out that he had developed the ideal type of locomotive for service on what he called "the track of the future"—one on which high tractive effort was achieved in a novel way.

Bearing his name, Fairlie's design employed the principle introduced by Horatio Allen in 1831—that of placing what amounted to two locomotives back to back. The twin boilers and central firebox and cab were treated as a single entity, but to provide flexibility on curves a trucklike cylinder and driving wheel assembly was pivoted beneath each barrel. The first of the double-enders, bought by the 23½-inch gauge Festiniog Railway in 1866, attracted hundreds of observers to the North Wales harbor town of Portmadoc. They came from Norway, Russia, Germany, France, Italy, Spain, and Brazil, to ride behind the

106

A gift horse presented to the narrow-gauge Denver & Rio Grande by England's Duke of Sutherland in 1873, the double-ended Mountaineer *was of a design developed by Robert Fairlie, locomotive superintendent of Ireland's Londonderry & Coleraine Railway. William Mason built a more formidable "Fairlie" in 1871.*

and Cabbage Cutters

diminutive 0-4-4-0 and study its action as it labored up a green valley underlaid with enough slate to give the line 90,000 tons of revenue shipments annually. The 39,000-pound *Little Wonder* handled six times its weight on the precipitous climb to the quarries, and rattled down again with 300-ton trains.

Enthusiasm for the "Fairlies" spread as far as India, and so did the passion for lilliputian railways. In America alone, more than seven hundred "slim gauges" were listed in various editions of *Poor's Manual of the Railroads* prior to 1900. At one time they served forty-two states, with Colorado boasting the greatest aggregate trackage—approximately 3,000 miles. However, the Irishman's curious machines never found favor in America, even on the narrow gauge lines for which they were designed.

An explanation is provided by an incident involving the Denver & Rio Grande. In 1873 the Duke of Sutherland traveled to Pueblo, Colorado, over the first completed section of the three-foot-gauge road, and when he returned to England he arranged to have a 30-ton "Fairlie" sent to the company. With it came a builder's representative, John Moulton, to do the final assembly work. He liked Colorado so well that he stayed on, and ran the double-ended *Mountaineer* when it was assigned to helper service at La Veta Pass. One day he overlooked an order and failed to pull onto a siding for a passenger train. Fortunately, there was no collision, but his error cost him a thirty-day suspension. Devotion to the "Fairlie" outweighed his resentment, and he took pains to explain to his replacement the proper use of its multitudinous controls. Increasingly bewildered, the new man finally said: "You keep the engine running and I'll take the thirty days."

William Mason did not anticipate the reaction of American crews to the complexities of double-ended locomotives, and in 1871 he designed and built a

F. W. Johnstone, a chief mechanical officer of the Mexican Central Railway, revived the double-ended arrangement with three engines constructed by the Rhode Island Locomotive Works in 1892. Of their designer, the technical editor Angus Sinclair wrote: "An engineer gifted with the inventive faculty runs the risk of pushing it to a rank crop that is difficult to harvest."

In 1917 the Baldwin Works turned out a fleet of diminutive double-enders for the French government. Throughout World War I they hauled troops and material up and down the trenches of the Western Front.

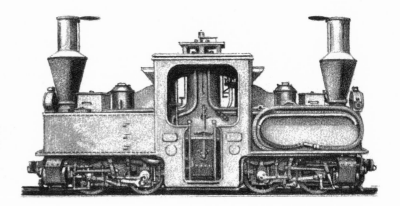

A fine example of Mason's artistry, the North Pacific Coast's Tomales, *employed a swiveling engine unit with a massive center bearing. This necessitated using externally mounted valve gear, and the builder chose a type invented by a Belgian master mechanic named Egide Walschaerts back in 1844.*

standard-gauge "Fairlie-Mason" weighing an impressive 81 tons. Named *Janus*, for the two-faced Roman god, this 0-6-6-0 was tested on the Boston & Providence and the Boston & Albany before the Lehigh Valley Railroad bought it to boost freight trains up a 1.65-percent grade east of Wilkes-Barre, Pennsylvania. Although admittedly powerful, the engine could carry only a limited amount of fuel in its flanking bunkers. That and the difficulty of getting coal down to the deck and onto the grates through an opening in the side of the firebox discouraged further orders, and in 1877 the *Janus* was scrapped without regret.

Mason's other unorthodox offering was the equivalent of an 0-4-0 and a stubby four-wheeled tender. However, the latter was a rigid extension of the cab, and the driving assembly swiveled on a center bearing attached to the bottom of the boiler. With this arrangement the engine could be run forward or backward with equal stability, eliminating turnarounds at terminals.

Intended for commuter service, the three-foot-gauge machine was the object of public admiration at Philadelphia's Centennial Exposition of 1876, where it hauled thousands of visitors over a track connecting the various exhibit buildings. Locomotive buyers were less enthusiastic, commending its fine workmanship but disapproving of the valve gear, which appeared altogether too simple to do its work well. The inventor, a Belgian named Egide Walschaerts, had found a good market for the valve gear abroad, but this was its first application in America.

Criticizing the various systems used to direct steam into and out of locomotive cylinders was then a popular preoccupation of railroaders—as was attempting to devise new linkages. Engineers and designers had known for a long time that some sort of variable control was needed for differing operating conditions. Letting the intake ports remain open throughout the length of piston strokes insured the maximum power needed at starting and on grades. But as engines picked up speed, the heavy charges were given

109

too little time to fully escape through the exhaust ports, and the resulting "back pressure" produced a bucking action. Thus at anything above a crawl it was desirable to admit steam during only a portion of the strokes. This not only insured smoother motion but allowed the steam to work expansively while it was trapped in the cylinders, developing more power in relation to the fuel and water consumed.

Unfortunately, the early gab-hook valve gears could not be adjusted to meet both requirements, and most builders compromised, limiting the intake to one half of the piston strokes, or what was called a "50-percent cut-off." In a few instances double sets of hooks were provided—one pair to be engaged at starting, and the other after the engine gained momentum.

Then, in 1842, two Robert Stephenson & Company employees, William Williams and William Howe, got into a well-publicized hassle, each claiming to have invented a gear which permitted an engineer to give the valves any action he chose. It was generally conceded that Howe, who was Williams's superior, pirated the young apprentice's arrangement. Overlooked was the fact that William James, whose Baltimore & Ohio contest entry had blown up ten years before, was the true originator of the mechanism. He had not only installed it on his ill-fated locomotive, but sent a set of drawings to an English builder, Forresters & Company, where they were apparently filed and forgotten.

Under the circumstances, Stephenson made no attempt to patent the gear, but used it so extensively that it was soon given his name. Its prime movers were two pairs of eccentrics mounted on an engine's main axle. Each pair controlled the action of one of the locomotive's two slide valves. In turn, one of each pair was set for forward running, the other for reverse operation. The far ends of the rods to which they imparted a push-pull motion were attached to the top and bottom of a crescent-shaped member called a

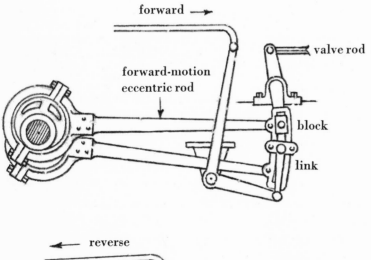

forward →

forward-motion eccentric rod

valve rod

block

link

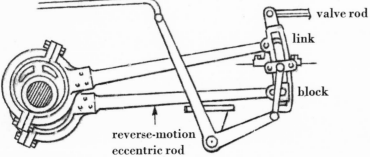

← reverse

valve rod

link

block

reverse-motion eccentric rod

The outstanding feature of the Stephenson valve gear was a pair of slotted links that could be lowered or raised by a bell crank. In the former position axle-mounted eccentrics, adjusted for forward running, applied the required "push-pull" motion to blocks within the links, and the blocks relayed it to the valves ahead. Conversely, when the links were raised, reverse-motion eccentrics delivered a "pull-push" motion to the blocks and valves. With the links half raised there was no valve movement, and by varying the positions above and below that point an engineer could control the amount of steam admitted to the cylinders for each stroke.

110

"link," whose central slot accommodated a sliding block connected to the valve rod. When the engineer's reversing lever was in a vertical position, both links were held at a height which placed the horizontal axes upon which they rocked at a level with the blocks, and those parts remained idle. But if the lever was thrown all the way forward, the links were lowered until the blocks were at the upper ends of the slots. There the full motion of the "forward eccentrics" was delivered to them and they passed it along to the valves. Conversely, when the links were fully raised by drawing the lever to the rear, the "reverse eccentrics" gave the blocks and valves comparably

long travel for backing up with maximum power. The beauty of the arrangement was the infinite choice of intermediate positions. A throttle artist could readjust the setting, notch by notch, until mere wisps of steam flicked into and out of the cylinders at high speeds.

This Stephenson gear served its purpose well, but its eccentrics and rods could not be fitted comfortably between the frames of Mason's centrally pivoted truck. Hence the adoption of the Walschaerts mechanism, all of whose parts were outside the wheels. Motion was taken from a half crank on each of the main drivers and transmitted to a link pivoted at its

In the Walschaerts gear the blocks, rather than the links, were lowered or raised to provide reversing, and to vary the amount of steam fed into the cylinders. The prime movers were half cranks on the main drivers, but union links and combination levers supplemented the action, opening the admission ports just before the pistons reached the ends of their strokes, to cushion the shock of reversal. Early engineers complained because the timing of this "lead" could not be adjusted to suit their personal whims.

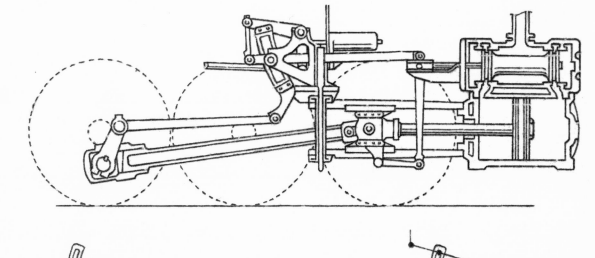

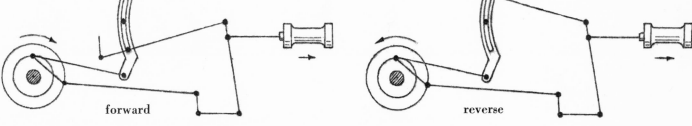

forward   reverse

midpoint on a fixed axis. With that hookup the block within the slot was raised and lowered to determine the valve's action.

American criticism of the Belgian design stemmed from a valve refinement called "lead," which permitted steam to enter the end of a cylinder a split second before it forced the piston in the opposite direction. This cushioned the shock of reversal and provided a fully open port for peak performance at the start of the next stroke. In the case of the Stephenson linkage the timing could be changed to suit the engineer, but the lead of the Walschaerts motion could not. Much was made of that relatively unimportant difference, and very little of the outside gear's virtues—greater accessibility, less dead weight, and reduced friction. It would take the huge locomotives of a distant day to force it upon the industry.

Curiously, Mason's failure to find a profitable market for his double-truckers was due to Matthias Forney, the man who later eulogized the Taunton builder's fine sense of styling. Forney deserved more than casual praise himself. His fatherless boyhood was a Pennsylvania Dutch version of the Horatio Alger story. Largely self-taught, he was seventeen years old when he entered Ross Winans's Baltimore plant as a drafting apprentice in 1852. From there it was a short step across the street to a more responsible job at the B&O's Mount Clare shops. The Civil War found him plying his ruling pen and triangle in the Chicago offices of the Illinois Central, where he first took note of the deplorable state of surburban traffic. While the railroads placed great emphasis upon the quality of the mainline passenger equipment, commuters rode in decrepit cars drawn by museum pieces.

An avid reader of technical publications, Forney knew that small locomotives of special designs handled trains in and around Europe's major cities. They carried reservoirs either on their sides or wrapped over their boilers, and their fuel bunkers were part and parcel of their cabs. These "tank engines" had only one drawback—as the water and coal went down less weight was carried by the drivers and the tractive effort decreased.

Forney had a better idea, and drew up plans for an 0-4-4T (Tank) type with the variable load imposed wholly upon the trailing truck. To that extent the arrangement resembled the one adopted by Mason,

but to avoid flexible steam connections he proposed fastening the driving assembly firmly to the engine bed and using flangeless main wheels to prevent binding on curves. His first drawings called for a vertical boiler, but he had time to work up plans for a larger horizontal-barreled machine while he waited for a response to his patent application. The government agency was too busy checking out inventions of potential military value to accommodate him until 1866.

Railroad managements were equally slow to give his efforts serious attention, but in 1872 two unforeseen circumstances opened the gates wide for the "Fairlie" type's acceptance. One was a nationwide epidemic of distemper which killed thousands of street railway horses. By focusing public attention on these animals, the plague touched off a campaign against the ways in which they were routinely treated. This, in turn, led to a demand for steam-powered elevated systems similar to a pioneering installation already in operation between the Battery and Central Park in New York City.

The other factor favoring the "Forneys" was their designer's decision to enter journalism. As the associate editor of the *Railway Gazette* he hammered away on the theme of mass transportation, and spent what time he could reworking his tank engine plans. Effectively promoted, more than three hundred of the machines were chugging over Manhattan's railroads in the sky by 1880, each drawing from five to seven cars.

That was only the beginning. Els in Brooklyn and Chicago clamored for Forney's "little giants," and major carriers including the New York Central; the New York, New Haven & Hartford; the Illinois Central; the Burlington; and the Rock Island belatedly ordered larger versions for suburban service. Produced by at least seven builders—Baldwin, Rogers, Cooke, and the Rhode Island, the Hinkley and the Brooks works—they exerted a greater affect upon metropolitan expansion than any vehicles previously devised. Yet they brought the inventor less profit than fame, for as he once wrote: "Manufacturers and purchasers found the engines most attractive the day my patents expired."

Forney's name was associated with another important contribution to the industry. In the early 1870s he came across a handbook published in Ger-

112

The Billerica & Bedford's Ariel *was a 2-foot-gauge "Forney" built by Boston's Hinkley Works in 1877. More often, engines of this type were equipped with two cow-catchers, or "pilots."*

many for the instruction of enginemen and shop mechanics. Unable to read German, Forney asked his editor, S. W. Dunning, for a translation. Forney had already considered writing such a work himself, being well aware that most American railroaders learned their trades the painful trial-and-error way. Not since the days of Isaac Dripps had anyone run an adequate training program.

The translation of one chapter was enough to convince Forney that the German handbook could not be adopted for domestic use. To his other projects, then, he added the authoring of Forney's *Catechism of the Locomotive.* Starting with a sketch of two apples, one halved horizontally and the other verti-

cally to show the differing appearances of the core and seeds, he stripped the mystery from mechanical drawings. Next, he analyzed the form and function of every one of a locomotive's parts, anticipating and answering 560 questions in the clearest possible language. Finally, he devoted a chapter to the personal habits and moral responsibilities of an engineman. A part of it read:

"The steady loud clatter which an engine makes while running has an injurious influence on the nervous system. In order to keep himself fresh and strong in his service, which is extremely exhaustive to body and mind, the runner must try to strengthen himself by regular, temperate living, and eating abundant

Draped in black bunting, and displaying a garlanded Brady portrait of the martyred president, the Cleveland, Columbus & Cincinnati Railroad's Nashville drew Lincoln's funeral train southward through Ohio in April, 1865.

Twenty-six years later, swords, cannons, and a drum were appropriate decorations for the presidential special assigned to onetime brigadier general Benjamin Harrison when he toured California on the Southern Pacific Railroad.

Seated in the ornate but generally musty cabs of inspection engines built between 1864 and 1908, high-ranking officials periodically evaluated their domains. The New York, Ontario & Western's trackwork may have appeared a bit unstable when viewed through the heat waves projected by old Number 23's split stack. Better vantage points were the "pulpits" on a New York Central curiosity completed in 1876, a year before Cornelius Vanderbilt died.

JAMES MILLHOLLAND

A cabbage cutter without equal was James Millholland's 12-drivered Philadelphia, *turned out by the Reading's own shops for pusher service on the Quaker City's short but demanding Falls grade. Because the 1863 curiosity could be stoked before each climb, it carried no coal. Nevertheless, its 50-ton weight was unequaled for 10 years.*

nourishing food. The common use of strong drinks, which undermines the mental and physical condition of men, should be avoided by a person occupying the exhaustive and responsible position of a locomotive runner. If in ordinary life a drunken man is unfit for any simple work, how shall a drunken runner or fireman undertake the difficult management of so great, so delicate and so costly a machine as a locomotive?"

Frequently revised, the *Catechism* became the bible of the industry and a comfortable source of income for a man who often claimed he preferred inventing to eating, and wrote out of the need to satisfy both appetites.

Discounting tank engines, locomotive design proceeded in two orderly post-Civil War directions—more powerful freight haulers and faster passenger

engines. The former were called "cabbage cutters" because their side rods swept so close to the ground at the lowest points in their long strokes. The Lehigh Valley Railroad took the lead in developing the big workhorses. In 1866 the master mechanic of the line's Mahanoy Division, Alexander Mitchell, designed a very large road engine which introduced a new wheel arrangement—the 2-8-0. Given the opportunity to bid on the construction, Matthias Baldwin declined, maintaining that the machine would be a colossal failure. Mitchell's Scotch temper flared but he remained canny. He said he had not asked for the Philadelphia builder's opinion, but if the job was too big for the plant he would continue negotiations with the Grant Locomotive Works in Paterson. Unaware that the rival firm had already turned down the order, Baldwin immediately reconsidered his decision.

REUBEN WELLS

Bearing the name of its designer, the Reuben Wells *first charged up the Jeffersonville, Madison & Indianapolis's 5.9-percent Madison Hill, in Indiana, in 1869. After conversion from an 0-8-0 to an 0-10-0, weighing 5 tons more than the* Philadelphia, *it appeared as shown.*

The veteran manufacturer died within weeks of the machine's completion in September, 1866. Conservative to the last, he nevertheless left his business firmly grounded upon sound engineering, fine workmanship, and efficient production methods. He had been the first in the trade to adopt assembly-line techniques, to use master patterns and jigs, to insure the interchangeability of parts, and to stock ample replacements as a service to his customers. The founder of a school for Philadelphia's black children and an ardent abolitionist, he lost his southern market during the late 1850s. Nevertheless, at the time of his death, nearly 1,500 of his engines were in use at home and abroad.

As for the "colossal failure," the 2-8-0 astonished both domestic and foreign observers who watched it amble up a 1.5-percent grade near Delano, Pennsyl-

vania, with a hundred empty coal cars weighing 340 tons. To commemorate the Lehigh Valley's recent merger with a number of feeder lines including the Beaver Meadow Railroad, the engine was christened the *Consolidation*—a name that was soon applied to all locomotives of its type.

Thereafter the Lehigh Valley's motive power men displayed a talent for introducing new wheel arrangements prematurely. Encouraged by the 2-8-0's success, Mitchell immediately ordered two 2-10-0s, or "Decapods," from one of the numerous Norrises (James), who had set up an engine works in Lancaster, Pennsylvania. Delivered in 1867, the *Bee* and the *Ant* outperformed the *Consolidation*, but they tracked poorly during back-up movements. To put an end to frequent derailments, one pair of drivers was later removed from each locomotive and re-

An abolitionist and staunch supporter of Abraham Lincoln, the master mechanic of the Lehigh Valley's Mahanoy Division, Alexander Mitchell, enlisted the aid of his barber to express his admiration for the sixteenth president.

Maintaining that it would be a colossal failure, Baldwin reluctantly built a 2-8-0 locomotive from Mitchell's drawings in 1866. Contrary to his prediction, the machine set the pattern for more than 33,000 of the workhorses constructed by American shops over a period of 45 years.

Introduced prematurely, the Lehigh Valley's "Decapods"—the Ant and Bee— were handicapped by the inferior trackwork of the 1860s, and jumped the rails so often that they were soon converted into 2-8-2s—another Mitchell "first."

Baldwin's saddle-tanked Uncle Dick *zigzagged up and down temporary switchbacks laid over Raton Mountain by the Santa Fe in 1878. The engine was named for Richens Lacy Wooton, the owner of a toll road whose rights to the route the company bought, at the old man's suggestion, for "six lifetime passes for my family, and $25 a month to keep the lot of us in groceries."*

placed with a two-wheeled trailing truck. This was probably forgotten by 1897, when the Baldwin Works manufactured what it claimed were the first 2-8-2s for Japan's Nippon Railway and gave the type a name: "Mikado."

The Lehigh Valley's other original contributions resulted from a policy of permitting its master mechanics at South Easton, Weatherly, Delano, Wilkes-Barre, and Sayre to build engines of their own designs. It was assumed that their knowledge of local operating conditions would be reflected in ideally customized locomotives, but the determination of each official to avoid paying the others the flattery of imitation often led to innovations of questionable value. This was demonstrated by Philip Hoffecker of Weatherly, who disregarded the known fact that single-axled guiding trucks were adequate for plodding freight locomotives and turned out three 4-8-0s in 1881 and 1882. Although they were handsome machines, their four-foot-diameter drivers hardly warranted the extra pair of stabilizing wheels ahead.

The Central Pacific had better luck with a much larger version of the type built at its Sacramento general shops late in 1882. Mechanical Superintendent A. J. Stevens was the designer, and after he watched his *Mastodon* hoist a 210-ton train up a 25-mile-long Sierra Nevada grade with a vertical rise of 3,900 feet, he placed an order with Danforth-Cooke for twenty more. They were remarkable in many ways, including their use of steam cylinders to actuate their reversing levers. The valve gear itself was a Stevens invention believed by a number of experts to be better than the Stephenson type, although it never achieved great popularity. Crews called it a "monkey motion," because the eccentric rods shuttled back and forth with a curious hop at the end of each stroke.

Heartened by the 4-8-0s' performance, Stevens built by far the largest locomotive of its day in 1883. The iron brute *El Gobernador* was a 4-10-0 weighing 73 tons without tender. It stood idle for a year while the road's trestles were strengthened to accommodate it. Unfortunately it remained in that condition throughout much of its short life, shopped and re-shopped far too often in relation to the work wrung out of it. Its principal value was as a tourist

119

That size was not the measure of success was the lesson learned by the Central Pacific when the awesome El Gobernador *broke down with disheartening regularity on freight runs in the High Sierras. If the 1883 giant had a virtue, it was the incentive it provided to build strong trestles to support its weight.*

attraction. Whenever large numbers of Easterners traveled through Sacramento on excursion trains they were properly awed by the sound and sight of the multiwheeled giant blasting past the depot with a long string of freight cars presumably bound for the mountains. Once the duffers departed, *El Gobernador* was returned to the enginehouse to have its fire dumped and await the next contingent.

As for passenger power, the Lehigh Valley again pointed the way to an original wheel arrangement, with the help of an independent designer, George S. Strong, who went to Wilkes-Barre in 1883 to try to interest Alexander Mitchell in his plans for a 4-4-2. Had the road's master mechanic bought the patent rights to the engine he would have been the earliest sponsor of the "Atlantic" type. However, the drawings incorporated too many untried features—a pair of tubular fireboxes placed side by side and connected to a single boiler; two sets of lightweight mainrods, each driving a pair of traction wheels; and steam valves of an unfamiliar pattern. Mitchell rejected the overall design but applied the valves to a new 4-4-0. They worked well enough to make him take a more serious view of Strong's twin furnace proposal, and in 1884 he built a locomotive incorporating the heating plant.

The *Duplex* was the world's first 4-6-2, a fact which attracted less attention than the curious fireboxes. They were of a corrugated construction, which had the virtue of combining unusual structural strength with expanding and contracting responses to temperature changes. Soon after the engine left the Wilkes-Barre shops it was run under its own steam to St. Paul, Minnesota, for exhibition at a master mechanics' convention. Back on the Lehigh Valley, it performed no better or worse than conventional locomotives and was finally converted into a ten-wheeler.

With the support of A. G. Darwin, a New Jersey financier, Strong continued to press for the adoption of his unusual machines, and two were actually built. One, the *Darwin*, produced by the Hinkley Locomotive Company of Boston in 1887, had a long and unsuccessful record as a demonstrator engine; and the other, manufactured by Schenectady in 1888, was sold to the Atchison, Topeka & Santa Fe. They deserve mention only because they were 4-4-2s, and as such preceded by more than six years an Atlantic Coast Line locomotive widely credited with introducing that type. Strong also prepared drawings for a 2-10-2 a decade before the wheel arrangement made its initial appearance on the Santa Fe.

In 1883 Philadelphia designer George S. Strong proposed using four lightweight mainrods, rather than two heavy ones, to stroke the driving wheels of an innovative 4-4-2. The object was to reduce the hammering action of the reciprocating parts, but anything gained in performance would have been canceled out by the added cost of maintaining the complex locomotive.

An unsuccessful demonstrator, Strong's 1884 Duplex took its name from two cylindrical fireboxes placed side by side behind a single boiler. The sections exposed to the flames were corrugated, providing inherent strength and permitting them to expand and contract without distortion in response to temperature changes. While the arrangement was adaptable to marine service, no advantage was found in applying it to locomotives.

Unsuccessful experimental engines usually disappointed no one but their designers, builders, and purchasers. However, there were exceptions, as noted by the ever outspoken editor of *Railway and Locomotive Engineering* in 1887. Wrote Angus Sinclair: "When we first heard of the Holman locomotive we supposed it to be the invention of a harmless crank who did not understand the principles of mechanics, but we now believe it has been, since its inception, an ostentatious machine designed to lure unwary capitalists into an investment which will be of the same value as throwing gold coin over Niagara Falls."

The engine he castigated had two pairs of elevated drivers, each delivering motion through intermediate wheels to a car truck below. In some miraculous way this was supposed to damp the reciprocating action of the mainrods and reduce the hammering effect on the rails. Frequent advertisements in Philadelphia newspapers announced that the Holman Locomotive Company of that city had been formed to sell the engines, and was offering $10 million in stock—par value $100—at a modest quarter of that figure.

Sinclair continued: "One painful case was pushed to my attention. Mrs. Marion French had sufficient money in United States bonds to produce her an income of $570 a year. Some idiotic friends advised her to invest in the Holman Locomotive Company's stock, assuring her that she would more than double her income without risk. Our washerwoman never loses a chance to ask me when the Holman locomotive will begin to pay dividends."

Those who in 1868 had put their faith and savings in a mechanism called the "atmospheric brake" made out better than Mrs. French. The inventor was a twenty-two-year-old Civil War veteran named George Westinghouse. He had read of the drilling machines being used by Germain Sommeillier to push a tunnel nearly eight miles long under Mont Cenis in the Alps. They were powered by compressed air, and he reasoned that a force capable of drilling holes in rock for blasting powder could also be used to stop trains.

In the first Westinghouse arrangement, a steam-actuated pump on the locomotive rammed compressed air into a large reservoir. When a valve in the cab was opened, part of the supply rushed back through pipes and hoses to a cylinder under each car.

LOCOMOTIVES WITH TWO-WHEEL GUIDING TRUCKS

TYPE	SYMBOL	NAME
2-2-0	△o O	
2-2-2	△o O o	
2-4-0	△o OO	
2-4-2	△o OO o	Columbia
2-6-0	△o OOO	Mogul
2-6-2	△o OOO o	Prairie
2-8-0	△o OOOO	Consolidation
2-8-2	△o OOOO o	Mikado
2-8-4	△o OOOO oo	Berkshire, Kanawha
2-10-0	△o OOOOO	Decapod
2-10-2	△o OOOOO o	Santa Fe
2-10-4	△o OOOOO oo	Texas

122

LOCOMOTIVES WITH FOUR-WHEEL GUIDING TRUCKS

TYPE	SYMBOL	NAME
4-2-0	◿ o o O	Six Wheeler
4-2-2	◿ o o O o	Bicycle
4-2-4	◿ o o O o o	
4-4-0	◿ o o OO	American
4-4-2	◿ o o OO o	Atlantic
4-4-4	◿ o o OO o o	
4-6-0	◿ o o OOO	Ten Wheeler
4-6-2	◿ o o OOO o	Pacific
4-6-4	◿ o o OOO o o	Hudson, Baltic
4-8-0	◿ o o OOOO	Mastodon
4-8-2	◿ o o OOOO o	Mountain
4-8-4	◿ o o OOOO o o	Northern, Greenbriar Dixie, Confederation
4-10-0	◿ o o OOOOO	
4-10-2	◿ o o OOOOO o	Overland
4-12-2	◿ o o OOOOOO o	Union Pacific

ARTICULATED LOCOMOTIVES

TYPE	SYMBOL	NAME
0-2-2-0	◿ O O	
0-4-4-0	◿ OO OO	
0-6-6-0	◿ OOO OOO	
0-8-8-0	◿ OOOO OOOO	
2-6-6-0	◿ o OOO OOO	
2-6-6-2	◿ o OOO OOO o	"Beyer-garratt"
2-6-6-4	◿ o OOO OOO o o	
2-6-6-6	◿ o OOO OOO o o o	Allegheny
2-8-8-0	◿ o OOOO OOOO	
2-8-8-2	◿ o OOOO OOOO o	Chesapeake
2-10-10-2	◿ o OOOOO OOOOO o	
4-4-6-2	◿ o o OO OOO o	
4-6-6-4	◿ o o OOO OOO o o	Challenger
4-8-8-4	◿ o o OOOO OOOO o o	Big Boy
2-8-8-8-2	◿ o OOOO OOOO OOOO o	Triplex
2-8-8-8-4	◿ o OOOO OOOO OOOO o o	Triplex

Until 1900, products of the Rogers Works had to be hauled through downtown Paterson, New Jersey, over tracks of a horsecar line to reach the nearest steam road connection. Here, the Texas & Pacific 256 approaches the City Hall.

There it drove a piston connected by rods and levers to the brakes, causing their "shoes" to press against the tires of the wheels.

The original installation, on a Panhandle Railroad passenger train running between Pittsburgh and Steubenville, Ohio, had not been in service long when it saved the first of countless lives. A farmer's wagon stalled on a crossing, the horses rearing in fright at the sight of the oncoming locomotive. Instinctively the engineer whistled for hand brakes, but before they could be manned a tug on a little brass lever sent fire streaming from the wheels as a force 16 times as great as that required to maintain speed brought the engine and its coaches to a safe stop.

Still, this "straight air brake" had three bad features. If there was a rupture in the system it would not work at all. Further, when cars became uncoupled on upgrades, only manual braking could keep them from rolling backward. Finally, compressed air was slow in reaching the rear cylinders of a long train.

Westinghouse solved two of these problems in 1871, when he brought out an "automatic air brake" which failed safe. The pump and main reservoir were unchanged, but each car carried a small auxiliary tank, and a mechanism called a "triple valve" which opened and closed passages by allowing one pressure to overcome another.

Under normal running conditions all of the reser-

124

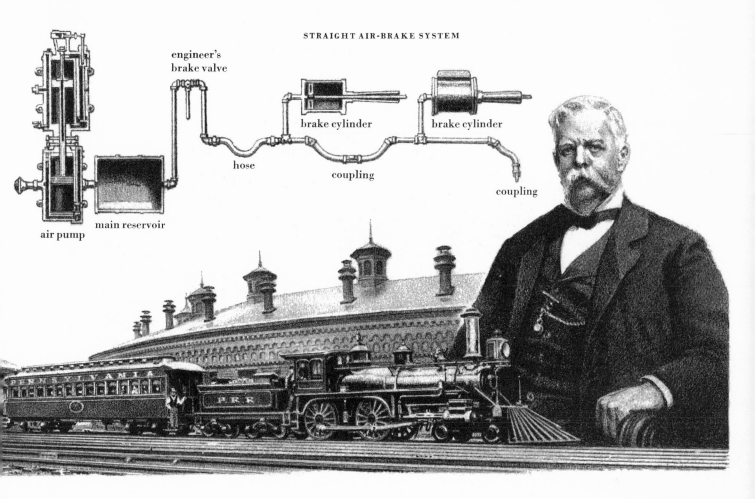

STRAIGHT AIR-BRAKE SYSTEM

engineer's brake valve

brake cylinder

brake cylinder

hose

coupling

coupling

air pump

main reservoir

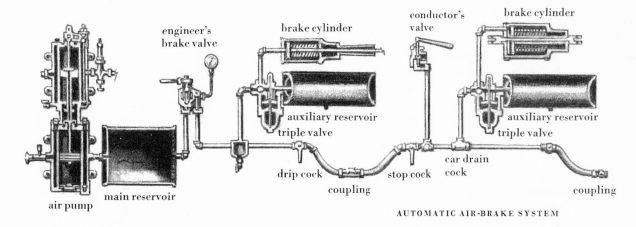

engineer's brake valve

brake cylinder

conductor's valve

brake cylinder

auxiliary reservoir

triple valve

auxiliary reservoir

triple valve

car drain cock

drip cock

coupling

stop cock

coupling

air pump

main reservoir

AUTOMATIC AIR-BRAKE SYSTEM

The first commercial application of George Westinghouse's straight air brake was to a Pennsylvania Railroad passenger engine. This 1869 system had a basic fault— any major leakage made it inoperative. Three years later the inventor introduced the automatic type, which failed safe when there was a rupture.

With a growing demand for huge volumes of compressed air, increasingly large pumps posed clearance problems, and in 1919 the Pennsylvania set a precedent for other roads by mounting two of them on the smokebox front of a full-boilered 2-8-8-0. Introduced too soon, the simple articulated Number 3700 proved too powerful for head-end work and was used as a pusher.

voirs, together with the pipes and hoses, collectively forming a continuous system called the train line, were fully charged, but the triple valves kept air out of the brake cylinders. For decelerations and full stops the engineer opened the control valve in the cab, letting some of the air in the train line escape to the atmosphere. The triple valve responded to the lessened pressure by permitting the more highly compressed air in the small tanks to flow to the brake cylinders, where it exerted a force equal to the reduction in the line. The brakes were released by closing the main valve again, giving the pump a chance to recharge the system. At the same time the triple valves shut off the passages to the cylinders and voided the air within them.

Smooth braking was insured by providing graduated escape ports in the control valve, each hole allowing a 15-percent reduction. Only in emergencies was the handle swept with a single motion through its arc, uncovering all of the openings at once. This drastic action was variously known as "dynamiting her," "dumping the air," or "big-holing the Westinghouse." A parted or blown-out hose produced the same effect, applying the full force to the wheels.

Whether "straight" or "automatic," air brakes represented a collectively huge capital investment, and the industry was slow to adopt them. In New England, where high speeds and dense traffic most warranted their use, they were ignored until a grim train wreck forced the issue. Running through dense fog on an August night in 1871, an Eastern Railroad express out of Boston plowed into a local that had stopped at suburban Revere. Twenty-nine persons were killed and fifty-seven injured. An outraged public and press denounced the directors as murderers, and the tragedy hastened the installation of air brakes on all passenger trains.

Freight conversions took longer. The reluctance of

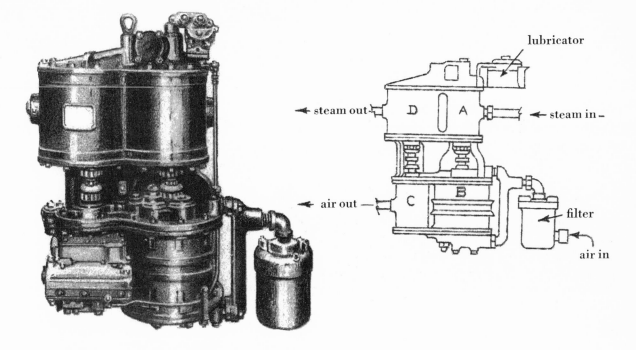

lubricator

← steam out

D   A

← steam in –

← air out –

C   B

filter

air in

Big Duplex pumps compacted as much as 150 cubic feet of air a minute and rammed it into main reservoirs at a pressure of 150 pounds to the square inch. In cylinders A and D, high- and low-pressure steam, respectively, compressed filtered air first to partial and then to full pressure in cylinders B and C.

many roads to provide the new brakes led to a twenty-year period during which the typical "merchandiser" or "drag" was an awkward blend of "air" and "non-air" cars. The latter were necessarily placed at the rear until regulations compelled freight car owners to provide pipes and hose connections which permitted the output of locomotive pumps to flow past them to any pneumatic equipment beyond. Either way, the free-wheeling cars surged violently forward during slowdowns.

Westinghouse owed part of his competition to the so-called "independent systems" which, curiously, used momentum as a decelerating force. All of their arrangements called for engines fitted with steam brakes. When the locomotives slowed down, the cars behind them bunched together, compressing spring-loaded buffers at their ends. In turn, the buffers shoved on levers which actuated the train brakes.

A more likely competitor was the Eames Vacuum

Brake Company of Boston. In its system, a steam-operated "ejector" took the place of a pump and drew air out of a bowl-shaped vessel under each car when a control valve was opened. That caused an India-rubber cover to be driven inward by the greater atmospheric pressure on its outer face, and the motion of the diaphragm was transmitted by rods and cams to the brakes.

In 1886 comparative tests of the three designs were conducted at Burlington, Iowa, by the Master Carbuilders' Association. Applied to a string of fifty boxcars weighing 1,000 tons, the independent type proved totally unacceptable, and neither the Eames nor the Westinghouse brakes could bring comparably long and heavy trains to satisfactory emergency stops, due to slow responses in their train lines.

The founder of the former company, Lovett Eames, finally settled for a market limited to urban railways, including the New York elevateds. However George Westinghouse went on to modify his automatic system in a manner which permitted air to be voided to the atmosphere not only through the engineer's control valve but at every triple valve. In the Burlington trials it had taken a third of a minute for the last of fifty cars to react to a reduction or release whereas, with the "quick-acting brake," the lag was only two and one-half seconds.

Designers could now draft plans for freight locomotives with the assurance that whatever tonnages they were capable of hauling would remain in full control on downgrades. Faster decelerations also made it possible to think in terms of 100-mile-an-hour passenger engines, and the closing years of the nineteenth century were marked by the construction of outstanding "high-wheelers." They were generally of the 4-4-0 type, handsomely exemplified by those turned out from plans of William Buchanan, motive power superintendent on the New York Central &

Hudson River Railroad. Head-ending the *Empire State Express* was his *999* which, on May 10, 1893, allegedly streaked over a mile of track near Batavia, New York, in 31.2 seconds. The unofficial record of 112.5 miles per hour was the subject of later controversy, but certainly the engine's 86-inch drivers and two-foot piston travel gave it the potential for extremely high speeds.

Similarly fast, a pair of Baldwin 4-4-2s built for the Atlantic City Railroad in 1896 regularly clipped off the 55½ miles between the New Jersey resort town and Camden at an average start-to-stop speed of 70 miles an hour. Like the locomotives of many roads within easy reach of eastern Pennsylvania's coal fields, they were of a design called "Camelbacks" or "Mother Hubbards," and owed their "humps" or "bustles" to the cheap waste anthracite they burned.

As early as 1850, a Philadelphia & Reading master of machinery, James Millholland, had designed a

Built between 1875 and 1886, Pennsylvania Class 1 "Consolidations" reflected a policy of standardization instituted by president Alexander J. Cassatt. From 1868 on, "family" characteristics, ranging from horizontally slatted cow-catchers to cabs of uniform design, effected substantial savings in the construction and maintenance of the system's formidable motive power fleet.

128

furnace especially for this fuel, placing it behind the drivers of a 4-4-0, where it extended outward beyond the rails to provide a large grate area. While similar arrangements were tried afterward, the cantilevered weight at the rear set up damaging lateral thrusts. The objectionable feature was eliminated during 1877-78, when the P&R's general manager, John E. Wootten, developed a similarly wide but relatively shallow firebox which could be placed above the driving wheels. One of two 4-6-0s equipped with the furnaces was sent abroad for demonstrations in France and Italy. Restricted right-of-way clearances in both countries made it necessary to remove the cab from the top of the firebox and bring it forward to a lower position straddling the boiler. Presumably everyone but the tallowpot was pleased, for thereafter that location became standard. As for the man with the scoop, he stood in lonely isolation on the tender, either completely exposed to the weather or provided with the most meager of shelters. The story goes that one "Mother Hubbard" fireman—some say it was a student and others a veteran drifter, or "boomer"—gave growing thought to man's inhumanity to man on a bitter winter night, and halfway up a long grade tossed his shovel into the fire, jumped off the engine, and watched the train disappear in a swirl of snow. How the engineer reacted when he ran out of steam is not recorded.

At the turn of the present century innovations of another sort were conspicuous at the head ends of most locomotives. Wood had long since become more scarce and costly than soft or hard coal, and the flaring balloon and diamond stacks long used to trap sparks and embers were becoming rare. The "straight" ones which replaced them actually tapered outward a bit at the top—roughly an inch to the foot—to allow for the expansion of escaping steam. Their bell-shaped lower ends were well within the smoke-

The fireboxes applied to the "Altoona" type of boilers of early PRR "Consolidations" were unusually low, making for spacious cabs. The brick arches used to lengthen the travel of flames and gasses were not installed until the turn of the present century.

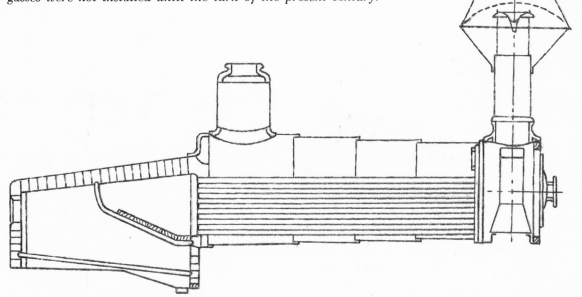

The number 999 became synonymous with speed when it was applied to a 4-4-0 with 86-inch drivers, designed by William Buchanan and built at the New York Central & Hudson River Railroad's West Albany shops in 1893. The high-wheeler was unofficially clocked at 112.5 miles an hour on May 10 of that year.

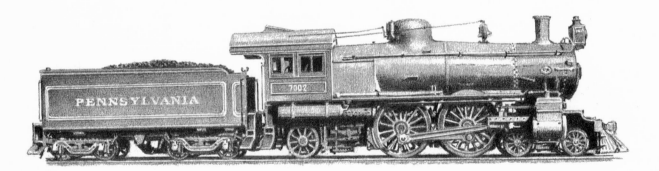

The Pennsylvania Railroad "Atlantic" 7002 racked up a long-enduring record when, on June 11, 1905, it burnished a straightaway west of Crestline, Ohio, at 127.1 (204.5 Km) *miles an hour. The engine was head-ending the Pennsylvania Special—later renamed the* Broadway Limited *—on its first 18-hour run from New York to Chicago.*

130

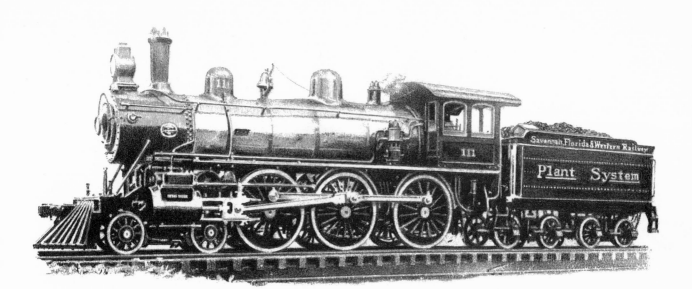

"I wouldn't do it again for a million dollars," drawled Plant System engineer Albert Lodge, after tooling this 10-wheeler 116 fog-blanketed miles from Jessup, Georgia, to Jacksonville, Florida, in 90 minutes. Highlighted by a 5-mile *77.33 MPH* stretch clipped off in 2.5 minutes, the performance wrested *120.0 "* a government mail contract from the rival Seaboard Air Line Railroad in March, 1900.

The Santa Fe's long-legged Number 510 *was the last of six engines assigned to the Death Valley Coyote—a special train chartered by Walter "Death Valley" Scott on April 9, 1905, for an unprecedented 44-hour-and-49-minute run from Los Angeles to Chicago. The eccentric desert millionaire helped the fireman stoke the locomotive across Illinois, and later said of the engineer, Charles Losee: "That fellah made the telegraph poles look like a fine-toothed comb!"*

CHARLES H. HOGAN

Starting as a waterboy for a section gang on the Auburn Road in 1865, and working his way up to the managership of the New York Central's Department of Shop Labor in 1930, Charles Hogan served the industry well for 65 years. After a brief stint as a Union Pacific fireman and engineer in the early 1870s, he returned to upstate New York, where his talent for measuring miles in seconds won him the opportunity to test the speed potential of the 999. Successive promotions included: traveling engineer (an adviser to less experienced runners), master mechanic, superintendent of motive power at Depew, and assistant superintendent of motive power, lines east, with headquarters at Albany.

BENJAMIN HAFNER

Known as "The Flying Dutchman," Erie engineer Ben Hafner had the unique distinction of being buried under wrecked locomotives no fewer than five times during half a century at the throttle. On each occasion it took hours to dig him out, but he emerged without injury to himself or his service record. He earned his nickname after scaring the wits out of a trainload of passengers on a run from Port Jervis to Jersey City in 1871. Despite seven stops, including one of 14 minutes for supper at Turner's, he covered the 89 miles in 2 hours. Blurted one white-faced gentleman, as he passed the cab: "I'd rather sail with the Flying Dutchman than to ride behind you!"

boxes below, and wire netting there deflected the flaming solids to the bottom of those boiler extensions.

As for the cylinders, ever-mounting operating pressures had called attention to the need for better valves. With few exceptions, the ones used from the beginning were of the sliding type, held firmly in place by the downward thrust of steam. As the force increased, the contacting metal surfaces abraded rapidly, and around 1870 experiments were made with arrangements intended to reduce the friction. They were not conspicuously successful until 1898, when the Brooks Locomotive Works of Dunkirk, New York, introduced a spool-shaped valve which shuttled back and forth in a cylinder, opening and closing ports in its periphery. Since the steam bore with equal pressure in all directions, this "balanced" type held up well and was almost universally adopted.

A final nineteenth-century development was a swing toward "compound" locomotives. These increased the energy derived from the fuel they burned by as much as 20 percent. They operated on the principle that after steam was released from one cylinder at roughly half its original pressure it could be made to exert equal force in another of twice its diameter.

On otherwise conventional engines, compounding systems took the following forms:

"Cross-compounds," or locomotives with a single high-pressure cylinder on one side and a low-pressure cylinder on the other. These dated back to 1887, when they were introduced by A. von Borries, the mechanical superintendent of Germany's Hanover Railroad, and T. W. Worsdell, who occupied a similar position on England's North Eastern Railway. Two years later a briefly popular domestic version was developed by Arthur J. Pitkin, chief engineer of the American Locomotive Company.

"Three-cylinder compounds," in which the third applied power to a crank at the center of the first driving axle, and either received steam from a pair outside the frames, or fed its own exhausts into them. Compounds of the former type were patented by F. W. Webb of the London & North Western Railway in 1878, and the latter owed their origin to the Northern Railway of France. Neither found favor in the United States.

Locomotives with two high- and two low-pressure cylinders. These included the "Vauclain compound," the "tandem compound," and the "balanced compound."

The first was invented in 1889 by the thirty-three-year-old general manager of the Baldwin Works, Samuel M. Vauclain—a second-generation motive-power man whose father had a hand in building *Old Ironsides*. The system called for a high- and a

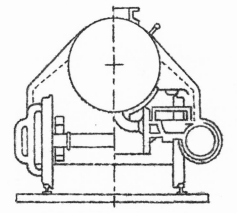

Engineer-journalist Zerah Colburn pointed the way to increased grate areas when he designed a group of 0-6-0s for the Delaware, Lackawanna & Western Railroad in 1855. By placing their fireboxes entirely behind the driving wheels he was able to give them an unprecedented width of over 7 feet.

133

For nearly 40 years Samuel M. Vauclain was a key figure at the Baldwin Locomotive Works. A son of Andrew Vauclain, who helped Matthias Baldwin put Old Ironsides together, "Big Sam" learned his trade in the Pennsylvania Railroad's Altoona shops, where endless hours of metalchipping left him with permanently clenched hands. From his first association with the world's largest locomotive-building plant in 1883 until he was appointed chairman of the board in the early 1920s, he was an innovative designer, as well as a shrewd salesman and tireless administrator. Among his earlier successes were 86 tandem compounds delivered to the Atchison, Topeka & Santa Fe beginning in 1893.

With the Vauclain compounding system, each cylinder casting incorporated a high- and a low-pressure cavity, and either could be placed at the bottom. In six rail-hugging rack locomotives built for the Manitou & Pikes Peak Railway in 1890, restricted clearances called for "upside down" positions.

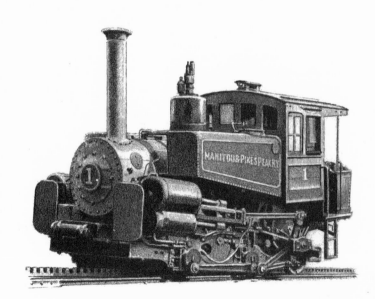

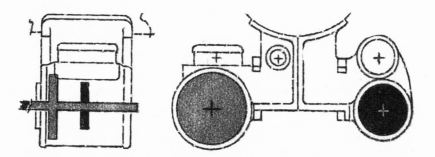

CROSS-COMPOUND

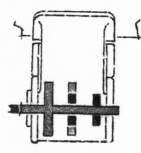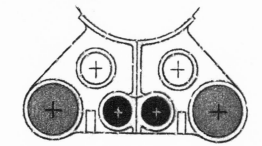

BALANCED COMPOUND

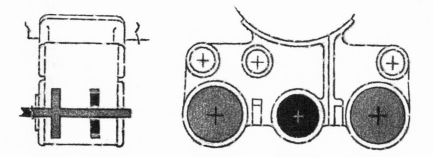

THREE-CYLINDER COMPOUND

Steam voided from a high-pressure cylinder produced equal power when it was directed into a low-pressure cylinder whose piston heads provided double the surface areas. Of the three arrangements shown, four-cylinder balanced compounds were the most popular.

A general manager of the Philadelphia & Reading, John E. Wootten, improved the stability of engines with wide furnaces by placing the grates above the rear drivers. When a machine of this type was sent abroad for display in 1877, the restricted tunnel clearances in Italy and France made it necessary to move its cab forward and downward. Thus was born the "Camelback" or "Mother Hubbard" arrangement.

low-pressure cylinder to be placed one above the other on each side of an engine, with the interconnected piston rods stroking a single mainrod. For fourteen years these compounds were vigorously promoted by the company.

The tandem compound also had a high- and low-pressure cylinder on either side and, as the name implied, the two were set end to end, permitting the pistons to be mounted on one rod. A pioneer installation tested by the Boston & Albany in 1883 was a

failure, presumably because of the inadequate size of the steam passages. Ten years later Baldwin constructed the first of eighty-six successful tandem compounds for the Atchison, Topeka & Santa Fe. This batch of 2-10-2s gave the wheel arrangement its universal name—the "Santa Fe" type.

Four-cylinder balanced compounds made their first appearance in the late 1870s, when Alfred G. De Glehn began turning them out for France's Northern Railway. In his system, high-pressure steam

High-bustled Atlantic City Railroad Number 1027 *wheeled the once fastest train in the world between Camden, New Jersey, and the popular seacoast resort town. The Baldwin "Atlantic" developed 1,450 horsepower at a speed of 70 miles an hour.*

Cab-dominated "Camelback" Number 1248 *was one of 20 Reading midgets used in switching service where tracks providing access to wharves and warehouses curved too sharply for 0-6-0s. The engine weighed 52½ tons.*

powered two axle cranks inside the frames, and the low-pressure cylinders drove external rods. The action was much smoother than that of cross-compounds, and by 1904 more than 1,500 of these engines were in use throughout Europe. In that year the Pennsylvania Railroad bought one and put it through its paces in fast passenger service.

Meanwhile, Vauclain developed a balanced compound which had the virtue of greater simplicity, because it eliminated one of the two sets of reversing gears and valves used by the Frenchman. Francis J. Cole, who had succeeded Arthur Pitkin as chief engineer of the American Locomotive Company, soon countered with a slightly different version, and both types found enthusiastic buyers until the high cost of maintaining them was weighed against an otherwise satisfactory 20 percent saving in fuel.

Oddly, the earliest form of compounding—and the only one which ever proved of lasting value—had yet to be tried in America.

12   The Mighty

An engine of unprecedented size and curious design was the object of mingled admiration and skepticism when it was displayed at the St. Louis Exposition of 1904. Rushed to completion by the American Locomotive Company just in time for the fair, the Baltimore & Ohio behemoth stretched 80 feet between couplers and tipped the beam at 240 tons. Watered and fueled, its boiler and firebox assembly alone weighed two-thirds as much as the Pennsylvania's De Glehn compound.

Twelve 56-inch wheels distributed its weight upon the rails, and for maximum traction all of them were powered. Arranged in a single group they could not have adjusted themselves to curves, so what amounted to two six-coupled engines, each with its own pair of cylinders, were connected in tandem beneath the barrel. The rear driving unit was bolted firmly to it, but the one ahead carried its share of weight on a transverse bearing plate, and was free to fan from side to side on crooked track. This was what disturbed the engine's critics. Stressing the obvious fact that at such times the boiler would be out of alignment with the rails up front, they predicted that its mass and momentum would hold the giant on a straight course to disaster.

Few domestic railroaders knew that nearly four hundred very much smaller engines of this "Mallet" type were already in service abroad. The design took its name from its inventor, Anatole Mallet, secretary and publications editor of the French Academy of Science. When that scholarly gentleman prepared his first drawings in 1874 he had no thought of setting a pattern for big engines. Rather, he felt that the arrangement would best meet the demands of the many narrow-gauge lines winding through the Pyrenees and Maritime Alps.

Apart from providing flexibility, Mallet's articulated setup invited compounding, and his plans

138

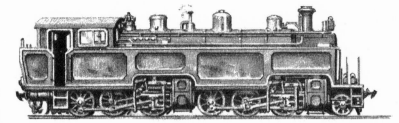

France's Anatole Mallet, the originator of the locomotives bearing his name, never received a sou from the American manufacturers who built more than 2,000 articulated compounds between 1904 and 1948.

Mallets

called for the exhausts from the second set of cylinders to be carried forward to the first through pipes and swiveling elbow joints. The worth of the system was demonstrated when a little 0-6-6-0 built to his specifications by the Creusot Works was tried out on the Bayonne & Biarritz Railway. As he had anticipated, whenever one driving unit lost its grip on the rails the flow of steam to the other increased, again balancing the power output. The only thing he overlooked was the reaction of Gascogne crews to a machine that did the work of two. Dedicated to full employment, they lost no time in damaging its parts and reputation.

Some ten years later Mallet collaborated with the Decauville Engineering Works in producing a basically similar locomotive for the French Army. Intended to draw artillery pieces and ammunition over portable tracks, the tiny 0-2-2-0 created a sensation during simulated war maneuvers outside Paris.

Among those witnessing its performance was George L. Fowler, who later revised several editions of Forney's *Catechism of the Locomotive*. He wrote:

"It was the first Mallet I ever saw and so small you could almost jump over it. The possibilities of the machine for light work were apparent in an instant. While I watched it, the engine was hauling a heavy cannon over a roadway that was being laid but a few minutes ahead of it. This was uneven country, and for the benefit of the test, soldiers were building bridges and laying track from material which had been torn up behind the locomotive as it passed. There were, altogether, only a few hundred yards of track, but it was laid so rapidly that the Mallet moved faster than I could walk. It was extremely unsteady, and the locomotive swayed back and forth, but either the forward or rear wheels always kept going."

The publicity given the trials led to substantial

The B&O's chief mechanical officer, James Muhlfeld, achieved the unique distinction of designing an experimental locomotive without faults when he adapted the overseas arrangement to American practice. His 80-foot-long Old Maud *outpulled a pair of 2-8-0s.*

orders for narrow-gauge Mallets, and at the turn of the twentieth century they were battling grades in Switzerland and Russia as well as France. By then Anatole Mallet was calling attention to the fact that conventional standard- and broad-gauge locomotives could not be made much larger without extensive improvements to existing trackwork, and he urged the adoption of his articulated design as a less costly alternative.

The proposal was ignored until 1903, when a new Baltimore & Ohio president, Leonor F. Loree, took a hard look at the number of 2-8-0s assigned to pusher service in the Alleghenies beyond Cumberland, Maryland. As much at home in a locomotive cab as an administrative office, he recalled some hours he had spent on the seatbox of a Fairlie double-ender in Mexico, and it occurred to him that dual-drive engines might be used to good advantage in the mountains.

Loree, a demanding boss, had insisted that the road's general manager, Clifford S. Simms, buy a house directly opposite his own in suburban Baltimore, so that the two could discuss business while walking to work together. On one of the extensions of the normal working day, Loree asked abruptly: "What do you know about Mallets?" At a loss for an answer, Simms could only assure him that all available data would be on his desk the following morning. Loree was impressed by the strong case the Frenchman made for engines twice as powerful as any yet produced, and at his request the B&O's chief mechanical officer, James Muhlfeld, undertook the formidable task of designing engine number *2400*— the controversial 0-6-6-0 exhibited at St. Louis.

The mighty Mallet silenced its critics when, after the Exposition, it was deadheaded to Connellsville, Pennsylvania, and tested on the line's 15-mile-long Sand Patch grade. Routinely, two heavy "Consoli-

The only Mallets ever to operate in Canada were five 0-6-6-0s built in the Canadian Pacific's Montreal shops in 1909 and 1911. Their cylinders were placed back to back to reduce condensation losses between them. A sixth engine in the series was equipped with four high-pressure cylinders, and thus, technically speaking, it was not a true Mallet.

dation" engines hoisted 2,000-ton trains to the summit, but the *2400* performed the same chore unassisted, while burning a third less coal.

Muhlfeld's attention to details had produced a phenomenon—an experimental locomotive without faults. Clusters of springs applied to the load bearing plate below the boiler held the first driving unit in firm alignment on straightaways and dampened lateral thrusts as the engine entered curves. Inadequate clearances prevented the use of inside valve gear, so Muhlfeld employed two sets of the external Walschaert type. To control them simultaneously and without effort, he provided an ingenious arrangement of levers connected to a double-acting piston housed in a small cylinder. Compressed air, directed against one face of the plunger or the other by adjusting a hand lever, lowered or raised the cumbersome radius rods and held them securely in the desired positions. An equally original device, called

an "intercepting valve," delivered high-pressure steam to all of the cylinders at starting. Then, as the need for tractive effort decreased, its passages were realigned for compound operation. Without the mechanism, Muhlfeld believed that engineers would be tempted to pour on full power at all times, and this would have overtaxed the boiler's capacity.

Not surprisingly, the men who tooled the *2400* up and down the big hill found its number too colorless for so personable a machine, and within months they gave it a name borrowed from that of a fabulously strong cartoon-strip mule. It became *Old Maud*, and retained the moniker until it was scrapped in 1938, long after the cartoon feature was forgotten.

Oddly, the Baldwin Works stole a march on *Old Maud's* maker, the American Locomotive Company, by being the first to profit from a lesson learned on the Sand Patch grade. Muhlfeld's object had been to produce a superior pusher engine, hence the absence

141

of leading and trailing wheels. Nevertheless, the *2400* clearly demonstrated the potential of articulated compound locomotives for sustained running with heavy trains, and in 1906 and 1907 Baldwin produced thirty 2-6-6-2s for the Great Northern Railway. Five were used as helpers, but the design of the others was modified for head-end service between Spokane and Leavenworth, Washington.

American Locomotive countered by delivering to the Erie Railroad three of the biggest "Mother Hubbards" ever built. They were 0-8-8-0s weighing thirty-eight more tons than *Old Maud*, and to generate the gases directly into their two miles of boiler flues and tubes they were given an unprecedented 100 square feet of grate area. The rule-of-thumb formula for determining the coal consumption of a locomotive working under load was 1½ pounds per square foot per minute. Thus the engines had a maximum combustion rate of 4.5 tons per hour, or twice what a competent fireman could handle.

Of seeming necessity, then, two shovel artists were assigned to each of the big pushers when they began nuzzling trains up an eight-mile grade from a division point at Susquehanna, Pennsylvania, to Gulf Summit, New York. What had not been anticipated was the extraordinary efficiency of the stoking teams. They soon found that while drifting back to the terminal after an ascent there was time for a single man to

spread enough fuel for the next short climb. Thereafter they split up the runs, one fireman working the hill while the other fortified himself for his turn at the scoop in a trackside saloon. An observing management quickly dropped the extra hands.

Lines using locomotives with more than 50 square feet of grate area in regular road service were less fortunate. There the only alternative to double stoking was some form of mechanical conveyer. Such devices were not new; as a matter of fact, James Millholland had applied one to a Philadelphia & Reading engine as early as 1850. It was described by the contemporary New York *Post* as "an endless chain of bars forming the bottom of the furnace, on which live coal blazes. The chain moves very slowly, not more than one inch a minute. At the end of the firebox it reverses itself and goes back underneath. The coal is laid in a hopper and the supply is regulated by a sluice slide."

Obviously, at that date Millholland's purpose was not to feed a huge furnace. Rather, he wanted to insure a clean exhaust by providing an even rate of combustion. He succeeded, but only at the expense of flexible locomotive performance. Other nineteenth-century mechanical stokers included one that pulverized coal and blew it through a firebox door, and another whose rotating blades paddled bituminous haphazardly over a fire. All were failures.

Erie engineers did not appreciate their close proximity to the stacks of their "Mother Hubbard" Mallets when the 0-8-8-0s blasted up the road's Gulf Summit grade east of Susquehanna, Pennsylvania.

The first step in the right direction came when inventors applied Archimedes' screws to conveyers. Placed in troughs and pipes and driven by small steam motors, these auger-like spirals of tough steel advanced coal from a tender and either forced it upward through a locomotive's grates or dropped it onto them from above. By 1910 stokers of both types worked well enough to replace the extra firemen on big engines.

Although larger furnaces sent greater volumes of gases through the tubes of engine boilers, gas temperatures remained the same. In effect, the larger furnaces produced more heat but not hotter heat. This posed a problem, for it had already been found that the emissions lost their steam generating heat some 22 feet ahead of a fire. Thus there was no point in extending a Mallet's water-filled, or "closed" boiler, section to the distant smokebox. Instead, a dry, or "open," cavity was placed between the two. There, after leaving the flues and tubes, the gases passed through the pipes of three auxiliary heaters. In one, the temperature of the steam on its way from the throttle valve to the rear driving unit was raised approximately 200 degrees. This did not increase its pressure, but in the terminology of the trade it was converted from "saturated" to "superheated" steam, which had greater volume and fluidity. Given these characteristics, it produced more work in relation to

the fuel consumed and created less back pressure. In addition, condensation losses were materially reduced. Another bundle of pipes reheated the steam fed to the forward cylinders, and a third brought the cold water flowing from the tender nearly to the boiling point before it was pumped into the barrel's closed section.

In 1910 it occurred to Samuel Vauclain that a Mallet's boiler could be treated as two entities, with a flexible joint connecting them at a point just ahead of the flues. This would make it possible to bolt each section to the driving unit beneath it, and the entire engine could then hinge on curves, eliminating overhang. The idea was prompted by the poor performance of a pair of passenger engines built by Baldwin for the Santa Fe a year earlier. In theory, their novel 4-4-6-2 wheel arrangement should have provided the stability and weight distribution required for fast running, but in practice they proved hard on the rails and themselves at speeds below the potential of their 73-inch drivers.

Vauclain believed that high-wheeled 2-6-6-2s of the hinged type he proposed would give and take less punishment, and the equally optimistic Santa Fe built one and purchased six from Baldwin over a two-year period. The first boiler joints were formed of fifty rings of resilient steel, each 75 inches in diameter and 10 inches wide, riveted together alternately

Believing that hinged boilers would give Mallets greater stability for high-speed running, the Santa Fe built one and purchased six from the Baldwin Locomotive Works between 1910 and 1912. When bellows connections formed of steel rings proved unsatisfactory, ball-and-socket joints were used. The locomotives failed to live up to expectations, but remained in service until the mid-1920s.

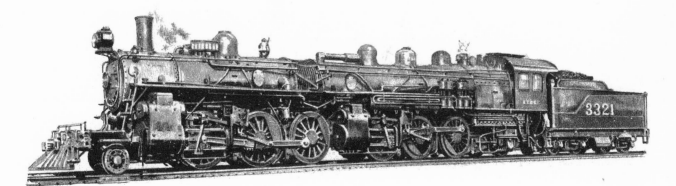

"Too many legs and not enough steam" was a familiar engineman's complaint about early Mallets. None warranted it more than the 24-drivered Triplexes designed by George R. Henderson, a consulting engineer employed by the Baldwin Works. The Matt H. Shay and two sister engines were delivered to the Erie Railroad in 1914 and 1916, and the Virginian Railway received a single 2-8-8-8-4 in 1919. While the boilers of that period were inadequate for the ambitious wheel arrangements, Henderson went on to propose Quadruplexes and Quintuplexes, and the Santa Fe seriously considered ordering a 2-8-8-8-8-2.

Matt H. Shay

Virginian 700

After a cartoon by Joseph Easley

"It took 7 miles of the Mississippi River to fill her boiler, and they cleaned her 42 acres of flues by running an old Erie engine with a snowplow through them." So ran the story of a mythical New Orleans & Fiddler's Green 4-18-0, concocted by an engineer who grew weary of listening to New York & Erie hoggers boast of the huge size of that system's 6-foot-gauge locomotives. The tall tale appeared in an early Railway Gazette.

on their inner and outer edges. These metal bellows provided the necessary flexibility until cinders accumulated in their folds of the joints. Then they burst apart on curves. A switch to huge ball-and-socket joints solved the problem, but the hinged engines rode no better than the rigid-barreled 4-4-6-2s and were soon retired.

Still venturesome, the railroad undertook an ambitious remodeling job in 1911. Ten chunky 2-10-2s hauled into its Topeka, Kansas, shops re-emerged as the world's largest locomotives—2-10-10-2s more than 120 feet long. In making the conversion the original cabs, fireboxes, water sections, and running gear were supplemented with boiler extensions, low-pressure cylinders, and high-capacity tenders supplied by Baldwin. Despite the engines' awesome proportions, the inadequate heating surfaces inherited from the 2-10-2s led to a chronic complaint by crews: "Too many legs and not enough steam."

The Mallets were just beginning to raise the echoes in Southern California's Cajon Pass when the Baldwin Works underwent a corporate change, and Vauclain assumed the vice-presidency. The firm's developmental work was assigned to George R. Henderson, a consulting engineer who saw no reason to limit an articulated locomotive's driving units to the customary two. By 1913 he held the patent rights to what he chose to call "Triplexes," "Quadruplexes," and "Quintruplexes." In each design he proposed using standardized cylinder and traction wheel assemblies, with either one or two of them placed beneath the tender.

Late that year the Erie ordered a 430-ton Triplex of the 2-8-8-8-2 type or what, in effect, was a trio of heavy "Consolidation" engines controlled by a single throttle. To provide the desired one-to-two compounding ratio, Henderson's plans called for the exhausts from a pair of high-pressure cylinders to feed four low-pressure cylinders of equal size. The steam vented from the latter was directed into two chimneys—the usual draft-inducing stack up front and a vertical pipe at the rear.

GEORGE FOX JOHNSON

Possibly the longest motive power career in America was that of George Fox Johnson, who in 1842 shaped horseshoes and nails in the shops of the Philadelphia & Columbia Railroad. Four years later he first fired and then drove the Rocket, *a Reading engine built in England. Impressed with his ability, Matthias Baldwin hired him as a locomotive messenger in 1848. In that capacity he delivered new machines to their purchasers, put them in working order, and instructed mechanics and engineers in their proper maintenance and operation. At the age of 88 Johnson ran his last engine, the Erie's 24-drivered* Matt H. Shay, *from the Eddystone plant to Susquehanna, Pennsylvania.*

Developing a starting tractive effort of 176,600 pounds, 10 Virginian 2-10-10-2s outshopped by the American Locomotive Company in 1918 were the most powerful steam engines ever built. In a widely circulated publicity photograph, the builder showed one of their boilers lying on its side with a four-drivered logging locomotive tucked in the firebox.

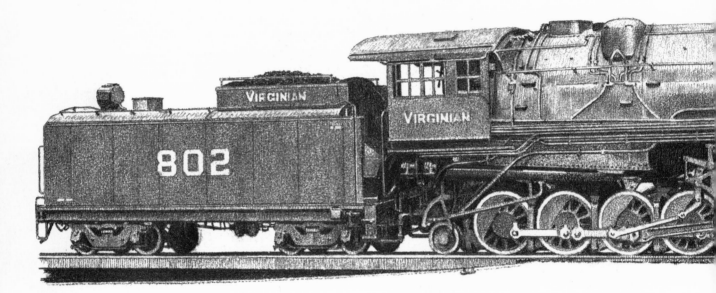

The 24-drivered Mallet left Baldwin's new plant at Eddystone, Pennsylvania, early in 1914. The Erie's president, Frederick D. Underwood, had established the policy of naming locomotives for engineers with outstanding service records, and gold lettering below the cab windows honored a veteran ballast scorcher on the road's Mahoning Division—Matt H. Shay.

Deadheaded to Susquehanna, the Triplex worked the Gulf Summit grade while the stage was set for a dramatic demonstration of its 160,000-pound tractive force. Over a period of several weeks loaded coal hoppers of the sturdiest construction were shunted onto sidings at nearby Binghamton, New York. Then

one morning the *Matt H. Shay* drifted into town and latched onto the accumulated cars—250 of them forming an 18,000-ton train. Assisted by two pushers the Mallet eased the long string into motion. Once clear of the yard it was on its own, spuming gray smoke from one stack and clear steam from the other. All went well for 17 miles, and officials crowded in the cab were no doubt dreaming of a new transportation era when a coupler suddenly let go, an air hose parted, and the train slammed to an emergency stop, plucking out a second coupler in the process. The railroad spectacular ended less than triumphantly, with two conventional Mallets lumbering

uptrack from Susquehanna to bring in the cars the Triplex had left behind.

In further tests, the *Matt H. Shay's* inadequate steaming capacity discouraged any thought of assigning the locomotive to long runs. A onetime Erie fireman later recalled without nostalgia his efforts to keep the big engine hot. Andrew Goobeck, in an article in *Railroad Magazine* in October, 1942, wrote: "I never worried about an explosion from excess pressure. We used to say that the best place for anybody to cool off on a summer day was behind the Matt Shay's firedoor. The needle on the steam gauge consistently pointed at the tallowpot's seat-

box, and I'll wager I hammered its casing more times than there are hopper cars in the State of Pennsylvania trying to get it to register a couple of extra pounds."

Henderson refused to admit defeat. In 1915 he submitted plans to the Santa Fe for a 2-8-8-8-8-2 with a jointed boiler. One of two cabs was to be placed ahead of the smokebox to give the engineer an unobstructed view of the track. In another, 75 feet behind it, the fireman would receive and acknowledge signals shouted through a speaking tube. Surprisingly, the railroad deliberated for a year before rejecting the proposed monstrosity.

In acknowledgment of his contributions to the industry, a handsome English-made "Rail Road Timekeeper," upper right, was presented to Horatio Allen upon the completion of the New York & Erie's line to Dunkirk, New York, early in 1851. Lower left: Casey Jones consulted an "American" watch only seconds before his 10-wheeled 382 carried him to glory 49 years later. Lower right: Key winders were the precursors of today's standard railroad watches, which must have bold Arabic figures, not fewer than 19 jewels, and hairsprings with five temperature-compensating positions. They can gain or lose no more than 20 seconds per week.

Pride in company engines was never more justified than in the case of the Norfolk & Western Railway, whose Roanoke, Virginia, shops produced latter-day locomotives of three superbly engineered designs: 4-8-4s for heavy passenger service, high-wheeled simple-articulated 2-8-8-4s for hotshot freights, and 2-8-8-2 Mallets to work coal drags over the southern Appalachians. Taking builder's photographs was more than a routine matter when the first engine of a new series left the railroad's 84-acre plant.

Meanwhile the Erie bought two slightly modified Triplexes which, like the *Matt H. Shay,* were effective only as pushers on the short Gulf Summit grade. Henderson's fourth and final offering—a 2-8-8-8-4 sold to the Virginian Railway in 1919—proved so inferior to ten 2-10-10-2s purchased from the American Locomotive Company in Schenectady a year earlier that within months it was truncated into a 2-8-8-0, and its rear driving unit used as the nucleus for a new "Mikado."

On the other hand, the 342-ton Schenectady products remained in service for twenty-seven years, moving 50,000 times their collective weight in coal out of the West Virginia mountains and down to tidewater at Sewalls Point, Virginia. The boilers of many narrow-gauge engines were no larger in diameter than the giants' forward cylinders—immense castings with 48-inch bores. The 2-10-10-2s exerted the greatest starting tractive force (176,600 pounds) of any steam locomotives ever built, and nearly a quarter of an acre of evaporative heating surfaces apiece gave them the capacity for sustained performance.

Powerful though they were, super-Mallets like these reintroduced the problem of high back pressures. Too, they rode hard, even at very low speeds, nosing heavily in response to the shuttling action of the massive pistons up front. What had once been the virtue of using steam twice became a handicap, and for a time it seemed that articulated engines would never be more than plodding workhorses.

151

13 Years of

The spectacular successes and failures of various Mallet designs overshadowed the steady progress made in improving nonarticulated locomotives during the same period. Here, innovations benefitting both forms of motive power were made without fanfare.

None had a more immediate impact than the invention of the single-axled trailing truck. As early as the 1840s the master mechanics of several New England roads had placed small wheels behind the drivers of 4-2-0s, but they were held in rigid alignment with the engine frames. The same was true of those applied to the first 4-2-2, or authentic "Bicycle" type, and of the original 2-4-2, or "Columbia," both of which were Baldwin products, sold to the Philadelphia & Reading in 1880 and 1892, respectively.

At the turn of the present century, however, designers developed a variety of subframe assemblies and trucks capable of shifting from side to side to accommodate themselves to curves. With these, wide grates could be placed below the tops of the driving wheels, and the correspondingly deepened fireboxes offered more than twice the cubic content formerly available for combustion. Since the boiler water absorbed about 85 percent of its heat through direct contact with the furnace walls and crownsheet, there was every reason to adopt the new arrangement.

Other ways were found to upgrade firebox performance, and again the past offered precedents. In 1857 George S. Griggs, a master mechanic on the Boston & Providence, had converted a group of engines from wood to bituminous burners by placing sloping shelves above their grates. Formed of firebricks supported by iron bars, the baffles forced the underlying flames to sweep far to the rear before they were drawn back over them and into the flues.

152

Vulcan Iron Works, Wilkes-Barre, Pennsylvania, offered a diminutive articulated locomotive for industrial service. The Dick Construction Company's Number 144 *came out of the shop in 1931.*

Glory

The lengthened travel provided more time for escaping embers to be burned, and the "brick arches" worked very well until—as happened too often— intense heat melted the bars. That problem was solved in a simple manner when they were reintroduced in 1900. Iron pipes took the place of the vulnerable supports, and water coursing through them not only protected the metal but improved the circulation in the boiler.

In 1916 another method of consuming embers before they reached the flues was borrowed from the past. In designing his culm-burning furnace, John Wootten had placed an open boiler section directly ahead of it, with a fire wall blocking off the lower half. In doing so he followed the example set by Isaac Dripps in building the *Monster* forty years before, but the combustion chamber worked better on the big "Camelbacks," and between 1916 and 1918

the arrangement was applied to conventional and articulated locomotives alike. By then it had the additional value of limiting the length of the flues beyond to an efficient 22 feet.

Mention has already been made of the primitive superheaters placed in the boilers of early Mallets. A more satisfactory type was designed by a German engineer, Wilhelm Schmidt, and in 1910 a group of accessory suppliers founded the Superheater Company of New York to promote it. The mechanism consisted of a reservoir, or "header," divided into two compartments, and a number of external tubes folded back upon themselves twice to form long double loops. The former occupied a portion of the engine's smokebox, with each loop fitted into the forward end of a boiler flue. Saturated steam entered one header compartment and rushed on through the flame-enveloped loops, where its temperature was

153

The Pennsylvania's Class K-4 "Pacific" Number 1737 was the prototype for more than 420 of the durable speed queens built by and for the system between 1914 and 1927. Only two railroads, the PRR and the Great Northern, routinely used fireboxes of the Belpaire type shown in cross section. Concentrically curved crownsheets and external shells were connected by staybolts of a single length, insuring uniform expansion and contraction of the assemblies.

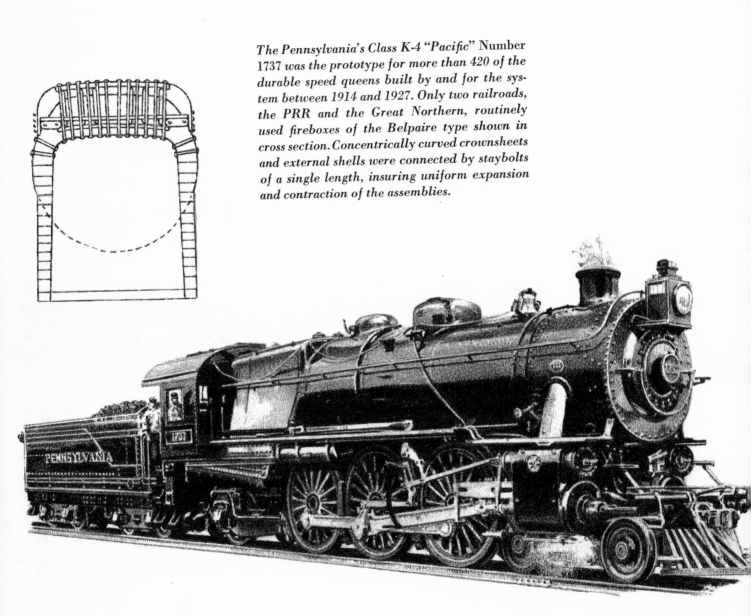

In an attempt to provide superior stability for four
fast passenger engines built in its shops in 1915, the
Reading equipped them with two-axled trailing
trucks. Poor design led to excessive lateral play and
within a year the machines were converted to 4-4-2s.
Wide Wootten fireboxes called for radial staybolts
of varying lengths.

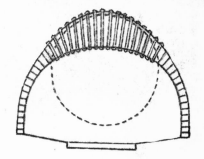

As boiler girths increased, locomotives swallowed their stacks and were enveloped by steam and smoke at high speeds, impeding crew visibility. Smokebox flanking metal wings relieved this condition by creating strong updrafts. A few systems, among them the Santa Fe and the Milwaukee Road, resorted to compressed air-actuated stack extensions, which could be lowered where clearances were limited. With or without such devices, operating officials frowned on black emissions of the type admired by rail photographers and artists.

substantially raised. After returning to the second compartment, the superheated supply was passed along to the throttle valve.

In time this Schmidt design dominated the market. Of more immediate importance, it wrote an end to the brief history of balanced compound engines by providing comparable fuel economy without the need for extra cylinders or moving parts.

Concurrently with these improvements, boilers grew to girths limited only by road clearances. These full-waisted locomotives came to be known as "pigs" or "hogs," and their engineers as "hoggers." The large locomotives created new problems. Stacks all but disappeared within smokeboxes, and their exhausts engulfed the fat barrels at high speeds. The intense draft slammed the eruptions against tunnel roofs, releasing showers of bricks, and single-track bores were so nearly plugged by big engines that their cabs became lethal gas chambers. Many years ago a Southern Railway brakeman, H. G. Monroe, described in *Railroad Magazine* the discomfort of his first trip on a "Mikado" through the long Braswell Tunnel in northern Georgia. He wrote:

The last trickle of daylight faded. The labored thunder of the exhaust slugged at our eardrums; the heat and smoke grew ever more intense. It was like slow baking in a Dutch oven.

We buried our faces in our caps and wads of wet cotton waste—coughing and choking. I had visions of stalling, and tried to steal a glimpse of the gauge. I thought of the water tank on the tender and wished I was in it up to my neck—and then some. About that time the drivers started to dance. But the hogger caught her, like a wayward wench being drawn to her feet by a true Southern gentleman.

We were suffocating, and yet we burrowed deep into coats and jumpers, trying to shut out the stifling heat and smoke fumes. My ears rang—or perhaps it was chimes. I vowed that if I ever got out of Braswell Tunnel I'd lead a sweeter, purer life. And then, suddenly, we were through, and Braswell Mountain was behind us.

Less dramatically, external auxiliaries had to be recontoured or moved to new positions. With boilers often more than nine feet in diameter, sand in the domes above could no longer flow by gravity to the rails below. One solution was to mount pairs of bins well to the sloping sides, but they obstructed an engineman's already restricted view of the rails ahead. In a later arrangement, compressed air jetting from a central pipe forced the sand outward and into the little receptacles, or "traps," which held predetermined amounts for each application.

The small Westinghouse pumps once bolted to the right sides of slim barrels had been supplanted by bulky Duplex compressors capable of compacting 150 cubic feet of air a minute to the 140-pound pressure at which it was delivered to the main reservoirs. Engines used in mountain service frequently carried two Duplexes mounted, for want of adequate clearances elsewhere, on smokebox fronts. Lowering locomotive bells was often mandatory, and this could be done only by moving their hangers to the head end, or setting them well to one side of a boiler's centerline. Even whistles were tilted forward or backward, and set in recesses.

This was the general condition of motive power when the federal government took over the operation of the railroads in 1918 as a World War I emergency measure. By then there were only three major independent builders—American, Baldwin, and the Lima Locomotive Company.

The last was a newcomer in name, incorporated two years earlier by the same group of accessory suppliers who had sponsored the Schmidt superheater. However, the western Ohio plant they acquired had been turning out engines since 1880, when, as Carnes, Agather & Company, it added to the manufacture of sawmill equipment the construction of a unique logging locomotive invented by a Michigan lumberman, Ephraim Shay. On the right side of the machine's vertical boiler a pair of upright cylinders powered a longitudinal crankshaft connected by flexible linkage and bevel gears to the wheels of two trucks. The "Shay" adjusted itself to the dips and rises of hastily laid track far better than direct-drive engines, and orders for others soon followed. Over a period of sixty-five years, marked by three changes in management, the "side-winders" evolved into twelve- and sixteen-wheeled huskies with horizontal boilers and three cylinders, developing 60,000 pounds of starting tractive effort. The building of conventional locomotives began in 1912, and the Lima Locomotive Company placed increased emphasis upon that phase of the business.

EPHRAIM SHAY

The locomotive design introduced by Michigan lumberman Ephraim Shay featured upright cylinders placed to the right of an offset boiler. The driving rods turned a train of shafts, universal joints, and bevel gears transmitting power to the wheels of two or more swiveling trucks. The setup combined high tractive effort with the flexibility required of engines operated on light and hastily laid industrial rails.

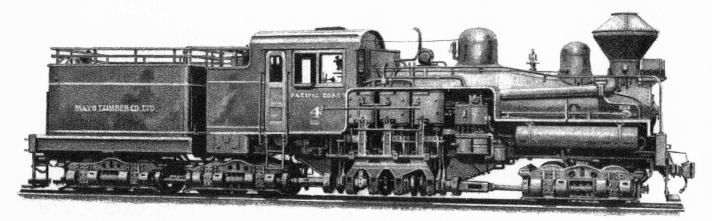

Primitive "Shays" evolved into the powerful "Pacific Coast" type developed by Lima in 1926. The last of the triple truckers was constructed 19 years later.

Together with railroad representatives and American and Baldwin engineers, Lima's designers comprised a committee appointed by the United States Railroad Administration to develop twelve standard types of engine for wartime service. These included a six-wheeled switcher, an eight-wheeled switcher, a 2-6-6-2, a 2-8-8-2, and a "light" and " heavy" version each of a "Mikado," "Santa Fe," "Pacific," and "Mountain" type. Only the last-named was of a comparatively new wheel arrangement—the 4-8-2—introduced by the Chesapeake & Ohio Railway, and built by American's Richmond, Virginia, plant in 1911.

Unlike many of the "plumber's nightmares" which

preceded them, the U.S.R.A. locomotives were well proportioned and pleasing in appearance. More to the point, large numbers of interchangeable parts were mass-produced, making for rapid production and minimum construction costs. In less than two years a total of 1,830 of them left the three builders' erecting shops.

The lesson which might have been learned from this efficient and economical policy was ignored when the railroads were returned to private control in 1920. It has often been said that General Motors' later success in driving steam locomotives from the rails was due in large measure to the refusal of its

Competing with "Shays" for geared locomotive sales, Heisler engines built in Erie, Pennsylvania, used pairs of inclined cylinders to stroke crankshafts centered beneath their boilers. One axle on each power truck was driven by gears, and connecting rods passed the motion along to the other.

Between 1888 and 1928 the Climax Manufacturing Company of Corry, Pennsylvania, was another aggressive competitor of the "Shay." The Class C model illustrated weighed 70 tons and was equipped with a spark-arresting stack for use on a logging road.

End view of a Climax truck with the bolster removed shows the staggered positions of the bevel gears.

Back-pedaling behemoths. The Southern Pacific's 4211 and 69 sister engines completed after 1940 weighed more than 500 tons with loaded tenders, and exerted a starting tractive effort of 124,300 pounds. Preheated crude oil was pumped 50 feet forward to feed the burners in their brick-floored fireboxes.

diesel-manufacturing Electro-Motive Division to cater to the individual whims of railroad mechanical departments. With a single line of well-designed units and a "take them at attractive prices or leave them" sales approach, EMD won the approval of expenditure-conscious managements.

In 1922 the Baldwin Works attracted attention with merchandising of another sort. The country was in the grip of a postwar economic slump, and the only activity at the firm's relocated plant in Eddystone, Pennsylvania, was the construction of fifty 2-10-2s ordered by the Southern Pacific during a previous boom. One by one the freight hogs rolled out of the

paint shop, ready for delivery but unclaimed by the purchasing road. The builder's new president, Samuel Vauclain, saw a parallel to the nation's economic doldrums in the vast amount of power immobilized on his company's storage tracks, and on May 26 he turned the symbolism to good account.

In response to his invitation, scores of industrial leaders, financiers, and politicians flocked to Eddystone for a colorful ceremony, complete with pretty girls, blaring bands, and a flag-draped speaker's platform. Behind the assemblage, twenty of the "Espee" engines were coupled heel to toe. Up front, a pair of Pennsylvania Railroad 2-8-2s added the drumming

Re-wheeling a 2-10-2 in the Santa Fe's San Bernardino, California, shops. A complete, or "Class 5," overhaul involved the checking of approximately 25,000 parts, making the necessary replacements, and applying updated auxiliaries. The result was a locomotive superior to the original machine.

162

of their air pumps to the festive din, waiting for a signal to pick up slack and deadhead the locomotive train over the first leg of a well-publicized run to the Pacific coast at Los Angeles.

As he admitted in his autobiography, *Steaming Up!* Vauclain had no fondness for formal attire. Nevertheless, frock-coated and black-tied, he rose to his six-foot-three-inch height and boomed: "This great demonstration originates in a desire to show the people of the United States of America that business is not dead in our country as it is in many other parts of the world. It has been done to inspire confidence, not only here but abroad, so that we may go forward to achieve our usual victory and have prosperity restored to us."

At that auspicious moment a telegram was thrust into his hand.

"I have here," he concluded, "a message from the President of the United States. It reads: 'My blessing on the *Prosperity Special;* may her speed be steadily maintained, and may God grant her a safe arrival.' Signed: 'Warren G. Harding.'"

Maintaining a steady speed was not the purpose of the *Prosperity Special,* however. Every portion of the run was made in daylight hours, and there were numerous layovers in Pennsylvania, Ohio, Indiana, Missouri, Kansas, Oklahoma, Texas, and California. At each stop local celebrities were on hand, prize-winning high school essays read, and cups of Prohibition-vintage beverages raised in optimistic toasts. What effect this had upon the country's swift return to normalcy could not be measured, but certainly no motive-power display ever won wider acclaim.

A year later the Chesapeake & Ohio gave articulated locomotives a long-term lease on the future by working up plans for a 2-8-8-2 in which high-pressure steam was fed to the four cylinders at all times. While attempts to eliminate the Mallet system of compounding had been tried twice before—once by the Canadian Pacific in 1909, and again by the Pennsylvania in 1919—it remained for the C&O's big "Chesapeakes" to prove that it was no longer necessary to conserve a boiler's output by using steam twice. It was true that the new breed of "simple articulated" engines could not develop the enormous tractive effort exerted by Mallets at starting, but freedom from the latters' objectionable back pressures permitted higher operating speeds. Between 1923 and

1926 the road acquired forty-five of the 2-8-8-2s, dividing the orders between American and Baldwin.

The designation "Chesapeakes" was a geographical misnomer, inasmuch as all of the locomotives operated out of inland Russell, Kentucky—either northward to Columbus and Toledo, Ohio, or eastward up the valleys of the Kanawha and New rivers to Hinton, West Virginia. To anyone unfamiliar with the big engines' steam distributing system, their popular nickname—"Simple Simons"—must have seemed equally inappropriate, for they were sharp performers and had an immediate impact on the industry. Plodding Mallets throughout the country

After heat-expanded tires were applied to driving wheels, they shrank to a firm fit. Here a worn tire is removed—again with the heat of burners on an encompassing ring of gas pipe.

163

The designation "Mikado" became highly unpopular soon after the last of six Lima-built 2-8-2s were placed in service by the Detroit, Toledo & Ironton in 1941, and throughout World War II all locomotives of that type were called "Mac-Arthurs." By any name the DT&I engines did credit to their manufacturer, whose plant they passed on their daily runs between the Rouge and Ohio rivers, hauling unprocessed iron ore one way and steel for Detroit the other.

Although neither the heaviest nor the most powerful "Berkshires" ever built, the Louisville & Nashville's 42 locomotives of that wheel arrangement had no peers in the matter of styling. Incorporating every advanced auxiliary and refinement known to the trade, they nevertheless retained an air of uncluttered elegance in keeping with the name trains they often handled over the Old Reliable's mountain districts in prediesel days. Orders, divided between Baldwin and Lima, were dated 1942, 1944, and 1949.

164

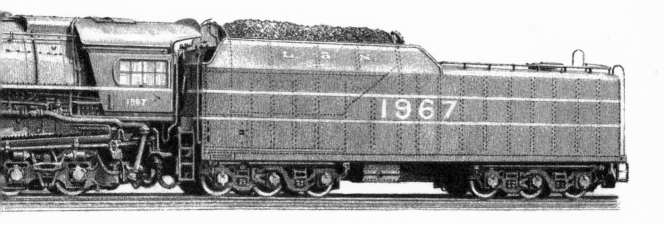

were trundled into railroad shops and upgraded by replacing their huge forward cylinders with high-pressure sets.

This was an extensive project for the Southern Pacific, which owned the world's largest and most unusual fleet of articulated locomotives. Known as "cab-in-fronters," the machines dated back to 1910. In the preceding year the road had bought two of the first four 2-8-8-2s ever built—capable Baldwin products almost identical in their specifications to a pair delivered to the Santa Fe. The Espee Mallets were assigned to service on the system's Overland Route and, more specifically, to heavy freight trains on the famous "Hill"—a tortuous stretch of track ascending the west slope of the High Sierras between Roseville, California, and Summit, Nevada. There the rails climbed 6,623 vertical feet in 89 miles, with a ruling grade of 2.65 percent. The sixteen-drivered giants raised impressive echoes in the canyons, and equally loud complaints from the enginemen who tooled them through more than 20 miles of snowsheds. Those long timber structures, which kept the line open when winter drifts piled from 50 to 200 feet deep in the passes, trapped smoke as effectively as tunnels, and the otherwise satisfactory engines were soon transferred to another district.

At about the same time, the Italian State Railways relieved a similar situation in the Alps with a number of locomotives whose boilers and cabs were reversed in relation to the undergear, placing crews ahead of the toxic stack emissions. Cylindrical water cars trailed the engines, and not-too-plentiful supplies of coal were stored in hoppers above the running boards. Closer to home, a little cab-in-fronter had chugged up and down California's 3-foot-gauge North Pacific Coast Railway for six years prior to 1905, when a careless fireman let its tubes burn out. Tunnel gas presented no problem on that road; rather the object of the design was to give the engineer a better view of a very crooked roadway. The NPC locomotive differed from the Italian machines in another respect, for it used crude oil as a fuel, and a generous amount of the heavy liquid was carried in a conventional tender, heated to the proper fluidity, and pumped forward to the firebox.

Between them, these engines offered a solution to the Southern Pacific's dilemma. The domestic locomotive, in particular, provided an attractive model

for the railroad, since most of its existing engines burned oil rather than coal. This meant that large oil-burning cab-in-fronters could be operated on the system with no more than the usual number of fueling stops. Under the supervision of Howard Stillwell, the company's mechanical department collaborated with Baldwin in working up plans for a back-pedaling 2-8-8-2, and fifteen of the bland-faced monsters were built and shipped west in 1910.

Apart from their curious appearance, the most noteworthy feature of the "AC"s (Articulated Consolidations) was the massive construction of the engine beds. This attempt to provide adequate crew protection in the event of head-end collisions probably had more psychological than practical value. But one thing is certain—the men up front rode through the snowsheds in greater comfort. Within a year, twelve passenger-hauling 2-6-6-2s, or "AM"s (Articulated Moguls), were added to the roster, and since speed was of no concern on the Hill they served their purpose well. The cab-in-fronter fleet continued to grow, both before and after the original engines were converted into simple machines and provided with four-wheeled guiding trucks to better absorb nose-heavy side thrusts on curves. During the closing months of World War II, when "Tokyo Expresses" were thundering westward by the thousands, more than 250 of them worked the Espee's stiffest grades, from Stein's Pass, New Mexico, to Cascade Summit, Oregon.

A nonarticulated renaissance of sorts began with the introduction of the 2-8-4 type in 1925. A pilot model, designed and built by Lima, was first tested on the Boston & Albany in February of that year. While a number of two-axled trailing trucks had been used in the past to improve stability, the principal purpose of the one applied to the demonstrator was to increase the size of the heating plant above. Its four wheels supported a stoker-fed firebox whose 337 square feet of evaporating surfaces exceeded those of the largest Mallets. An 8-foot-diameter boiler generated dry steam at the then high pressure of 240 pounds to the square inch. The valve gear differed from the Walschaerts design, employing a combination of small levers, rather than links and sliding blocks, to control the action of the pistons in a pair of 28-by-30-inch cylinders. The motion of this Baker gear was somewhat less smooth, but the wearing

166

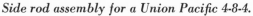

Side rod assembly for a Union Pacific 4-8-4.

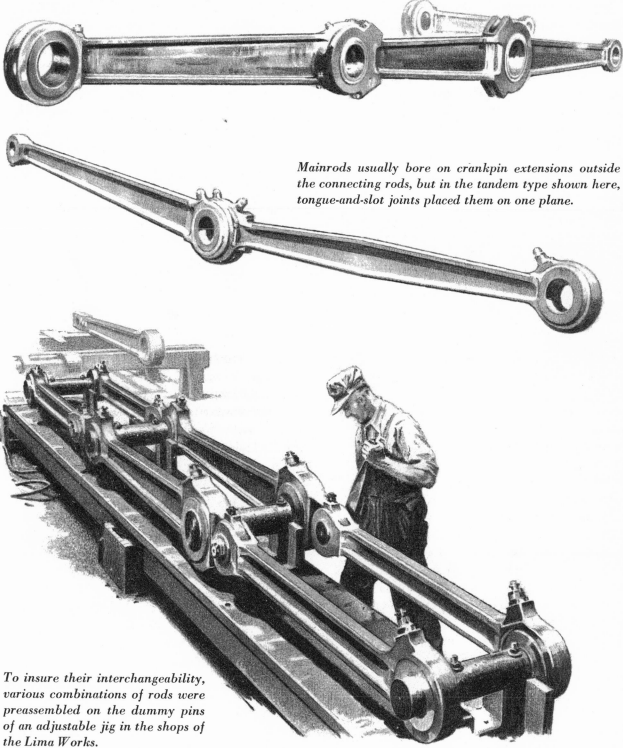

Mainrods usually bore on crankpin extensions outside the connecting rods, but in the tandem type shown here, tongue-and-slot joints placed them on one plane.

To insure their interchangeability, various combinations of rods were preassembled on the dummy pins of an adjustable jig in the shops of the Lima Works.

Latter-day cabs were dwarfed by the bulk of the boilers ahead, the running gear below, and the tenders trailing them. When engineers notched up their throttles, the rivet-blistered cubicles resounded with dissonant bangings, hissings, and crunchings. These Erie men rode the business end of an S-3 "Berkshire" towering 16 feet 4 inches above the rails.

areas were limited to inexpensively replaced pivotal bearings. The relative merits of the two mechanisms remained a subject for inconclusive debate until the last days of steam power.

The experimental *A-1* promptly distinguished itself on a 55-mile run from Selkirk Yard, near Albany, to North Adams Junction, Massachusetts. Coupled to a 2,296-ton merchandiser, it eased onto the high iron 47 minutes after one of the B&A's "Mikados" left the same terminal with a 1,691-ton train. Blasting upgrade into the Taconic Mountains, the demonstrator overtook the 2-8-2 in a little over an hour and lazied to a stop at the junction 10 minutes ahead of it.

Culminating a round of similar tests throughout the country, the *A-1* turned in its finest performance on the Milwaukee Road, where it head-ended the sixteen-car *Olympian* the entire distance from Chicago to Seattle—2,188 miles across the prairies and over the Rockies, Bitterroots, and Cascades. At that time the longest regular engine runs in the world were the Santa Fe System's 603-mile passenger assignments between Winslow, Arizona, and Los Angeles, all handled by Baldwin-built 4-8-2s.

Lima's bid for sales paid off. The Boston & Albany ordered fifty-five of the 2-8-4s and gave them their generic name—"Berkshires." The Illinois Central bought fifty, including the *A-1*, and before the year was out the Texas & Pacific accepted delivery of ten 2-10-4s basically similar to the 2-8-4s but with extended boilers and 29-by-32-inch cylinders. In each case the locomotives were equipped with small auxiliary steam engines which engaged their rear trailing truck axles. Designed for use at starting and low speeds on heavy grades, the two-cylindered "boosters" added more than 12,000 pounds of tractive effort to that provided by the driving wheels ahead.

The staunchest advocates of the "Berkshire" and "Texas" types were a group of roads being welded into a transportation empire more extensive, if less publicized, than those created by the earlier Vanderbilts, Jim Hill, and Edward H. Harriman. The quiet men behind the operation were the Van Sweringen brothers—Oris P. and Mantis J. In 1916 these young real estate developers had bought the New York, Chicago & St. Louis (Nickel Plate) from the New York Central, only because the long-neglected and unwanted line was up for sale for less than it would have cost them to build an interurban system from Cleveland, Ohio, to an outlying suburb they were promoting.

With the Nickel Plate came the services of an able operating official, John J. Bernet, who did such an effective job of converting it into a profitable property that his employers spent the next fourteen years acquiring similarly rundown railroads, all of which he and comparably qualified administrators revitalized. By 1930, when a congressional committee took note of the Van Sweringens' holdings and laid the groundwork for antitrust proceedings, their vast domain included the NYC&StL, the Pere Marquette, the Erie, the Chesapeake & Ohio, the Missouri Pacific, the Texas & Pacific, and the International–Great Northern, together with fifteen subsidiaries. The network added up to 28,500 Class I route miles, or one out of every eight in the United States.

Transferred to the presidency of the Erie in 1927, Bernet wryly observed that he had nothing better to work with than wide clearances—the result of the road's having originally been laid to a 6-foot gauge. The antiquity of the company's rolling stock was matched by that of its 1,500 locomotives. They averaged an unimpressive 66 miles per engine per day, at a maintenance cost of 36 cents a mile, or half again the usually acceptable figure.

Within two years the new administrator saw to it that 427 of the venerable kettles were scrapped and hundreds of others modernized. The slack was taken up by ordering 105 "Berkshires" from American, Baldwin, and Lima. Weighing from 27 to 40 tons more than the *A-1*, these 3300s and 3400s matched its tractive effort with drivers ¾ foot higher. The 70-inch wheels permitted better counterbalancing, and the husky freight haulers rode smoothly with wide-open throttles.

Moving on to the Chesapeake & Ohio in 1929, Bernet pressed for the formation of an Advisory Mechanical Committee to pool the network's engineering talent. The proposal met with the Van Sweringens' approval and the C&O became the first beneficiary.

Sold on large nonarticulated locomotives, the AMC reevaluated the performance of the line's 2-8-8-2s. The simple articulateds had racked up enviable records in mountain service but, their superiority to Mallets notwithstanding, they could not be run at the speeds invited by the easy gradients north of Russell,

169

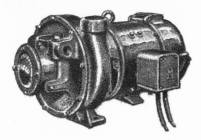

Turbines quickly replaced the reciprocating engines first used to drive electric headlight generators. The unit's 32-volt direct current output ranged from 500 to 1,000 watts.

Most latter-day headlights were centered on smokebox fronts. Hoods and flagstaffs embellished those applied to the Southern Railway's green and gold "Pacific" and "Mountain" engines.

Generators were frequently placed just ahead of cabs, where, in theory, they were exposed to a minimum of abrasive grit and grime.

The positions of Pennsylvania headlights and generators were reversed in the early 1940s to place the latter farther from the stacks and make them more accessible for servicing.

A typical headlight, equipped with a glass reflector, 200-watt lamp, and illuminated number boards. Incandescent lamps were preceded by arc lights, whose intense beams could not be dimmed.

The upper of two headlights recessed in the silver smokebox fronts of the Southern Pacific's Class GS-4 4-8-4s projected oscillating beams to warn motorists of the engine's approach.

Placing two small seal-beam headlights in one housing was a 1938 development. If one failed, the other provided adequate illumination.

With the coming of the Mallets, headlights were mounted on the pilots of the forward driving units to keep the beams in reasonable alignment with curving track. The Chesapeake & Ohio liked the arrangement, which placed the point of greatest light intensity below an opposing engineer's direct line of vision, and all of its later engines —including this "Hudson"—carried the lamps under their chins.

Complying with a 1942 War Production Board ruling that all new locomotives must be of tried-and-proven designs, the Pennsylvania chose the Chesapeake & Ohio's 12-year-old 2-10-4s as prototypes for 125 keystone-emblazoned J-1s. The 493½-ton giants emerged from the company's Juniata shops at the rate of three a week.

Kentucky. A Baldwin-built "Berkshire"—the Erie's S-3 *Number 3377*—was brought down to the coal road's nearby Huntington, West Virginia, shops and prepared for comparative tests with the "Chesapeakes." Heavy trackwork permitted a greater amount of the engine's weight to be placed on the drivers, and the equalizing system was adjusted to provide it. At the same time, the safety valves were set to pop at a pressure of 265 rather than 250 pounds.

While the 2-8-4 failed to handle the 10,500-ton drags to which the hinged engines were routinely assigned, its otherwise superior characteristics encouraged the committee to draft plans for a 2-10-4 incorporating the most impressive specifications yet drawn up for a rigid-frame locomotive. These included a grate area of 121.7 square feet, heating

surfaces totaling nearly a fifth of an acre, 29-by-34-inch cylinders, 69-inch drivers, and a booster-supplemented tractive effort of 108,625 pounds. Together with their tenders, the engines each were to weigh 490 tons and stretch 111 feet between couplers. An order for forty of the "Texas" types was placed with Lima, and the giants rolled out of its plant at the rate of better than three a week in the fall of 1930.

With all their parts scaled up harmoniously, it was impossible to appreciate the immense size of the 2-10-4s unless a "Chesapeake" stood conveniently near. Tight tunnel clearances east of Russell had limited the heights of the 2-8-8-2s to a shade over 15 feet and that, combined with their relatively low drivers, created an illusion of abnormal length. Yet

174

Turntable pits were the hubs of multistall roundhouses. As many as 44 tracks radiated from them, and the largest of the rotating bridges were 135 feet long. With roller bearings applied to their center pivots, two 35-horsepower electric motors provided enough power to turn 600-ton locomotives. Here, at the Norfolk & Western's Shaffers Crossing terminal in Roanoke, Virginia, a restive 2-6-6-4 awaits its signal to clump onto the outbound irons.

King Louis XIV and his courtiers literally took a turn in the Gardens of Versailles when a tramway was installed on the palace grounds in 1714.

the largest of the lot were only 7 feet longer than the "Texas" types and weighed 54 tons less.

New performance standards were set when the big Limas laid their smoke banners across Ohio's midriff drawing 160-car coal trains bound for Toledo's docks. The 13,500-ton assignments called for helpers only at starting and on a short grade out of Columbus. Elsewhere the superb machines maintained the operating speeds demanded by Bernet, and the 2¼ hours allotted them for terminal servicing and turning was proof of their high availability.

It might be added that 12 years after the 2-10-4s first thundered over the accommodating route to the Great Lakes they were paid the high tribute of imitation. World War II was imposing an unprecedented burden on America's railroads, and the need for large

numbers of new locomotives became acute. There was neither time nor precious steel to devote to unproven designs and, in compliance with a War Production Board ruling, construction was limited to engines patterned after existing power. The hard-pressed Pennsylvania System selected the C&O's aging but still remarkable behemoths as the prototypes for 125 Class J-1 and J-1a 2-10-4s built by its Juniata shops and by Baldwin between December 1942 and the end of 1943. The PRR versions differed only in their slightly increased weights and boiler pressures, the use of sixteen-wheeled tenders of a type that the road had already developed, and minor appliance and styling changes. While the matter is debatable, there are those who still maintain that no finer freight engines ever burnished "Pennsy" rails.

175

Three-cylindered "Union Pacific" 4-12-2s left impressive service records etched with sand on mountain rails in Wyoming, Utah, Idaho, and Oregon. Worked to full capacity, their fuel consumption was a modest 7 tons an hour. With the coming of the "Challengers" and "Big Boys," they were reassigned to Nebraska runs.

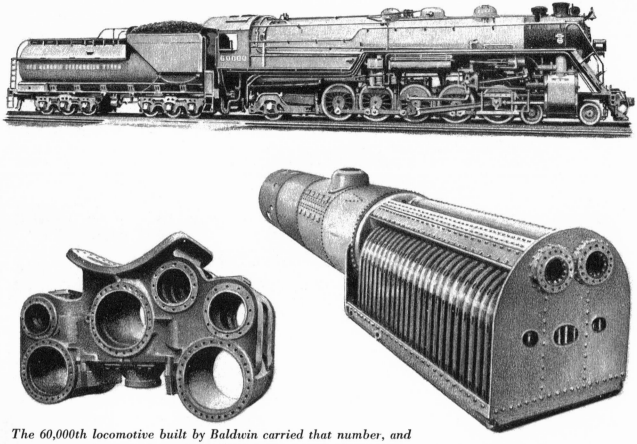

The 60,000th locomotive built by Baldwin carried that number, and was an experimental three-cylinder 4-10-2. Forty-eight 4-inch water tubes on each side of its firebox provided circulation from a "mud ring"—a hollow, rectangular frame encompassing the grates—upward to a pair of drums connected to the boiler's water section.

Returning to the early impact of Lima's *A-1* on the industry, the responses of the American Locomotive Company and the Baldwin Works were predictably prompt. In 1925 the former proposed, as a logical successor to the "Santa Fe" type, a 4-10-2 powered by three cylinders receiving steam directly from the boiler. With the mainrods stroking outside pins and an axle crank placed 120 degrees apart, the torque would be improved, and the uniformly spaced exhausts promised a more even rate of combustion. Both the Southern Pacific and the Union Pacific invested in these "Overlands," and despite the added cost of maintaining inside connections the locomotives gave good accounts of themselves, burning fuel conservatively in relation to the increased tonnages they handled.

Characteristically, the UP was back within a year demanding larger, faster, and more powerful three-cylinder engines with six pairs of 67-inch drivers and a weight, including tender, of 403½ tons. The first of the wonderfully ugly "Union Pacific" types left American's Dunkirk, New York, plant in April, 1926, and after testing it took its place in regular freight service on runs between Cheyenne, Wyoming, and Ogden, Utah. By then the measure of a locomotive's worth was a realistic figure obtained by multiplying the tonnage assigned to the engine by the number of miles it traveled in an hour. On that "ton-miles per hour" basis, the *9000* and other 4-12-2s showed an 80 percent gain over the plodding Mallets they replaced. Watching them hammer up either slope of the Wasatch Range with their triple exhausts

Horatio Allen's 2-2-2-2s of 1831 excepted, the B&O's 5600 was the first American locomotive to combine two independent driving units with a single rigid engine bed. Designed by the road's chief mechanical officer, George H. Emerson, and constructed at the Mount Clare shops in 1937, the 386-ton 4-4-4-4 went the disheartening way of all engines equipped with water tube fireboxes.

"Every time we sent her out a machine shop had to go with her." That was a D&H veteran's unflattering evaluation of a triple-expansion "Mastodon," the L. F. Loree, built to the railroad's specifications by the American Locomotive Company in 1933. Steam at 500 pounds pressure was first fed to a small cylinder under the engineer's side of the cab. The exhaust was directed to an intermediate cylinder on the fireman's side and, finally, to two low-pressure cylinders up front.

In 1934 the New York Central streamlined one of its eye-filling Class J-1e "Hudsons" and assigned it to the crack Commodore Vanderbilt. A year later the undergear was revamped by applying lightweight main and side rods to new sets of drivers of the Scullin disk type. Mechanical improvements notwithstanding, the result was a locomotive with the esthetic charm of an inverted bathtub.

By 1938 the Central had called upon a New York industrial designer, Henry Dreyfuss, to develop distinctive cowlings for 10 Class J-3a "Hudsons" head-ending the Twentieth Century Limited. The effect was so pleasing that the Commodore engine was returned to the railroad's West Albany shops and given the same treatment. It was again stripped of its shroud in 1945 for easier maintenance.

buffeting one another in unseemly haste, it appeared unlikely that they would ever be "bumped" by more impressive locomotives.

Baldwin's bid for customer approval took a somewhat different form. Then in its ninety-fourth year, the firm drew attention to the 60,000th locomotive built in its shops by giving it that number. The handsome, if unorthodox, 4-10-2 was a demonstrator, and the sales promotion rationale was this:

1. The best available valve and cylinder lubricants broke down at superheated steam temperatures above 700 degrees Fahrenheit.

2. Since it was impractical to use steam at higher temperatures, further increases in operating pressures would result in a reduction of heat content per pound of steam. It followed that nothing was gained in thermal efficiency.

3. Higher pressures were desirable, and they could be accompanied by improved thermal efficiency if greater use were made of the expansive properties of steam. This meant a return to compound operation.

Based upon that logic, the 360-ton *60000* was provided with a water tube firebox combined with a conventional boiler generating 350-pound steam, and the output was fed to one high- and two low-pressure cylinders.

Improved fuel economy notwithstanding, the locomotive did not live up to expectations. The objectionable features of three-cylinder compounding reasserted themselves, and the water tube firebox proved even more troublesome. The advantages of eliminating thousands of staybolts and providing increased heating surfaces with two cylindrical drums and four banks of pipes were more than offset by the arrangement's inadaptability to rapid temperature changes. These did not occur in marine or stationary plant installations, but every variation in locomotive speed increased or reduced the draft and its effect upon the fire's intensity. Leaking flue joints at the forward ends of conventional fireboxes were not uncommon, and an engine could generally work its way over the road in spite of them. But when water spurted from the *60000's* overhead tube and drum connections, steam filled the cavity and drowned out the coals. If the demonstrator served a worthwhile purpose, it was to give officials of the roads testing it fair warn-

ing of the trials in store for those who later pinned their hopes on that form of heating system.

While the *60000* was making its unsuccessful sales tour, the New York Central's mechanical department conducted experiments of its own with a reworked 4-6-2. Mainline passenger traffic was heavy, and a growing number of "overnighters" were being dispatched in two or more sections. As the posh flyers roared east and west, observation platform riders watched without concern the three-mile-distant headlights trailing them at 80 miles an hour. The rails linking New York with Chicago and St. Louis had become, in effect, a high-speed conveyer belt, and intermediate station stops called for rapid decelerations and reaccelerations to ensure its smooth action. Ever-improved air brakes met the former demand, but increasing train weights taxed the capacities of the system's largest "Pacifics." Equally fast but substantially more powerful locomotives were needed.

Word was out that the Milwaukee Road had developed plans for a 4-6-4 and obtained cost estimates from both American and Baldwin. Paul W. Kiefer, the Central's able chief engineer of motive power and rolling stock, recognized the design's potential, and was further impressed by the performances of the Boston & Albany's new "Berkshires." The object of the tests he supervised throughout the fall of 1926 was to determine the tracking and load-bearing characteristics of a four-wheeled trailing truck replacing the 4-6-2's single-axled assembly.

Predicated upon the results, and taking full advantage of the massive carrying unit's benefits—commodious grates, improved circulation, and ample space for an effective booster engine—drawings and specifications were prepared for a 4-6-4 and turned over to the American Locomotive Company. In a well-publicized ceremony on February 14, 1927, the first of the machines emerged from the Schenectady plant, draping itself, as it came out of the erecting shop, with bunting that had been stretched across a doorway providing far more headroom than the New York Central's clearances. The road had always been handicapped in that respect, and the engine's height was limited to a shade over 15 feet. With 79-inch drivers and a full boiler, the stack and domes were necessarily squat, and that, combined with a firebox-hugging cab and full-throated head-

Too large to pass through the B&O's Baltimore tunnel, 16-foot-high 4-8-4s en route from the Baldwin Locomotive Works to the Santa Fe in 1941 were ferried across the mouth of the Patapsco River on car floats. Engine messengers accompanied new power on such trips, eating and sleeping in their cabs.

Between 1929 and 1945, the Rock Island acquired 75 dual-service 4-8-4s—the largest number of that type owned by any American railroad. Intended primarily for freight runs between Kansas City, Missouri, and Dalhart, Texas, the final series of American Locomotive Company products had 74-inch drivers and exerted a tractive force of 67,000 pounds. A pair of 18-quart mechanical lubricators pumped oil to 64 wearing surfaces.

The dean of his craft, Otto Kuhler styled the cowlings for six 395-ton "Hudsons" assigned to the Milwaukee Road's incomparably swift "Hiawathas" in 1938. Streamlining had little functional value at normal operating speeds, but it served its purpose well when Number 100's 84-inch drivers reeled in the miles at the rate of one each 30 seconds.

The largest steam passenger locomotive ever built, the Pennsylvania's 140-foot-long 6100 made its debut at the 1939-40 New York World's Fair. If the pretentious and trouble-plagued 6-4-4-6 had a virtue, it was its tastefully restrained streamlining—the work of industrial designer Raymond Loewy.

The ankle-length shroud applied to the PRR Number 3768 in the early 1930s did stylist Loewy less credit. Static sheet metal could not match the inherent beauty of flashing spokes and dancing rods.

Small smoke-lifting wings applied to a final series of Boston & Maine 4-8-2s in 1941 were nicknamed "ear muffs"—appropriate when the Baldwin beauties battled snow in the Berkshire Hills. Many motive power esthetes considered "Mountain" types the most handsomely proportioned of all steam locomotives.

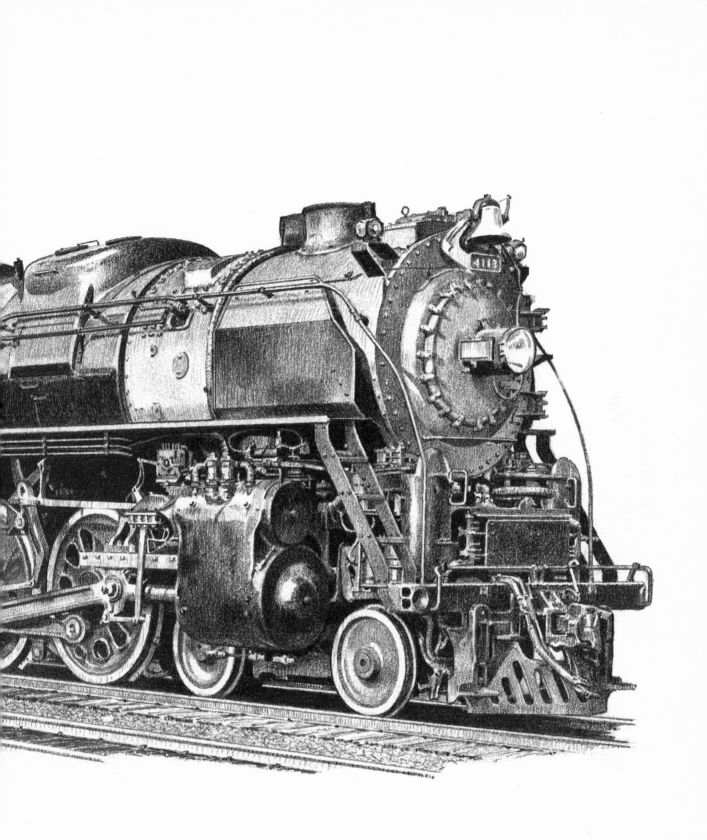

end treatment, created an effect of speed and power bursting at the seams.

The impression was substantiated when the *5200* and *274* "Hudsons" of periodically modified design were placed in systemwide service. Their booster engines enabled them to accelerate as many as twenty standard-weight cars with a rapidity more characteristic of electric than of steam locomotives, and when they traced the eastern shore of the river whose name they bore, streaked through the Mohawk Valley, and swept tornadolike across the flatlands beyond, the modulated chuckle of their exhausts was music to knowledgeable ears—for fiercely barking stacks were not, as popularly supposed, a sign of tremendous power but of overly restrictive steam passages.

The "Hudsons" were sparing of fuel; 75 tons of coal, reduced to small chunks before it was jetted onto the grates, satisfied their needs on runs between Harmon, New York, and Chicago. To provide space for 46 tons, the largest tenders ever applied to them carried only 16,000 gallons of water, a permissible reserve on a road whose practice was to replenish the tanks from track pans placed between the rails. However, it had previously been necessary to decelerate to 45 miles an hour before an engineer approaching one of the slender troughs could safely signal to his fireman: "Scoop down!" At higher speeds the shovellike mechanism hit the water with the impact of a battering ram and either was ripped from the underframe or rammed a geyser into the reservoir. In the latter case, compacted air blew off the manhole cover above, and while the cars behind were washed down in a dramatic fashion, the tank remained virtually empty. Along with other improvements, then, the scoops were reinforced, and with large chambers vented by air ducts mounted on the tops of the tenders, the engines picked up their thousands of gallons of water while thundering over the pans at 80 miles an hour.

The popularity of the 4-6-4s spread to other roads, and just as "Berkshires" had pointed the way to 2-10-4s, the "Hudsons" suggested the possibilities of 4-8-4s. In 1921 a two-axled trailing truck had been applied to what would otherwise have been one of fifteen identical "Mountain" type locomotives built by Baldwin for the Santa Fe. Since the grate area was not increased, the only gain was slightly im-

proved stability, and the wheel arrangement excited no interest in the industry. But the success of a Northern Pacific 4-8-4 design developed in 1927 led other railroads to place orders with all three major builders. There was some resistance to the generic designation "Northern," particularly in the Deep South, where the name "Dixie" aroused warmer sentiments. The Canadian National called the engines "Confederations," and on the Lehigh Valley, the Delaware, Lackawanna & Western, and the Chesapeake & Ohio they were "Wyomings," "Poconos," and "Greenbriars," respectively.

The most definitive 4-8-4 was a demonstrator designed and produced by American for the Timken Roller Bearing Company in 1930. The firm was actively soliciting railroad business, and a substantial number of passenger cars and tenders were equipped with its products. A few applications had been made to locomotive guiding and trailing trucks, but the bolt-assembled engine frames and crossmembers then in general use did not provide the complete rigidity required for similar installations on driving axles. There, any skewing action would have damaged the sophisticated bearings. In the demonstrator, however, Timken was given precisely what was needed—an entire engine bed, cast in one unit, of tough and inflexible steel.

With all its running parts turning freely on the company's "antifriction" bearings, the locomotive became a commuter stopper when, at selected metropolitan terminals, three pretty young flappers pulled it several feet along rails flanked by press reporters and photographers. More productively, *Number 1111*, better known as the *Four Aces*, latched onto a dozen Pennsylvania Railroad coaches at Altoona and hoisted them over the Alleghenies without assistance, clipping three minutes off the system's best-scheduled time in the bargain. Tests on thirteen other carriers were similarly impressive, and Timken not only expanded its market but recovered the investment when the machine was bought by the Northern Pacific in 1933.

As was generally the case with latter-day steam power, 4-8-4s reached their most formidable proportions in the West, with the largest—thirty giants constructed by Baldwin for the Santa Fe in 1944— each stretching more than 120 feet between couplers and tipping the beam at 439½ tons. Of the Union

For more than 10 years the Northern Pacific's 12 "Yellow-stones" were unequaled in size and weight. Built in 1928 and 1930, the 556-ton 2-8-8-4s were given 182 square feet of grate area to meet the combustion demands of low-grade bituminous mined by the railroad at Colstrip, Montana. Burned at the rate of a third of a ton a minute, the fuel evaporated 15,000 gallons of water an hour.

Reluctant to adopt diesel power, the Pennsylvania poured $35 million into steam locomotives of four-cylinder, rigid-frame designs. With one exception they were of the 4-4-4-4 and 4-4-6-4 types. Fifty-two of the former—"shark nose" T-1s—produced by Baldwin and the Juniata shops in 1942 and 1945, supplanted the system's venerable "Pacifics" in passenger service west of Harrisburg, Pennsylvania.

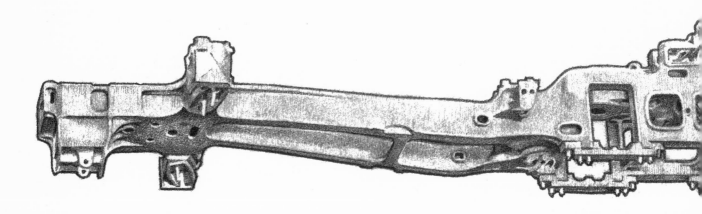

A T-1's engine bed was a foundry masterpiece, with its main frames, transverse braces, pivoted bearing plates, cylinders, saddles, and air pump brackets formed as a single unit. A foreman at the General Steel Castings Corporation boasted: "The only things we can't cast integrally here are an engineer and fireman."

Airlifting a partially assembled T-1 was a task for a pair of 200-ton traveling cranes. Completed and fired up, these machines were capable of maintaining 100-mile-an-hour speeds, on level track, with a dozen 73-ton Pullmans.

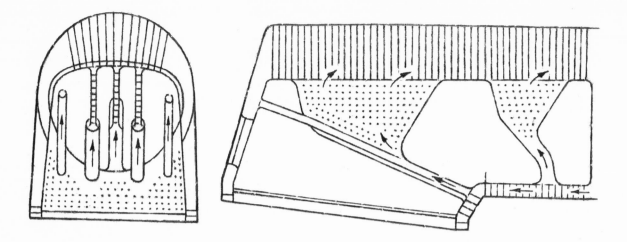

Thermic syphons shaped like flattened funnels induced the circulation of water from the bottom to the top of the boiler, thence forward, downward, and back to re-entry at their stems.

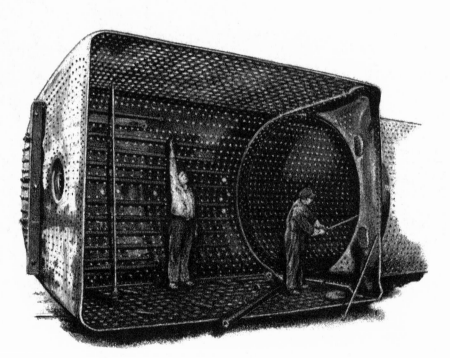

Laid on its side, the outer shell of a C&O "Allegheny" type's firebox stood 10½ feet high. Thousands of perforations were required for the staybolts.

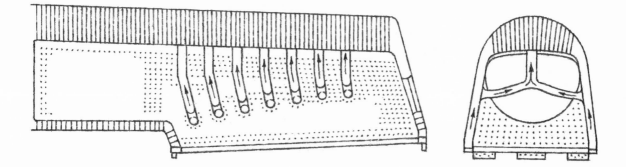

Shaped like inverted T's, circulators did triple duty, keeping water in constant movement, bracing the firebox, and providing supports for the brick arch that lengthened the distance flames traveled.

The early discovery that a thin blanket of air above a bed of coals was a black-smoke deterrent led to periodic attempts to provide overdrafts with orifices in the firebox sides, or "water legs." The variation shown employed compressed air piped from the engine's main reservoir. The drum-shaped jets, nicknamed "bazookas" or "top hats," muffled the objectionable shrieking common to all such systems, but in doing so failed of their main purpose.

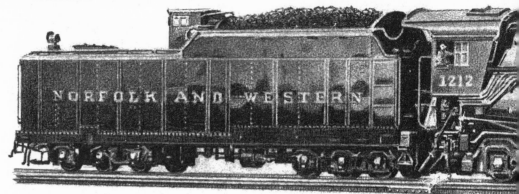

Company-built classics—the Norfolk & Western's dual-service 2-6-6-4s. When a small Kentucky boy asked one of their runners, "Where do you git them enjines at?" the reply was a straight-faced: "Sonny, we dig them out of the mountains."

Monarchs of the Wasatch Range. The Rio Grande's 4-6-6-4s were the heaviest and most powerful locomotives of the "Challenger" type ever constructed. Weighing 332½ tons without tender, they developed 105,000 pounds of starting tractive effort.

Engines of war. Two days after Pearl Harbor, the first of 60 "Alleghenies" was delivered to the Chesapeake & Ohio. Its six-wheeled trailing truck alone supported a weight equal to that of the New York Central's 999 and tender. (p. 130.)

DENVER & RIO GRANDE WESTERN

A pair of diesel competitors built by General Electric in 1938 were given their baptism of fire on the Union Pacific a year later. Prime power was produced by turbines (left) receiving 310-pound-pressure steam from semiflash-type boilers. Air-cooled condensers permitted 700-mile runs without water stops, and electric traction motors provided high torque at starting and finely graduated control. Offsetting those advantages, the machines cost three times as much as conventional locomotives of comparable power, and their complexity led to frequent breakdowns. They were scrapped in 1942.

Pacific's comparably capable, if slightly less heavy, final series, bought from Alco in the same year, one remains in operating condition today. The Southern Pacific's Lima-built "GS [General Service]–3" class rounded out an awesome trio. Designed to handle the system's strikingly handsome "Daylight" trains, their streamlined cowlings blazed with broad expanses of orange and red when they were placed in service in 1942.

By then, attempts to "pretty up" the iron horse were well under way, and much was made of the fact that head-end air resistance was materially reduced at high speeds. Less attention was directed to another and often greater retarding force—a crosswind that forced the wheel flanges on the far side of a locomotive and trailing cars against the inner faces of the leeward rails. Thus when deep skirting was applied to an engine, it increased the surface areas exposed to such thrusts, unless the metal work was curved to "spill" the air upward, downward, or in both directions. This was done more often abroad than on domestic applications.

As had always been the case, improved locomotive performance led first to the operation of heavier trains where easy grades permitted, and then to a demand for still more powerful machines to match their tonnage ratings in the mountains. Thus the popularity of the 2-8-4s, the 4-8-4s, and the 2-10-4s hastened, rather than retarded, the development of more capable articulated engines. A long step in the right direction was taken when, in 1929, the Northern Pacific introduced the 2-8-8-4 type with the first of twelve 558-ton behemoths, designed to work 4,000-ton freights coming off the prairies over a continuous 216-mile district extending from Mandan, North Dakota, to Glendive, Montana.

At that time the road was using fuel scooped from its open-pit diggings at Colstrip, Montana—subgrade bituminous so low in heating units that firemen claimed it burned best when the miners left broken pickax handles in it. Because it was consumed very rapidly, unusually large beds of coal and high-capacity automatic stokers were required, and the "Yellowstones" were given 182 square feet of grate area, fed by "iron firemen" capable of handling 20 tons of the brown stuff hourly. Within that time the furnaces, together with 2½ miles of boiler flues, could evaporate 15,000 gallons of water. American built the original machine and Baldwin produced eleven in 1930.

That only three other railroads—the Southern Pacific, the Duluth, Missabe & Iron Range, and the Baltimore & Ohio—ever became customers for "Yellowstones" was due in large measure to the more flexible characteristics of two innovative types brought out soon afterward. Both owed their origins to a pair of Baldwin 2-6-6-2s delivered to the B&O in 1931. Provided with 70-inch drivers, these were the first high-wheeled articulated locomotives placed in service since the Santa Fe's less-than-successful ventures three decades earlier. One had a water tube firebox, inviting the accompanying troubles, and both nosed excessively at speeds below those for which they were designed. Still, they suggested the possibility of equipping basically similar engines with four-wheeled trailing trucks to improve their stability, and in 1935 both the Pittsburgh & West Virginia and the Seaboard Air Line turned to the Eddystone plant for 2-6-6-4s. With the deep fireboxes permitted by the arrangement and resulting gains in combustion chamber length, the locomotives lived up to expectations; but they were hardly a match for the first of fifty heavier and more sophisticated versions of the same type built for the Norfolk & Western Railway in its own Roanoke, Virginia, shops between 1936 and 1949. Operating at a boiler pressure of 300 pounds to the square inch, these long-barreled brutes regularly handled 175 coal hoppers and gondolas from Williamson, West Virginia, to Portsmouth, Ohio —trains so long that the engine moved nearly 200 feet before the slack in the couplings behind played out and the 1¼-mile-distant caboose began to roll. Again, their 70-inch drivers enabled them to maintain the fastest speeds permitted in mountain territory with twenty-coach sections of the road's swank *Pocahontas* and *Cavalier*.

Hard on their heels came the first of eighty-five "Challengers," or 4-6-6-4s, engineered by the Union Pacific and outshopped by American. Somewhat more stable than the 2-6-6-4s, machines of this type became the most popular of the latter-day articulateds, attaining what many connoisseurs contended were the most handsome of contours in twenty built for the Delaware & Hudson at Schenectady, and unquestionably the most awesome displays of plumbing as well as the greatest weight and tractive effort—

199

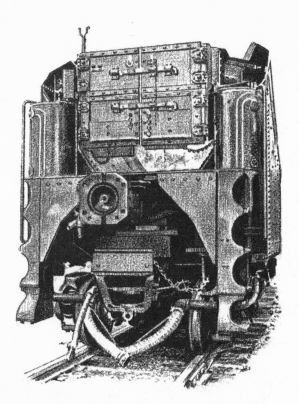

The front end of a Pennsylvania "Decapod" locomotive's tender, showing, from top to bottom: the coal gates, the deck, the automatic stoker connection, the chafing plate and pocket for the coupler, or "drawbar," the two water hoses, and the air hose.

Forty-seven feet long and 15 feet high, the largest of the Union Pacific "Centipede" tenders carried 25 tons of coal and 25,000 gallons of water.

200

ORE AND OHIO

"Vanderbilt" tenders derived their name from that of the rail magnate on whose network of roads they were first used extensively. The cylindrical reservoirs were structurally stronger per pound of dead weight than rectangular compartments of the same capacity, and it was claimed that the water within them surged less violently in response to canting on curves, making the cars more stable.

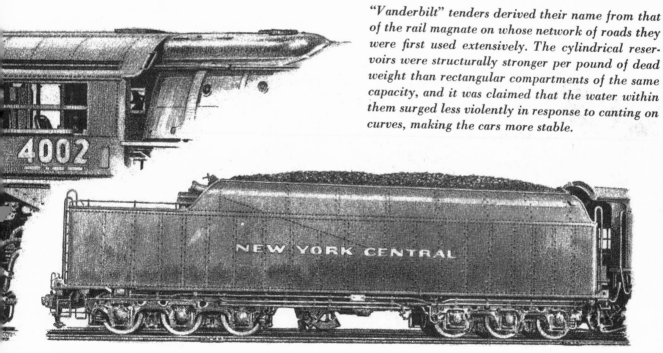

4002

NEW YORK CENTRAL

The 43-ton-capacity coal compartments of tenders applied to many New York Central "Hudsons" and "Mohawks" required replenishing only once on runs between Harmon, New York, and Chicago. The system's extensive use of track pans and scoops accounted for their relatively small (15,000 gallons) water capacity.

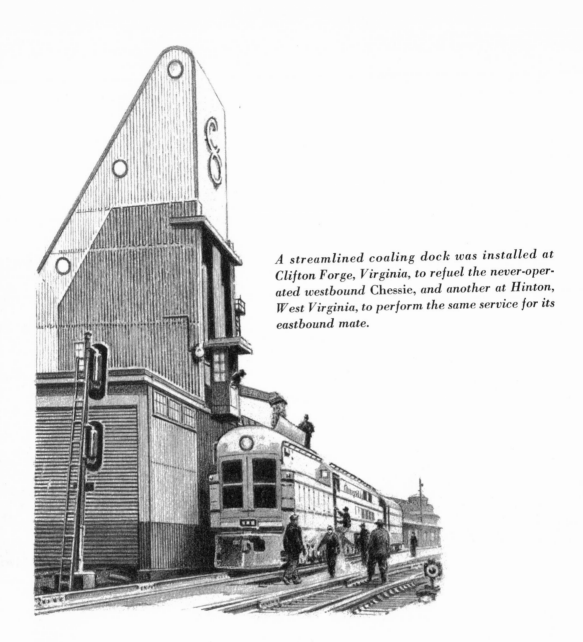

A streamlined coaling dock was installed at Clifton Forge, Virginia, to refuel the never-operated westbound Chessie, *and another at Hinton, West Virginia, to perform the same service for its eastbound mate.*

518 tons and 105,000 pounds, respectively—in ten monsters bearing Baldwin builder's plates.

Never long content with the Union Pacific's currently most productive motive power, the road's president, William Jeffers, had only to give the word and Otto Jabelmann, vice president of the system's Research and Development Department, was always ready with a sheaf of data pertinent to a new design. That was the way it happened in 1941, when tonnages handled between Omaha, Nebraska, and Cheyenne, Wyoming, encouraged the adoption of

locomotives of unprecedented size to buck the Wasatch Mountains to the west. Completely detailed plans were turned over to American within six months, and half a year later the first of twenty of the 604½-ton "Big Boys" backed on to its initial revenue train. Developing a tractive effort of 135,375 pounds, these 133-foot-long machines cost $265,174 apiece—not a bad bargain at a per-pound rate of less than 22 cents. The engines were deliberately "overbuilt" to withstand the punishment of 80-mile-an-hour speeds, and during World War II they occasionally

Reluctant to bite the hand that fed it, the coal-hauling Chesapeake & Ohio invested in three of the world's all-time-heaviest locomotives in 1939 and 1940. The service for which the 617-ton steam turbine–electrics were intended—handling a streamliner (to be named the Chessie) *between Washington, D.C., and Cincinnati —never materialized, and the overly complex engines themselves might better have remained in the planning stage. They were sold for scrap metal in 1950.*

topped 70 with heavy troop trains. However, they were at their vocal best when they drummed up Weber Canyon out of Ogden, punctuating each beat of their exhaust with a towering black exclamation mark.

The Chesapeake & Ohio put on comparable spectaculars in the East with a fleet of Lima-built 2-6-6-6s delivered to the road between the Decembers of 1941 and 1948. Weighing a shade over 600 tons, they created an illusion of greater bulk than the "Big Boys," thanks to their equipment-burdened smoke-box fronts and pilots, exceptionally large trailing trucks, and twin sand domes of 5-ton capacity. As the line's 2-10-4s had bumped the "Chesapeakes" from demanding runs a dozen years before, so the new "Alleghenies" took over their assignments. Increased clearances made it possible to operate the 16-foot-high articulateds from Russell both northward to Toledo and east to Hinton, West Virginia, and they proved as adaptable to varying terrain as the "Big Boys."

The 4-8-8-4s and the 2-6-6-6s were the last of the

To dream the impossible dream proved costly when Baldwin and the Pennsylvania Railroad collaborated in designing a direct drive steam turbine locomotive in 1944. Efficient only when run at high speeds, the 501-ton 6-8-6 accelerated too slowly to maintain schedules involving any number of intermediate stops.

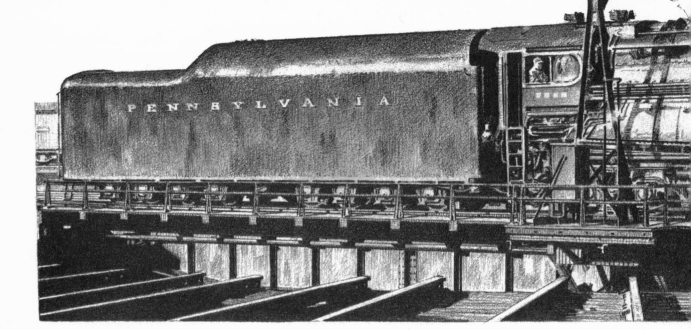

The 6200's transmission unit was mounted on the second and third pairs of driving wheels.

View of the unit with the two turbines in place and the rotor and gearbox covers removed.

The axle-mounted main driving gears nearly matched in weight the flanking traction wheels.

Large forward-motion turbine.

Small backward-motion turbine.

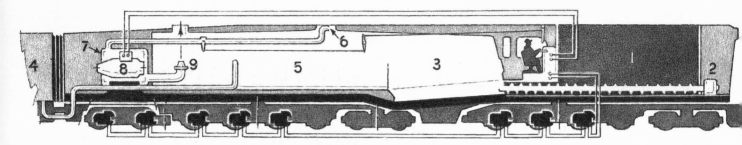

Schematic arrangement of the steam turbine–electric. Coal (1) was transported by an Archimedes screw, driven by a stoker motor (2), to the firebox (3). Water from the tender (4) flowed forward to the boiler (5). Steam entered an intake port (6) and passed through a throttle-governed delivery line to a turbine (7) geared to two flanking generators (8). The exhaust created a draft for the fire as it blasted from a nozzle (9) and into the smokestack. Direct current of 600 volts was fed to eight traction motors from a control stand in the cab.

truly great steam locomotives. Later-day engines of unconventional or modified design were only marginally successful. Duplex machines with two independent driving units sharing a single engine bed largely eliminated the rail-damaging hammer blows caused by heavy reciprocating parts, but at the cost of higher maintenance. The same disadvantage discouraged the widespread adoption of cam-operated poppet valves of the type used in internal combustion engines, despite the fact that they opened and closed steam ports more rapidly than the balanced type. An otherwise finely engineered direct drive turbine locomotive proved what should have been anticipated—that prime movers of this kind operate effectively only at high and fairly constant speeds, making them unsuitable for the rapid accelerations and decelerations demanded in train handling. Finally, three attempts to combine steam turbines with electric generators and traction motors proved costly to General Electric, the Chesapeake & Ohio, and the Norfolk & Western when the expense of building the machines ran out of all proportion to their power output.

The attractions of diesel-electric power—high starting torque, the elimination of numerous servicing facilities, more hours of engine availability each day, and greater cleanliness—wrote an end to the years of glory. Nevertheless, the reciprocating locomotive had served the nation well for 120 years. It had tied the economies of young seaboard cities together with endless miles of smoke ribbons. It had labored over three transcontinental mountain ranges to carry settlers west and to tap the riches of the prairies, the desert, and the deep ravines. It had introduced new concepts of speed and power, and hastened the development of an even faster means of communication—the telegraph. Overlooked, perhaps, was the fact that in wooing youngsters from both farms and urban areas to stoke its hungry maw, it had placed a country-wide accent on mechanics.

Its most appealing attribute, however, was its almost human behavior. Aside from its iron belly and lungs, its pulsebeat, and its highly articulate mouthings, the locomotive was a headstrong machine from the moment it was outshopped. Its behavior was well-mannered or stubborn, depending in large measure upon the hand at the throttle. Again, some engines were avowed killers, while others would tear their hearts out on tasks beyond their capabilities. The great French novelist, Emile Zola, summed it up well when, in *The Human Beast,* he wrote:

Somewhere in the course of manufacture, a hammer blow or a deft mechanic's hand imparts to a locomotive a soul of its own.

Named for the legendary black giant who bored blasting holes faster than a steam drill with the mighty blows of his 12-pound hammer, the Norfolk & Western's Jawn Henry differed from the Chesapeake & Ohio's steam turbine–electrics in its use of a marine-type furnace and boiler. Maintenance costs were disappointingly high.

Glossary

ADHESION — The grip of wheels upon the rails, determined largely by the weight imposed upon them.

AIR BRAKE — A brake operated by compressed air.

"AIR" CAR — A railroad freight car equipped with air brakes. (*See* "non-air" car.)

"ALLEGHENY" TYPE — A 2-6-6-6 locomotive developed by the Chesapeake & Ohio in conjunction with the Lima Locomotive Works in 1941.

"AMERICAN" TYPE — A 4-4-0 locomotive. The first of this type was proposed by George Escol Sellers in the 1830s. Henry R. Campbell was the first to build one. Before 1900, American manufacturers produced 25,000 of the type, or three to one of any other kind.

APRON — A flat hinged metal plate used for a standing place between a locomotive and tender. *Also* sheet metal skirting, if any, under a locomotive's runningboard.

ARTICULATED LOCOMOTIVE — A locomotive with two driving wheel assemblies, each powered by a set of cylinders. The leading assembly supported the front end of the locomotive and was pivoted to the one behind.

"ATLANTIC" TYPE — A 4-4-2 locomotive. George S. Strong first proposed the wheel arrangement in 1883, and two were actually built from his drawings in 1887 and 1888, preceding by more than six years an Atlantic Coast Line locomotive widely credited with introducing this type.

ATMOSPHERIC BRAKE — The first brake operated by compressed air, invented by George Westinghouse in 1868. Also called a "straight air brake," it was the predecessor of his automatic air brake.

ATMOSPHERIC ENGINE — A low-pressure engine developed by Thomas Newcomen in 1705.

AUTOMATIC AIR BRAKE — Invented by George Westinghouse in 1871, this air brake is applied automatically by a rupture in the system or by train separation.

AUXILIARY RESERVOIR or AUXILIARY TANK — A cylindrical reservoir which holds compressed air supplied by the main reservoir, for use in operating the air brakes on locomotives, tenders, and cars.

AXLE OFFSET — A ridge or shoulder formed by reducing the diameter of that portion of an axle upon which a wheel either turns or is pressed, thus preventing the wheel from moving further inward on the axle.

BACKHEAD — The back end of the boiler, in which the fire door is placed.

BACK PRESSURE — The pressure remaining when a piston exhausts steam, against which the steam taken in must work.

BALANCED COMPOUND TYPE — A steam locomotive

with two high- and two low-pressure cylinders. Developed in France in the 1870s, its smooth action made it popular in Europe. In the United States, Samuel M. Vauclain and Francis J. Cole each developed versions of the engine, but high maintenance costs outweighed their fuel economy.

BALLAST — Broken stone or gravel placed in a road-bed to provide a sturdy surface for the track and to facilitate drainage.

"BALLAST-SCORCHER" — A fast-driving engineer.

BALLOON STACK — A chimney resembling the man-carrying balloons of the nineteenth century. The lower section was shaped like an inverted cone, and the one above it was cylindrical, topped either by a shallow dome formed of wire screening or by a third section tapering inward again and similarly capped with screening.

"BARREL" — Common railroad parlance for a boiler.

BEARER — Any small wheel, either on a truck or attached directly to a locomotive's frame, which supports weight but to which power is not applied.

BEARING — A load-carrying part upon which an axle or pivot turns or moves.

BEARING BLOCK — A metal part bored to receive an axle or pivot.

"BERKSHIRE" TYPE — A 2-8-4 locomotive introduced by the Lima Locomotive Works in 1925. The name was derived from its early use by the Boston & Albany in the Berkshire Hills.

"BICYCLE" TYPE — A 4-2-2 locomotive produced by the Baldwin Works in 1880.

"BIG BOY" — Any one of a fleet of Union Pacific 4-8-8-4 articulated locomotives built by the American Locomotive Company between 1941 and 1944. The largest conventional steam locomotives ever built, they weighed 604½ tons and exerted a tractive effort of 135,375 pounds.

"BIG-HOLING THE WESTINGHOUSE" — In an emergency, uncovering all the openings in the control valve of an air brake system at the same time, thus applying its full force.

BLENKINSOP RACK — See rack rail.

BLIND TIRE — A ring of iron or steel, encompassing a driving wheel center, that has no flange. This permits it to adjust itself to rail curvatures without binding.

"BLOOMER" TYPE — A 2-2-2 high-wheeler designed in England in the midnineteenth century. Its name derived from the fact that there were no framing members or rods outside the driving wheels, leaving them as exposed as the legs of the feminists in the briefs introduced by Amelia Bloomer.

BOILER — A metal container in which water is converted into steam by the heat from a firebox.

BOLSTER — A wooden or steel beam placed across the frame of a truck to receive the weight of the engine.

"BOOMER" — A nineteenth- and early twentieth-century term for a railroad worker who drifted from job to job.

BORE — The inner diameter of a cylinder, or, loosely, the cylinder cavity.

BRAKE CYLINDER — An iron cylinder containing a piston operated by compressed air to apply the air brake.

BRAKE HOSE — A flexible tube which connects the brake pipes between cars.

BRAKE PIPE — An iron pipe connecting the engineer's brake valve with the air brake apparatus on the cars behind.

BRAKE SHOE — A crescent of metal that drags against the tread of a wheel when the brake is applied.

BRICK ARCH — A sloping baffle made of firebrick, placed in a furnace to provide more time for embers to burn before they reached the flues. George S. Griggs applied brick arches to locomotive furnaces as early as 1857, but they did not achieve popularity until 1900.

BRIDGE WALL — A water-filled partition partially separating a forward extension of the furnace from the coal-burning section.

BROAD-GAUGE LINE — A track wider than the standard gauge of 4 feet 8½ inches.

BUMP — To replace or demote.

BURY FIREBOX — A furnace with a hemispheric top, invented by the English designer Edward Bury in the early 1830s. Structurally strong, it was popular until increasingly large locomotives required fireboxes with larger grate areas.

CAB — A shelter on a locomotive for the enginemen, usually at the back end of the boiler. Cabs came into being about 1843.

"CABBAGE CUTTER" — A freight hauler, so called because its main and side rods swept close to the ground at the lowest points in their long strokes.

CABBAGE HEAD STACK — A chimney with a bulbous top that served as a repository for wood ashes.

"CAMELBACK" or "MOTHER HUBBARD" TYPE — A locomotive with the cab on top of the boiler. The term should not be confused with "Camel," which referred to the much earlier engines designed by Ross Winans.

"CAMEL" TYPE — An 0-8-0 engine developed by Ross Winans in the 1840s, which gave the appearance of a dromedary with a rider on its back because of the placement of the steam dome and the engineer's controls in front of the furnace. The term was also applied to the Baltimore & Ohio's first ten-wheelers.

CHAIR — A clamp, made of iron or steel, that supports a rail.

"CHALLENGER" TYPE — A high-speed 4-6-6-4 articulated locomotive, equally competent in freight and passenger service. It was introduced by the Union Pacific Railway in 1936.

"CHEESE" BOILER — Developed by Phineas Davis for his *York*, this upright boiler consisted of a water jacket surrounding a central furnace, and a shallow drum suspended above the grates. The drum, when viewed through the fire door, was thought to resemble a cheese, thus giving the entire assembly its name.

"CHESAPEAKE" TYPE — A 2-8-8-2 simple articulated locomotive first used by the Chesapeake & Ohio Railway after World War I. It was soon adopted by practically every railroad confronted with stiff grades and heavy traffic.

CHILLED RIM — The periphery of a cast iron wheel toughened by a process introduced by Ross Winans in the 1830s, using an iron mold rather than one made of sand. When the molten iron contacted the mold, it solidified almost at once, producing treads and flanges of extremely hard and wear-resisting crystalline texture.

"THE CITY OF IRON HORSES" — Paterson, New Jersey, so called because no other city matched its locomotive output in the last half of the nineteenth century. Before 1900, more than 10,000 of the 60,000 engines built in the United States were manufactured there.

"CLOCK" — A circular steam gauge mounted on the backhead of the boiler, first used in the late 1850s.

"COLUMBIA" TYPE — A 2-4-2 locomotive. The first engine of this type was produced by the Baldwin Works in 1892.

COMBUSTION CHAMBER — A space in a boiler where combustion is promoted and additional heat obtained from the gasses before they enter the fire tubes. The combustion chamber theory was originally introduced by Isaac Dripps in the 1830s with the *Monster*, but was not made practical until a hundred years later.

COMPOUND TYPE — A steam locomotive using steam released from one cylinder in a second cylinder.

CONNECTING ROD — *See* mainrod.

"CONSOLIDATION" TYPE — A locomotive of the 2-8-0 wheel arrangement, built primarily for freight service. The first engine of this type was designed in 1866 by Alexander Mitchell of the Lehigh Valley Railroad.

COUPLER — A mechanism used to connect the individual cars and locomotive of a train.

"CRAB" TYPE — A nickname for an engine developed by Ross Winans in the 1830s. Its main and side rods stroked in opposite directions, suggesting the motion of a crab.

"CRAMPTON" TYPE — A locomotive with a single pair of driving wheels from 7 to 8 feet in diameter, developed in England in the midnineteenth century. Although these engines were very fast, inadequate weight on the drivers gave them poor traction. The *John Stevens*, designed by Isaac Dripps in 1847, was the first American version of this type.

CRANK — A device attached to a shaft, one end of which is free to rotate about the shaft's axis, used to convert rotary to reciprocating motion or vice versa.

CRANK DISK — *See* crank web.

CRANKED AXLE — A driving axle provided with cranks inside the wheels mounted upon it to which the mainrods transmit motion.

CRANKPIN — A short cylindrical piece attached to a crank on a driving wheel or joining the two disks, or webs, of a crank axle. It transmits the reciprocating motion of the piston to the driving wheel.

CRANK WEB — One of two flat steel pieces of circular or other shape attached to the driving axle, between which is the crankpin.

CROSS-COMPOUND TYPE — A steam locomotive with a high-pressure cylinder on one side and a low-pressure one on the other, the second cylinder using the steam exhausted by the first. The cross-compound was introduced in 1887 by A. von Borries of Germany and T. W. Worsdell of England. An American version was developed in 1889 by Arthur J. Pitkin.

CROSS-STRINGER — A transverse beam bolted to the longitudinal stringers forming the underlayment for the plates or strap iron rails of early track. Cross-stringers held the longitudinal members in parallel alignment.

CROSSTIE — A wooden beam laid at right angles to and beneath rails for support. In the 1830s wooden crossties were used by Robert L. Stevens as a stopgap measure until more stone could be quarried for the Camden & Amboy Railroad track then being laid across New Jersey. The wooden ties were found to have greater resiliency and thus permit higher operating speeds.

CROWNSHEET — The roof of the firebox.

CULM — The screenings of refuse coal.

CUP WHISTLE — A small locomotive whistle employing steam. Popular in England in the 1830s, it was first used in America on a 4-2-0 constructed by Thomas Rogers in 1837. The idea for the whistle originated in a Welsh iron foundry, where one had been devised to signal the beginning and end of the working day.

CYLINDER — A chamber with circular ends and parallel sides through which a piston is driven.

CYLINDER HEAD — A metal cover on the end of a cylinder.

"DEADHEAD" — A locomotive hauled by another.

"DECAPOD" TYPE — A 2-10-0 freight locomotive introduced in 1867 by a Lehigh Valley master mechanic, Alexander Mitchell.

DIESEL ENGINE — An internal combustion engine using compressed air to ignite fuel injected into the cylinder, where a piston is actuated by the combustion and expansion.

DIVISION POINT — One of a number of sections of a large railroad, run as an independent entity to the extent of having its own fleet of locomotives, engine and repair shops, officials, and clerical and operating personnel.

"DOG-LEG" — Railroad parlance for a sharp reverse curve in the track. The term's basis is the comparable crooked appearance of a dog's hind legs.

DOUBLE-ACTING ENGINE — An engine in which steam is directed alternately into the two ends of a closed cylinder, eliminating unpowered return strokes of the piston.

DOUBLE-ENDER — A locomotive able to run in either direction. Robert Fairlie of Ireland designed the most widely adopted double-ender in 1866, an 0-4-4-0 that had twin boilers with a central firebox and cab, and a trucklike cylinder and driving wheel assembly beneath each barrel for flexibility.

"DRAG" — A slow freight train.

DRIVING AXLE — An axle on which the driving wheels of a locomotive are mounted.

DRIVING BOX — A housing containing the bearing for a driving axle.

DRIVING UNIT — An assembly of cylinders, valve gear, rods, driving wheels, and brakes mounted on or attached to an engine bed.

DRIVING WHEEL — One of the wheels of a locomotive that is connected to the main or side rods and transforms the engine's power into traction.

"DUMPING THE AIR" or "DYNAMITING HER" — Uncovering all the openings in the control valve of an air brake system at once in an emergency, to apply its full force.

DUPLEX AIR COMPRESSOR — An air compressor, developed about 1910, capable of compacting as much as 150 cubic feet of air a minute to the 140-pound pressure at which it was delivered to the main reservoirs. The Duplex contained two steam cylinders and two compound air cylinders.

ECCENTRIC — A circular plate with a slightly off-center hole, mounted on a driving axle. Eccentrics were used on most early locomotives to actuate the valve gear mechanism controlling forward and backward motion.

EJECTOR — A device for exhausting air in a vacuum brake, used in the latter nineteenth century.

ENGINE BED — The underframe assembly of a locomotive.

EQUALIZER — A beam that connects two axle springs to distribute the weight of the car or locomotive evenly.

"FAIRLIE-MASON" TYPE — An 0-6-6-0 double-ended locomotive built in 1871 by William Mason of Taunton, Massachusetts, for standard-gauge lines. Because of the limited amount of fuel it could carry and the difficulty of getting coal onto the grates, only one, the *Janus*, was ever built, and it was scrapped in 1877.

"FAIRLIE" TYPE — An 0-4-4-0 double-ended locomotive designed for narrow-gauge lines by Robert Fairlie of Ireland in 1866. The first "Fairlie" in America was used by the Denver & Rio Grande Railroad in the 1870s, but it did not find favor because of its complexity.

FEEDWATER HEATER—An auxiliary heater, invented about 1910, which brought cold water from the tender nearly to the boiling point before being pumped into the boiler.

FIREBOX — The furnace in which fuel was burned to convert water into steam in the boiler.

FIREBOY — *See* fireman.

FIRE DOOR — The door in the firebox through which fuel was thrown on the fire.

FIREMAN — One who stoked the fire, maintained the water level in the boiler, and, in early days, applied the handbrake on the tender.

FIRE TUBE or FLUE — A tube in a steam boiler through which hot gasses pass to heat the surrounding water.

"FISH BELLY" — A short-span rail whose lower surface undulated, providing greater thickness between the ties than above them, for uniform strength.

FLANGE — A rim projecting at right angles from the inside edge of a locomotive wheel to guide it along the track. Earlier, when wagons moved along the rails, the flanges were located on either the outer or the inner edges of the rails themselves.

FLATCAR — A freight car with no sides, ends, or covering.

FLEXIBLE BOILER — A boiler with two parts connected by a flexible boiler joint, developed by Samuel M. Vauclain in 1910 for high-wheeled 2-6-6-2s.

FLEXIBLE BOILER JOINT — A connection between the two parts of a flexible boiler which allowed the forward end of the boiler to swivel when the locomotive rounded a curve, or accommodate itself to dips and rises. Samuel M. Vauclain invented the first flexible boiler joint in 1910.

FLUE — *See* fire tube.

FLY-BALL GOVERNOR — An automatic device to decelerate by centrifugal force an engine running above a desired speed.

FLYWHEEL — A large, heavy wheel on an engine crankshaft to convert shuttling action to a smooth rotative force.

"FORNEY" TYPE — *See* "tank" type.

"FRICTION WHEEL" DESIGN — A wheel-and-axle assembly that rotates as one. Introduced by Ross Winans in the 1830s, the assembly is misnamed, since it reduces friction rather than increasing it.

FUEL BUNKER — A compartment in a locomotive for storing fuel. *Also* the coal section of a tender.

GAB HOOK — Part of the valve-gear mechanism on early locomotives.

GEAR TRAIN — A group of gears with intermeshed teeth, used either to increase or reduce rotative speed, or to relay motion from one shaft or axle to another.

"GIG-TOP" — A shelter on top of a fuel car for the brakeman, the upper section of which was canvas stretched over hickory bows. The first gig-top was on the *Stevens*, built in the 1830s.

GOVERNOR — An automatic device to limit speed.

"GRASSHOPPER" TYPE — The first American engine of this type, the *Atlantic*, was developed in 1832 by Phineas Davis. The "grasshopper," an extremely powerful engine for its time, derived its name from the motion of its walking beams and the long rods, which resembled a locust's hind legs.

GRATE — Parallel bars, usually of cast iron, to hold fuel at the bottom of a firebox.

HALF CRANK — An L-shaped axle projection functioning as a crank but having only one side member at right angles to the axle. A familiar example is the half crank on which a pedal of a bicycle is mounted.

"HAYSTACK" BOILER — A boiler whose most conspicuous feature was a large dome above the furnace resembling a haystack. Officially it was named the Bury boiler, for its designer.

HAZLETON BOILER — An early nineteenth-century upright boiler that applied the heat of a central fire to a water jacket whose inner wall was covered with studs exposed to the flames. The boiler, developed in Hazleton, Pennsylvania, was more practical for stationary engines than for a moving locomotive, whose jouncing often caused ruptures.

HEAD END — The front of a locomotive or train. To "head-end" is to pull a train.

HEADER — A reservoir divided into two compartments and occupying part of the smokebox. It was used in a superheater designed by Wilhelm Schmidt in Germany in 1910.

"HELPER" — An extra locomotive used to assist trains on steep grades or with extra-heavy loads.

HIGH-PRESSURE ENGINE — An engine using pistons driven directly by the expansive force of steam.

HIGH-WHEELER — A locomotive with extra-large driving wheels for higher velocities, popular in the last half of the nineteenth century. The first high-wheeler, the "Crampton" type, had driving wheels 7 to 8 feet in diameter. Near the end of the century the quick-acting brake brought about the construction of outstanding high-wheelers, generally of the 4-4-0 type.

"HOG" or "PIG" — A locomotive with an extra-large boiler, introduced about 1910.

"HOGGER" or "GRUNT" — The engineer on a "hog" or "pig."

HOPPER CAR — A freight car with its floor sloping to one or more doors, designed for unloading the contents (such as coal or ore) by gravity.

"HORSE'S NECK" — The term was applied specifically to the two upright rocker arms mounted at the front of Isaac Dripps's *Monster*. As they nodded in response to the engine's piston thrusts, they suggested the neck action of a team of plodding horses.

"HUDSON" TYPE — A 4-6-4 locomotive. The Milwaukee Road developed the first plans for an engine of this wheel arrangement several years before the New York Central put the type into production and gave it its generic name in 1927.

IMPULSE TURBINE — A rotary engine driven by steam jets directed at its blades.

INCLINED PLANE — An inclined track on which trains are raised or lowered to another level.

INDEPENDENT SYSTEM — A braking system of the latter nineteenth century using momentum as a decelerating force. The engines were equipped with steam brakes, and when they slowed down, the cars behind them compressed spring-loaded buffers as they bunched together. In turn, the buffers actuated the secondary brakes.

INJECTOR — An appliance without activated parts, by which water could be added to the boiler when the locomotive was not in motion. Invented in 1852 by Henri Giffard for his unsuccessful dirigible, the injector was first produced for steam engines in England in the latter part of the decade.

INTERCEPTING VALVE — A device invented by James Muhlfeld in the early 1900s for use on his Mallet-type *2400*, or *Old Maud*. It delivered high-pressure steam to all the cylinders at starting, and as the need for tractive effort decreased, its passages were realigned for compound operation.

"IRON FIREMAN" — An automatic stoker.

"JIMMY" — A four-wheeled coal car.

JOINTED BOILER — *See* flexible boiler joint.

JOURNAL BOX — An iron or steel box enclosing the journal of a truck axle, the journal bearing, and the lubricant for the journal.

"KETTLE" — Any small locomotive.

"KILLINGSWORTH" TYPE — A four-drivered locomotive originally designed by George Stephenson to haul coal from the Killingsworth, England, mines. Use of this type spread to continental Europe.

LAGGING — An insulative covering laid in sections on the outsides of a boiler and cylinders to prevent loss of heat.

LATERAL-PLAY AXLE — An axle that permitted flanged wheels to move to one side or the other, accommodating themselves to curves. In later installations the axle boxes shifted with them, bearing against the resistance of coil springs to provide improved stability.

LEAD — The amount that a valve moves at the beginning of a piston stroke.

LEAF SPRING — A long multiple spring composed of several layers of spring metal bracketed together.

LINK — In a valve gear, a crescent-shaped piece of metal with a central slot which accommodated a sliding block connected to the valve rod.

LOW-PRESSURE ENGINE — An early engine in which steam at hardly more than atmospheric pressure was driven into an upright cylinder, then condensed, to create a vacuum beneath the piston, which had been raised to the top of the cylinder by a counterbalanced lever, or "walking beam."

MAIN RESERVOIR — A cylindrical steel tank in which compressed air is stored for use in the air brake system.

MAINROD or CONNECTING ROD — A large rectangular iron or steel rod which transmitted the motion of the piston and piston rod to the driving wheels of a locomotive.

MALLET TYPE — An articulated compound locomotive designed by Anatole Mallet of France in the 1870s for narrow-gauge lines. The first American Mallet was the *2400*, nicknamed *Old Maud*, a powerful 0-6-6-0 designed by James Muhlfeld in the early 1900s.

"MASTODON" TYPE — A 4-8-0 locomotive introduced by the Lehigh Valley's Philip Hoffecker in 1881, and improved by A. J. Stevens of the Southern Pacific a year later. Novel features of the latter's engines included the use of steam cylinders to actuate the reversing levers, and the Stevens valve gear, called a "monkey motion" by the crews.

"MERCHANDISER" — A freight train transporting other than bulk commodities.

"MIGHTY MOGUL" — A name misapplied by journalists to any extremely large engine in the nineteenth century. It was derived from Eastwick & Harrison's "Mogul" type of locomotives—2-6-0s built for the St. Petersburg & Moscow Railway in the 1840s.

"MIKADO" TYPE — A 2-8-2 locomotive. While the Baldwin Works was widely credited with producing the first engines of this type for Japan's Nippon Railway in 1897, the Lehigh Valley had converted a "Decapod" into a 2-8-2 in the 1860s.

"MOGUL" TYPE — A 2-6-0 locomotive first constructed by Eastwick & Harrison for the St. Petersburg & Moscow Railway in the 1840s. The type soon found favor in the United States.

"MONKEY MOTION" — Crew name for the type of valve gear designed by A. J. Stevens for his *Mastodon* in 1882, because the eccentric rods shuttled back and forth with a curious hop at the end of each stroke.

"MOTHER HUBBARD" — *See* "Camelback" type.

"MOUNTAIN" TYPE — A heavy 4-8-2 locomotive first built in 1911 and used for fast freight and passenger service.

"MUD DIGGER" TYPE — A group of 0-8-0s built by Ross Winans in the 1830s. The engines were typified by unprecedented grate areas of 17 square feet and cast iron drivers with chilled rims. The name referred to the fact that their hammering action caused clay to well up between the ties in wet weather. A few of the engines were in service until 1865.

NARROW-GAUGE LINE — A track narrower than the 4-foot 8½-inch standard gauge.

"NON-AIR" CAR — A freight car without air brakes. During the latter part of the nineteenth century many railroads were reluctant to equip their freight cars with expensive air brakes. This led to a mixture on freight trains of "air" and "non-air" cars.

OFFSET-HEADED SPIKE — The most commonly used rail fastener. The head is forged entirely on one side of the spike and bears down on the upper surface of the rail's broad base.

"OUTSHOP" — To produce a locomotive—literally to turn it out of the shop.

"PACIFIC" TYPE — A 4-6-2 locomotive which derived its name from a group built by Baldwin for the New Zealand Railways in 1901.

"PICKLE BOTTLE" BOILER — A large vertical boiler developed by Phineas Davis for his *Atlantic* in 1832.

"PIG" — A locomotive with a full boiler, introduced about 1910. Also called a "hog."

PILOT or "COW-CATCHER" — A triangular frame curved around the lower part of the front of a locomotive to remove obstacles from the track.

PILOT BEAM — A crossbar placed at the front of an engine to absorb shocks and support the pilot.

PISTON — A thick, snug-fitting metal disk that slides back and forth within the cylinder. In early "low-pressure" engines, pistons were driven by steam at little more than atmospheric pressure, the steam having been introduced into the cylinder, then condensed, to create a vacuum beneath the piston. In "high-pressure" engines, pistons were driven by the expansive force of the steam.

PISTON ROD — An iron or steel rod attached at one end to the center of a piston and at the other to a moving block, or crosshead, and by which the piston moves the drivers.

"PLANET" CLASS — Developed by England's most important locomotive builders in the 1830s, George and Robert Stephenson, this locomotive applied the power of inside cylinders to a single driving axle. A modified version of this class was *Old Ironsides,* built in the United States in 1832 by Matthias W. Baldwin.

PLATE — An early form of rail with a flange on its outer or inner side to restrain the wheels of mine cars.

PLATE WHEEL — A wheel whose center was a disk, or plate, rather than spokes radiating from a hub.

"PRAIRIE" TYPE — A 2-6-2 locomotive, popular principally in the Midwest. While a number of high-speed "Prairies" were built, they proved less popular than "Pacifics."

"PUSHER" — A locomotive used to help trains up steep grades by pushing from behind.

QUADRUPLEX TYPE — A Mallet articulated compound locomotive with four driving units, designed by George R. Henderson about 1915.

QUICK-ACTING BRAKE — A modification by George Westinghouse of his automatic air brake for quicker responses at the rear of a train.

QUILL — A whistle.

QUINTRUPLEX TYPE — A Mallet articulated compound locomotive with five driving units, designed by George R. Henderson about 1915.

RACK RAIL — Either a running rail with iron pins projecting from its outer surface, or a toothed third rail between the conventional rails. Locomotives with power-driven gear wheels engaged the pins or teeth to prevent slipping.

RAILHEAD — The end of a railroad line.

RATCHET WHEEL — A toothed wheel that turned in one direction and was prevented from being turned in the other by a short metal pivoting piece.

REACTION TURBINE — A turbine in which released steam or gas rotates the member from which it is ejected.

"REAL ESTATE" — Railroad lingo for coal, and more particularly fuel of an inferior grade.

RECIPROCATING ENGINE — A piston type of engine.

REDUCTION GEAR — Two or more gears that reduce the input speed to a lower output speed in order to gain more power.

RETURN-FLUE BOILER — A steam-generating system in which the distance that flames and gasses travel is increased by giving the flues through which they pass a 180-degree bend at the end of a boiler farthest from the fire and bringing them back through the water section.

ROCKER ARM — An arm pivoted at some point along its length, which receives motion at one of its ends and transmits it to a connected part at the other.

ROCKING BEAM — A beam pivoted at some point along its length, and used either to transmit power or to serve as an equalizer.

"ROLLED THEIR OWN" — The proud claim of the relatively few railroads that built their own locomotives instead of purchasing them from independent manufacturers.

ROLLING STOCK — The wheeled vehicles, other than locomotives, owned and used by a railroad.

"RUNNER" — A locomotive engineer.

RUNNINGBOARD — The narrow platforms on the sides of a boiler, providing convenient access to many parts on the superstructure of the engine.

RUNNING GEAR — Those parts propelling a locomotive, together with their supporting frames.

SAFETY VALVE — A valve on a boiler which lets steam escape when it exceeds a certain predetermined pressure.

"SAMSON" CLASS — Designed by George and Robert Stephenson, England's premier locomotive builders in the 1830s, a number of these engines were bought by American railroads, principally those serving New England.

SAND DOME — A bin filled with sand, straddling a boiler top, for the purpose of sanding the rails to achieve more traction.

SANDER — A mechanism attached to a locomotive for the purpose of sanding the track in front of the driving wheels for added traction. Its origin in 1836 is attributed to an unidentified Pennsylvania engineer, inspired by a plague of grasshoppers whose crushed bodies greased the rails. Not until the 1840s, however, was a commercial sander used. On later locomotives sand was also applied to the rails behind the drivers for backup movements.

SATURATED STEAM — Steam that contains liquid droplets.

SCHMIDT SUPERHEATER — A superheater consisting of a two-compartment reservoir and numerous external tubes. Saturated steam entered one compartment and passed through the tubes, where it was heated, to the second compartment, from which the superheated steam passed to the throttle valve. The design wrote an end to balanced compound engines by providing comparable fuel economy without the need for extra cylinders or moving parts.

SETSCREW — A screw by which a valve opening can be regulated.

"SHAY" TYPE — A logging locomotive invented by Ephraim Shay in 1880, which adjusted itself to the irregularities of hastily laid track by the flexible linkage and bevel gears connecting its longitudinal crankshaft and the wheels of two trucks. Nicknamed a "side-winder," it evolved over a period of sixty-five years into husky twelve- and sixteen-wheeled locomotives.

SHOE — See brake shoe.

SHOULDER — See axle offset.

SIDE ROD — A steel rod that connects the crankpins of any two adjoining driving wheels on the same side of a locomotive to distribute the power from the mainrod to the driving wheels.

"SIDE-WINDER" — See "Shay" type.

SIMPLE ARTICULATED LOCOMOTIVE — A locomotive in which the cylinders receive steam at full boiler pressure, as opposed to a compound articulated locomotive.

SINGLE-ACTING PISTON — A piston that exerts a thrust in only one direction, relying upon a counterbalancing weight, accumulated momentum, or the action of another piston, or pistons, for its unpowered return strokes.

SLIDE VALVE — A valve that admits steam to and ex-

hausts it from a cylinder.

SLIDING AXLE — See lateral-play axle.

SMOKEBOX — The forward portion of a boiler ahead of the water section.

SMOKESTACK — An iron or steel chimney attached to the top of a smokebox, through which smoke and gasses are discharged.

SPUR GEAR — A flat gear with broad transverse teeth on its periphery.

STACK — See smokestack.

STANDARD-GAUGE LINE — A track with the inner faces of its rails spaced 4 feet 8½ inches apart.

STATIONARY ENGINE — A steam engine placed in a permanent position.

STAYBOLT — A bolt threaded at both ends, screwed through the inner and outer plates of a firebox to hold the plates several inches apart.

STEAM BRAKING — Reversing the valve gear in order to decelerate an engine. This type of braking risked blowing out the cylinder heads, but enginemen used it for many years in emergencies. Mounting boiler pressures and heavy train tonnages eventually put an end to the practice.

STEAM DOME — The vertical chamber on top of a steam boiler in which steam accumulated.

STEAM PUMP — See injector.

STEPHENSON GEAR — A valve gear that enabled an engineer to run an engine forward or backward, and to regulate the time during which steam was admitted to the cylinder. Used extensively by Robert Stephenson, one of whose employees had designed it in 1842, the gear had actually been invented ten years earlier by William James, who had sent drawings of it to an English company where they had been filed and forgotten.

STOKER — A device for adding fuel to the firebox. Although mechanical stokers had been tried as early as 1850, all were failures until the early 1900s, when Archimedes' screws were applied to conveyors. By 1910 stokers were efficient enough to replace extra firemen on big engines.

STRAIGHT AIR BRAKE — See atmospheric brake.

STRAP IRON — In railroad service, a flat iron bar mounted on a wooden stringer and used as a running rail.

STRINGER — A timber laid in the earth or on stone ties, to whose upper surface iron plates, or running rails, were applied.

STROKE — Reciprocating movement, such as that of a piston rod.

SUNFLOWER STACK — A smokestack with a wide mouth shaped like an inverted cone.

SUPERHEATED STEAM — Steam directed through auxiliary coils in the flues to increase its temperature. This gave it greater volume and fluidity, enabling it to do more work in relation to the fuel consumed. The advantage of using superheated steam was recognized soon after the turn of the present century.

SUPERHEATER — An auxiliary heater that produces superheated steam.

"TALLOWPOT" — A nickname still in use for a fireman. In the midnineteenth century during nonstop journeys of any great distance, the fireman had to make his way forward on the running-board to replenish the lubricating tallow in the valve chambers.

TANDEM COMPOUND TYPE — A steam locomotive with a high- and low-pressure cylinder set end to end on each side, with the pistons mounted on one rod. In 1893, ten years after the failure of the system in a test, the first of eighty-six tandem compounds was constructed for the Atchison, Topeka & Santa Fe Railroad. *See also* compound type.

TANK ENGINE — A locomotive with compartments for carrying its own fuel and water. Although small tank engines were used in Europe in the midnineteenth century, their tractive effort decreased as the water and fuel were consumed. Matthias Forney improved on them in the 1860s with his 0-4-4T (Tank) type, which imposed the variable load wholly on the trailing truck.

"TANK" TYPE — Any locomotive carrying fuel and water in bins and tanks that are an integral part of it, rather than in a separate tender. Tank engines designed by Matthias Forney gained wide acceptance on New York City's elevated railroads after a nationwide epidemic of distemper killed thousands of railway horses in 1872, and later was used extensively for the suburban lines of large cities.

TENDER — A railroad car stocked with fuel or water for the running of the engine.

"TEXAS" TYPE — A 2-10-4 locomotive, first used on the Texas & Pacific in 1926. The originating firm —Lima—built a total of 141 of them for the T&P, Chesapeake & Ohio, Chicago Great Western, and Kansas City Southern.

THREE-CYLINDER COMPOUND TYPE — A steam locomotive in which the third cylinder either received steam from a pair of cylinders outside the frames, or fed its own exhaust into them. The first kind originated in England in 1878 and the second in France. Neither was popular in the United States.

THROTTLE — The combination of equipment by which the amount of steam admitted to the cylinders is controlled.

THROTTLE VALVE — A device for regulating the supply of steam from the boiler to the cylinders.

TONNAGE RATING — The number of tons of train weight a locomotive of a certain class could handle on a particular division.

TORQUE — The turning power of a shaft or wheel.

TRACK ILLUMINATOR — A flatcar covered with a thick layer of sand on which rested an iron brazier filled with blazing pine knots. This was the original headlight, used for the first time in 1831 in South Carolina.

TRACTION INCREASER — A mechanism for transferring part of the weight of a fuel car from one of the trucks to the driving wheels in order to increase traction in starting. In 1834 E. L. Miller devised a levering mechanism which was used extensively in Baldwin locomotives until George Escol Sellers invented an automatic mechanism a few years later.

TRACTIVE FORCE — The amount of effort exerted by a locomotive in turning its wheels. It is predetermined by a formula involving five factors: operating boiler pressure less 15 percent, piston area, length of stroke, driving wheel diameter, and weight upon drivers.

TRAILING TRUCK — The truck under the firebox of a locomotive and behind the driving wheels, used to carry part of the engine weight.

TRAIN CAPTAIN — Any early-day train conductor.

TRAIN LINES — The brake pipes and brake hoses.

TRAMWAY — Any railway operated by horsepower.

TRAP — A receptacle receiving sand from a sand dome

218

and holding a predetermined amount for each application to the track.

TRIPLE VALVE — A mechanism connected to the brake pipe, the auxiliary reservoir, and the brake cylinder, which regulates the intake, exhaust, and equalization of compressed air in the brake system.

TRIPLEX TYPE — A Mallet articulated compound locomotive with three driving units, one of which was placed beneath the tender, designed by George R. Henderson about 1913.

TRUCK — A swiveling wheeled frame carrying a portion of a locomotive or car to guide it in turning sharp curves.

TRUMPET STACK — A chimney shaped like an elongated inverted cone.

UNDERCARRIAGE — Early term for a locomotive's frame assembly and running gear.

VALVE — A movable lid covering an opening, the movement of which permits or prevents the passage of steam.

VALVE GEAR — A mechanism for directing steam into and out of the cylinders, by which a locomotive is run backward or forward.

VALVE ROD — A steel rod which communicates the motion of an eccentric rod to a valve.

VAPOR JACK — A cylinder and piston arrangement used in Ross Winans's *Carroll of Carrollton* to lift part of the boiler weight from the leading and trailing trucks and apply it to the driving wheels for improved traction at starting and on grades.

VAUCLAIN COMPOUND TYPE — A steam locomotive with a high- and a low-pressure cylinder, one above the other, on each side, with interconnecting piston rods stroking a single mainrod. It was invented in 1889 by Samuel M. Vauclain. *See also* compound type.

"VIBRATING FRAME" — The name Andrew Eastwick gave to a crude equalizing system applied to his *Hercules* in 1836. The driving wheels were mounted on a separate carriage which teetered up and down to adjust them to dips and rises.

The system functioned effectively only when the rails rose and fell in unison.

"WAGON-TOP" BOILER — A boiler in which the part linking the water section and the firebox was elevated gradually by a conical section to provide maximum height above the crownsheet.

WALKING BEAM — A counterbalanced lever.

WALSCHAERTS GEAR — A valve gear performing the same functions as others, but one of the first to be mounted outside the wheels for convenient servicing. Designed in Belgium in the midnineteenth century, the value of this gear was not recognized until much later.

"WARMING SHELF" — A shallow shelf above the fire door where tallow for lubricating the sliding valves was kept melted in a long-spouted tin or copper can.

WATER JACKET — An arrangement of outer and inner metal shells surrounding a fire and protected by a curtain of water between them.

WEB — *See* crank web.

WHEEL BASE — The distance between the points of contact with the rails of the first and last pairs of wheels or, if so noted, between the first pair of locomotive wheels and the last pair of tender wheels.

WHYTE CLASSIFICATION — A system of classifying locomotives by the wheel arrangements, suggested by F. M. Whyte and adopted in the twentieth century. An eight-wheel American type, for example, would be designated 4-4-0, meaning an engine with four guiding wheels, four driving wheels, and no trailing wheels.

WRAPPER SHEETS — The outer shell of a firebox, and the metal sheets covering the lagging on a boiler.

WRIST JOINT — A joint providing flexibility in only one direction, as in the case of the human wrist.

"YELLOWSTONE" TYPE — A 2-8-8-4 articulated locomotive introduced by the Northern Pacific Railroad in 1929.

YOKE — A member that connects two parts located on opposite sides of a third, which it must straddle.

Bibliography

BOOKS

Black, Robert C., III, *The Railroads of the Confederacy*, University of North Carolina Press, Chapel Hill, 1952.

Bruce, Alfred W., *The Steam Locomotive in America*, W. W. Norton & Co., New York, 1952.

Colburn, Zerah, *Locomotive Engineering and the Mechanism of Railways*, William Collins Sons & Co., London and Glasgow, 1871.

Cooley, Thomas M., *The American Railway*, Charles Scribner's Sons, New York, 1889.

Forney, Matthias N., *Catechism of the Locomotive*, The Railroad Gazette, New York, 1874, and subsequent editions.

Harlow, Alvin F., *The Road of the Century*, Creative Age Press, New York, 1946.

————, *Steelways of New England*, Creative Age Press, New York, 1947.

Hungerford, Edward, *The Story of the Baltimore & Ohio Railroad*, 2 vols., G. P. Putnam's Sons, New York and London, 1928.

Johnson, Ralph P., *The Steam Locomotive*, Simmons-Boardman Publishing Company, New York, 1942.

Kratville, William W., *Big Boy*, Barnhart Press, Omaha, Nebraska, 1963.

Marshall, James, *Santa Fe, The Railroad that Built an Empire*, Random House, Inc., New York, 1945.

Mott, Edward Herold, *Between the Ocean and the Lakes*, John S. Collins, New York, 1899.

Neal, D. H., *Recent Locomotives*, 2nd edition, The Railroad Gazette, New York, 1886.

Shuster, P.; Huddleston, E. L.; and Staufer, A., *C & O Power*, Alvin Staufer, Carrollton, Ohio, 1965.

Sinclair, Angus, *Development of the Locomotive Engine*, Angus Sinclair Company, New York, 1907.

Sipes, William B., *The Pennsylvania Railroad*, P.R.R. Passenger Dept., 1875.

Trumbull, L. R., *A History of Industrial Paterson*, Carleton Herrick, Paterson, New Jersey, 1882.

Vauclain, Samuel M., and May, Earl Chapin, *Steaming Up!*, Brewer, Warren, & Putnam, New York, 1930.

Woods, Arthur T., *Compound Locomotives*, R. M. Van Arsdale, 1891.

PERIODICALS

Modern Railroads
Railroad Magazine
Railway Age
Trains

Index

Italic page numbers refer to illustrations.

A-1, 169, 178
"AC"s (Articulated Consolidations), 166
Adhesion, 78
Aeolipile, 2-*3*
Aeolus (sailing car), *22*
Air brakes, 21, 124, *125,* 126
Albany & West Stockbridge Railroad, 70
"Allegheny" type of locomotive, 196-97, *203*
Allen, Horatio, 18, 21, 32, *35,* 82, 106
Altoona boilers, *129*
America (locomotive), 21
America (locomotive), 64
American Locomotive Company, 77, 78, *90,* 138, 141-42, *148-49,* 151, 157-58, 163, 169, 178, *179,* 182, 190, 199, 202
American Steam Carriage Company, 58
"American" type of locomotive, 64, 75
"AM"s (Articulated Moguls), 166
Andrew Jackson (locomotive), *30, 98*
Andrews, James J., *104-5*
Andrews, L. R., 90, 93, 101
Ant (locomotive), 117, *118*
Anti-trust proceedings against Van Sweringen brothers, 169
Ariel (locomotive), *113*
"Articulated Consolidation" (AC) type of locomotive, 166
"Articulated Mogul" (AM) type of locomotive, 166
Artillery hauler, 5, 7

Atchison, Topeka & Santa Fe Railway, 120, *134,* 136
Atlantic (locomotive), *29,* 31, 121
Atlantic City Railroad, 128, *137*
"Atlantic" type of locomotive, 120
Atmospheric brake, 122, 124, 126-27
Atmospheric engine, *4*
Austria, 62
"Automatic air brake," 124, 126, 128
Ayres, Henry (Poppy), 99, 101

Baker gear, 166
"Balanced compound" locomotive, 133, *135,* 136-37, 157
Baldwin, Matthias W., 50, *51,* 52-54, 56-64, *74,* 90, 112, 116-17, *118, 134,* 136, *147, 178, 204-5*
Baldwin & Whitney, 72, 75
Baldwin Locomotive Works, 87, *108, 134,* 142-43, 147-48, 152, 157-58, 162, 163-66, 169, 174-82, 190, 199
Balloon smokestack, 44, *45*
Baltimore, 18, *84*
Baltimore & Ohio Railroad, *22, 23,* 24, 57, 79, 199
    "American" type of locomotive for, 75
    expansion of, 75
    4-6-0s on, 79
    Jackson destroys locomotives of, 80
    Long employed by, 58
    Rainhill Contest of, 25-31
    "17-Mile Grade" of, 79
    Whistler aids, 69
    Winans and, 71

Baltimore & Susquehanna Railroad, 71
Bank of the United States, 56
Bayonne & Biarritz Railway, 139
Beam, flexible, *74*
Bearer wheels, 77
Beaver Meadow Railroad, 64-66, 117
Bee (locomotive), 117, *118*
Bellcasting, *92*
Bells, 88-89, *90,* 91-93, 157
Belmont Plane, 60, *61*
"Berkshire" type of locomotive, *164-65, 169,* 169-74, 182-190
Bernet, John J., 169, 175
Best Friend of Charleston (locomotive), 33, *34,* 35
Bevel gears, *159*
"Big Boy" type of locomotive, *176-77,* 202-3
Birmingham Coach, *13*
Birmingham & Gloucester Railway, 62
Blenkinsop, John, *9,* 11
Blenkinsop rack, 11
Blood, Aretas, 90
"Bloomer" type of locomotive, 78
Boilers:
    Altoona, *129*
    cheese, 27, *28*
    haystack, 53-*54*
    Hazleton, 28, 31
    hinged, *143*
    horizontal, 14, 26, 35, 38, 75
        Trevithick improves, 9
    multitubular arrangement in, 12-*14*
    pickle bottle design for, 72

Boilers (cont.)
  return-flue arrangement for, 11-12, 14
  two flue-filled water sections in, 58
  vertical, 29, 31, 72
  wagon-top, 94, 102, 103
  water-tube, 18
Bonaparte, Joseph, 42
Bonaparte, Napoleon, 7
Borries, A. von, 133
Boston, 84
Boston (locomotive), 70
Boston & Albany Railroad, 109, 136, 166-69, 182
Boston & Lowell Railroad, 68-69
Boston & Providence Railroad, 69, 109
  cabs on, 97
Boston & Worcester Railroad, 70
  night travel by, 83
Bradley & McAlister, 86
Braithwaite, John, 14
Brakes:
  air brakes, 21, 125
    automatic, 124, 126, 128
    straight, 124, 126
  atmospheric, 122, 124, 126-27
  steam, 60, 127
Branca, Giovanni, 2-3
Branca's turbine, 4
Brandt, John, 63-64
Broadway Limited, 130
Brooks, Chauncy, 79
Brooks, James, & Company, 64
Brooks Locomotive Works, 112, 133
Brother Jonathan (locomotive), 39-40, 53
Brunton, William, 11
Buchanan, William, 128, 130
Buffaloe (locomotive), 75
Bury, Edward, 53, 54, 71
Bury firebox, 54

Cab, 97, 98, 99, 100, 101-3
Cab seats, overhanging, 100
Cabbage cutters, 116
Cabbage head smokestack, 44, 45
"Cab-in-front" locomotive, 166
California-Nevada Railroad Historical Society, 83
Cam-operated poppet valves, 206
Camden & Amboy Railroad, 40-44, 47, 48-49, 76-77
"Camel" type of locomotive, 79-80
"Camelback" type of locomotive, 128, 136, 153
Cameron, James, 63-64
Campbell, Henry R., 59, 64, 66
Canadian National Railway, 190
Canadian Pacific Railway, 141, 163
Cannonball Express, 96
Caps, 45
Carmichael valve gear, 46, 48

Carnes, Agather & Company, 157
Carroll, Charles, 71
Carroll of Carrollton (locomotive), 78
Cassatt, Alexander J., 128
Catechism of the Locomotive, Forney, 113, 116, 139
Cavalier, 199
Centenary Pageant (B&O), 23
"Centipede" type of locomotive, 200-1
Central Pacific Railroad, 119
"Challenger" type of locomotive, 176-77, 196-97, 199
Charters for railways, 18
Cheese boilers, 27, 28
Chesapeake (locomotive), 73, 79
Chesapeake & Ohio Railway, 158, 163, 169, 171, 172-73, 190, 196-97, 203-6
"Chesapeake" type of locomotive, 163, 174, 203
Chessie, 202, 203
Chicago, Burlington & Quincy Railroad, 113
Chicago, Rock Island & Pacific Railway, 39
Childs, Ezekiel, 27-28, 50
Chilled rims, 75
Church, William, 13
Cincinnati, 84
Clark, John T., 36
Climax Manufacturing Company, 159
"Clock," 98
Coal-gas lamp, 5
Cog-railway system, 9
Colburn, Zerah, 5, 133
Cole, Francis, 137
Colorado, 107
Columbia (locomotive), 71
Combustion chamber, 49, 58
Commodore Vanderbilt, 180-81
"Compound" locomotive, 133
Compressors, Duplex, 157
"Confederation" type of locomotive, 190
Consolidation (locomotive), 117, 118, 128
Cooke, 112
Cooper, Peter, 24-25, 27, 101
Costell, Stacey, 27-28, 50
Counterbalances, 64
Cow-catcher, 44
"Crab" type of locomotive, 72
Crampton, T. R., 76
Crampton engines, 76-78
"Cross-compound" locomotive, 133, 135
Croton Aqueduct, 39
Cugnot, Nicholas, 5, 6, 7, 11
Cup whistle, 93, 94, 95, 99
Cylinders:
  Cugnot's, 6
  outside, 94

Danworth-Cooke company, 94
Darlington, rail line between Stockton and, 13
Darwin (locomotive), 120
Darwin, A. G., 120
Davenport, Joseph, 97
Davis, Phineas, 26-27, 28, 30, 31, 50, 71-72
Daylight, 199
Death Valley Coyote, 131
"Decapod" type of locomotive, 117, 118, 200
Decauville Engineering Works, 139
DeGlehn, Alfred G., 136
Delaware (locomotive), 21, 24
Delaware & Hudson Company, 20, 35
Delaware, Lackawanna & Western Railroad, 79, 133, 190
Denver & Rio Grande Railway, 107, 175
Depression, economic, 162-63
Detmold, C. E., 24, 33
Detroit, Toledo & Ironton Railroad, 164-65
DeWitt Clinton (locomotive), 36, 37, 42
Diamond smokestack, 45
Direct drive turbine locomotive, 206
"Dixie" type of locomotive, 190
"Documents . . . Advantages of Railways and Steam Carriages . . . ," 17
Double-acting engine, 5
Double-ended locomotive, 106-7, 107-8, 112
Dowlais plant, 93
Dreyfuss, Henry, 180-81
Dripps, Isaac, 42, 44-47, 48, 49, 76-77, 113, 153
Duluth, Missabe & Iron Range Railway, 199
Dunning, S. W., 113
Duplex (locomotive), 120, 121
Duplex compressors, 127, 157

E. L. Miller (locomotive), 54, 55, 90
Eames, Lovett, 127
Eames Vacuum Brake Company, 127
"Ear muffs," 188-89
Eastern Railroad, 126
Eastwick, Andrew, 67, 75, 90
Eastwick & Harrison, 67, 75
Eiford, "Dutch," 95, 97
Eight-wheeled switcher, 158
El Gobernador (locomotive), 119-20
Electric generators, 206
Electric headlights, 86
Electric power, 206
Electro-Motive Division of General Motors, 158
Elephant (locomotive), 75
Elevated railways, 112

Emerson, George H., *179*
Empire State Express, 128
Engine beds, 64
Engines:
    atmospheric, 4
    double-acting, 5
    high-pressure, 5
    Murray's cog, *9*
    reciprocating, 5
England (locomotive), 62-63
Equalizer, diagram of, *66*
Ericsson, John, 14
Erie Canal, 18, 36, 39
Erie Railroad, 142, *144-45*, 151, 169-74
Evans, Oliver, 16-17

Fairlie, Robert, 106, *107*
"Fairlie-Mason" type of locomotive, 109
"Fairlie" type of locomotive, 106-7, 112
Feedwater pump, 56
Festiniog Railway, 106
Firebox, Bury, *54*
"Fish bellies," *38*, 40
Fitch, John, 16-17
Flangeless tires, 72, *73*
Flexible beam, *74*
Fly-ball governor, 5
"Flying Dutchman," *132*
Forced-draft arrangement, 11
Foresters & Company, 110
Forney, Matthias N., 103, 112, *113*,
    114-16, 139
"Forney" type of locomotive, 112, *113*
Foster, Rastrick & Co., 21
Four Aces (locomotive), 190
4-2-0, etc., *see under* Locomotive types
Four-way valve, *6*
Fowler, George L., 139
France, 63, *108*
Freeman, Mrs. Mary B., 97
French, Mrs. Marion, 122
Friction-wheel design, 71
Fuel box, *133*
Fuller, Capt. William A., *104-5*

Gab-hook valve gears, *46*, 110
Gallatin, Albert, 17
Gallows turntable, *175*
Garrett & Eastwick, 66
Gartner, *30*, 31
Gear wheels, power-driven, 11
Gears:
    bevel, *159*
    poppet, 206
    running, 103
    Stephenson, 110-11
    valve, *109, 111*
        Baker, 166
        Carmichael, 48
        gab-hook, *46*, 110
        Walschaerts, 111-12
General (locomotive), *102, 104-5*

General Electric, *198*, 206
General Motors, 158
George Washington (locomotive),
    60, *61*, 62
Georgia Railroad, 87
Giffard, Henri, 98-99
Gig-top, 44
Gillingham, George, 72
Gladiator (locomotive), 75
Goobeck, Andrew, 149
Gowan & Marx (locomotive), 67, 75
Granite Railway, 21
Grant Locomotive Works, 94, 116
"Grasshopper" type of locomotive,
    29, 30, 31, 71, *98*
Great Northern Railway, 142
Great Western Railway of Canada, 90
"Greenbriar" type of locomotive, 190
Griggs, George S., *45*, 152

Hackensack (locomotive), *91*
Hackworth, Timothy, 11, *12*, 14, 63, 88
Hafner, Benjamin, *132*
Half-crank arrangement, *54*
Hall, Adam, 36
Hall, E. L., 83
Hamel, 99, 101
Harding, Warren G., 163
Harkness, Anthony, & Son, *84*
Harriman, Edward, 169
Harrison, Joseph, 59, *65, 66*, 67, 75, 90
Harrison, William Henry, 114
Hayes, Samuel, 79
Haystack boilers, 53-54
Hazleton boilers, 28, 31
Headlights, *83, 85, 170*
    acetylene, *86*
    electric, 86
    oil, 83-86, *87*
    Pennsylvania Railroad, 87
Hedley, William, 11, *12*
Heisler type of locomotive, *159*
Henderson, George R., *144-45*, 147,
    149, 151
Henry Ford Museum, *37*
Herald (periodical), *99*
Hercules (locomotive), *65*, 66-67,
    75, 90
Hero of Alexandria, 2
Hiawatha (locomotive), *101*
"Hiawatha" type of locomotive, 186-87
Hibernia (ship), 40
High-pressure engines, 5
Hill, Jim, 169
"Hill" (of Southern Pacific route), 166
Hinged boilers, *143*
Hinkley Locomotive Company, 112,
    113, 120
Hoffecker, Philip, 119
"Hog" type of locomotive, 157
Hogan, Charles, *132*
"Hoggers," 157

Holman Locomotive Company, 122
Homfray, Samuel, 8-9
Horizontal boilers, 9, 14, 26, 35, 38, 75
Horse treadmill engine, 23
Howe, William, 110
Hudson (locomotive), 21, 24
Hudson River, 18
Hudson River Railroad, 84
"Hudson" type of locomotive, *180-81,
    186-187*, 190, *201*

Illinois Central Railroad, 112, 169
Impulse turbine, *3*
"Injector," 99
Intercepting valve, 141
International–Great Northern
    Railroad, 169
"Iron Czar," 67, 70-71
Italian State Railways, 166

Jabelman, Otto, 202
Jackson, Andrew, 56
Jackson, Stonewall, 80, *81*
James, J. H., 94
James, William T., 27-28, 31, 110
Janus (locomotive), 109
Jawn Henry (locomotive), 207
Jeffers, William, 202
Jervis, John B., 18, 21, 36, 38, *39*, 40,
    42, 53, 71
John Bull (locomotive), *38-39, 42, 43,
    44*, 53, 59, 68-69
John Stevens (locomotive), 76-77
Johnson, George Fox, *147*
Johnson, George W., 27-28
Johnston, F. W., *108*
Jones, Casey, 96, *150*
Juniata shops, *172-73*, 175

Kiefer, Paul W., 182
"Killingsworth" type of locomotive, 13
Krudener, Baron, 24
Kuhler, Otto, *186-87*

L. F. Loree (locomotive), *179*
Lake Erie & Mad River Railroad,
    94, *95*
Lancaster (locomotive), *55*, 56, 64
"Lead," 112
Lehigh Coal & Navigation
    Company, 64
Lehigh Valley Railroad, 80, 109,
    116-17, 119-20, 190
Lenses, concentrating light with, 83
Lickey Incline, 62-63
Lightning (locomotive), 77-78
Lima Locomotive Company, 157-58,
    166-69, 169-75, 203
Lincoln, Abraham, 93, *114*
Little Wonder (locomotive), 107
Liverpool & Manchester Railway,
    14, *15*, 94
Locomotion No. 1 (locomotive), 13-14

Locomotive run, world's first, 8-11
Locomotive sander, 86-*88*
Locomotive types, 122-23
    0-4-0, 106, 109, *137*
    0-4-4T, 112
    0-6-0, 87-88, *133, 137*
    0-8-0, 78, *117*
    0-10-0, *117*
    0-12-0, *116*
    0-2-2-0, 123, 139
    0-4-4-0, 107, 123
    0-6-6-0, 109, 123, 139-40, *141*
    0-8-8-0, 123, *142*
    2-2-0, 70, 122
    2-2-2, 78, 122
    2-4-0, 122
    2-4-2, 122, 152
    2-6-0, 67, 122
    2-6-2, 122
    2-8-0, 116-17, *118*, 122
    2-8-2, 119, 122, 162, *164-65*, 169
    2-8-4, 122, 166-69, 174, 199
    2-10-0, 117, 122
    2-10-2, 120, 122, *134*, 136, 147, 162
    2-10-4, 122, 169, *172-73*, 174-75, 190,
        203
    2-2-2-2, *179*
    2-6-6-2, 142-43, 158, 166, 199
    2-6-6-4, 123, *174, 196-97*, 199
    2-6-6-6, 123, 203
    2-8-8-0, 123, *126*, 151
    2-8-8-2, *151*, 158, 163-66, 169-74
    2-8-8-4, *151, 191*, 199
    2-10-10-2, 123, 147, *148-49*, 151
    2-8-8-8-2, 123, 147
    2-8-8-8-4, 123, *144-45*, 151
    2-8-8-8-8-2, *144-45*, 149
    4-2-0, 64, 75, 94, 123, 152
    4-2-2, 123
    4-2-4, 78, 123, 152
    4-4-0, *59*, 64, 66, 75, 120, 123,
        128-29, *130*
    4-4-2, 120, *121*, 123, 128, *137*
    4-4-4, 123
    4-6-0, 79, 123, 129
    4-6-2, 120, 123, 182
    4-6-4, 123, 182-90
    4-8-0, 80, 119, 123
    4-8-2, 123, 158, 169
    4-8-4, 123, *151, 167, 171, 183,*
        184-85, 190, 199
    4-10-0, 119, 123
    4-10-2, 123, *178-82*
    4-12-2, 123, *176-77*, 178
    4-4-4-4, *179, 192*
    4-4-6-2, 123, 143, 147
    4-4-6-4, *192*
    4-6-6-4, 123, *196-97*, 199
    4-8-8-4, 123, 203
    6-2-0, 77
    6-8-6, *204-5*
    6-4-4-6, *186-87*

Locomotives, numbered, *see under*
    Numbered locomotives
Lodge, Albert, *131*
Loewy, Raymond, *186-87*
Londonderry & Coleraine Railway, 106
Long, Col. Stephen H., 58-59, 69
Loree, Leonor F., 140
Losee, Charles, *131*
Louisville & Nashville Railroad, *104-5*
Lowell (locomotive), 70

"MacArthur" type of locomotive,
    164-65
McConnell, J. E., 76, 78
McKay, Donald, *90*
McKay, Nathaniel, *90*
McKay & Aldus, *90*
McLean, Louis, 72
McNeil, William Gibbs, 69
Mallet, Anatole, 138, *139*, 140
"Mallet" type of locomotive, 138-40,
    142, 143, *144-45*, 148, 151-53,
    163-66, 166, 169, 171, *178*
Manchester Locomotive Works, 90
Manitou & Pikes Peak Railway, *134*
Martin, Joshua, 84
Martinsburg, Virginia, terminal, *81*
Mason, William, 101, *103*, 106, *107*,
    108, *109*, 111-12
Master Carbuilders' Association, 127
Mastodon (locomotive), 119
"Mastodon" type of locomotive, 80
Matt H. Shay (locomotive), *144, 147,*
    148-49, 151
Matthew, David, 36, 39
Mechanical stoker, 142-43
Mechanical Traveller (locomotive), *11*
Meginnes, Joseph Widrow, 97, *99*
Mehaffey, A., 56, 60
Mercury (locomotive), 75
Merrimac (locomotive), 70
"Mikado" type of locomotive, 119, 151,
    157-58, *164-65*, 169
Mill Dam Factory, 70
Miller, E. L., 33, 35, 53, 60, *62*
Millholland, James, *101, 116*, 128, 142
Missouri Pacific Railroad, 169
Mitchell, Alexander, 116-17, *118*, 120
Mohawk & Hudson Rail Road, 36, *37*,
    38-39, 59
"Mohawk" type of locomotive, *201*
Monitor (ship), 14
"Monkey motion," 119
Monroe, H. G., 157
Monster (locomotive), 47, *48-49*, 58,
    153
Moore & Richardson, *84*
Moorson, Capt., 62
"Mother Hubbard" type of locomotive,
    128-29, *136, 142*
Mott, Edward Herold, *Between the*
    Ocean and the Lakes, 97, 99, 101

Mott, Jordan L., 87, *88*
Moulton, John, 107
"Mountain" type of locomotive, 158,
    170, 188-89, 190
Mountaineer (locomotive), *107*
"Mud Digger" type of locomotive,
    75, 78
Muhlfeld, James, *140*-41
Multitubular boiler, arrangement,
    12-*14*
Murat, Madam, 42
Murdoch, William, 5, 11
Murray, Matthew, *9*, 11

Nashville (locomotive), *114*
Nathaniel Wright (locomotive), *84*
National Road, 18
Neversink (locomotive), *55-56*
Neville, James, 12
New Brunswick, railway between
    Trenton and, 18
New Jersey Railroad & Transportation
    Company, 94
New York Central & Hudson River
    Railroad, 128
New York Central Railroad, 84, 112,
    115, 130, 169, 182, *196-97*
New York, Chicago & St. Louis
    Railway, 169
New York City, 18
New York & Erie Railroad, 79, 84, 95
    cabs of, 98
    Meginnes joins, 97-98
    Number 102 of, *102*
New York & Harlaem Railroad, 87
New York, New Haven & Hartford
    Railway, 113
Newcastle & Frenchtown Railroad, 58
Newcastle mechanics, 68
Newcastle Works, *12*
Newcomen, Thomas, 3-4
Newcomen's engine, *4*
Nicholas I, 67, 70-71
Nikolai Pavlovich, 67, 70-71
Niles & Company, *84*
Nippon Railway, 119
Norfolk & Western Railway, *151*, 199,
    206
Norris, Edward, 77-78
Norris, James, 117
Norris, Messrs., Brothers, 76-77
Norris, Richard, 77
Norris, Septimus, *73*, 77-79
Norris, William, 58-60, *61*, 62-64, 75
Norris six-wheeler, 60, 97
Northern Pacific Coast Railway, 166,
    190, 199
"Northern" type of locomotive, 190
Novelty (locomotive), 14, 16
Numbered locomotives:
    23: 115
    100: 186-87

Numbered locomotives (cont.)
    102: 102
    111: 131
    144: 153
    382: 94
    510: 131
    700: 145
    999: 196-97, 130
    1027: 137
    1111: 190
    1248: 137
    1737: 154
    2400: 140-42
    3300s: 169
    3400s: 169
    3700: 126
    3768: 186-87
    4211: 160-61
    5200: 190
    5600: 179
    6100: 186-87
    6200: 204
    7002: 130
    9000: 187
    60000: 182

Oil headlight, 83-86, *87*
Old Ironsides (locomotive), *52, 53,* 67, 133, *134*
Old Maud (locomotive), *140,* 141
Olympian, 169
Orange (locomotive), 97
Oruktor Amphibolis (ship), 16, *17*
Overhanging cab seats, *100*
"Overland" type of locomotive, 178

"Pacific" type of locomotive, *154, 158, 170,* 182
Panhandle Railroad, 124
Panic of 1837, 62, 64, 67, 72
Paterson, New Jersey, *94-95*
Paterson & Hudson River Rail Road, 94
Patrick (locomotive), 70
Peale, Benjamin Franklin, 50-51
Peale, Charles Willson, 50
Pennsylvania, 57
Pennsylvania Public Works Commission, 54-56, 60, 63
Pennsylvania Railroad, 44, 79, 87, *126, 128, 130,* 137, 162-63, *170, 172-73,* 175, *186-87,* 190, *192, 200, 204-5*
Pennsylvania & Reading Railroad, 44
"Pennsylvania Society for the Promotion of Internal Improvements," 18
Pennsylvania Special, 130
Pen-y-Darran line, 8, *10*
Pere Marquette Railway, 169
Persia, 67

Petsch, Julius, 35
Philadelphia:
    Centennial Exposition (1876), 109
    railway between Susquehanna River and, 18
Philadelphia (locomotive), *116-17*
Philadelphia & Columbia Railroad, 24, 54, 59-60, 63
    Baldwin hired by, 56
    coaches of, *57*
    Long employed by, 58
    successor to, 79
Philadelphia, Germantown & Norristown Railroad, 50-53, 64, 67
Philadelphia & Reading Railroad, 55, 67, 79, 152
    Meginnes leaves, 97
Phoenix (locomotive), 35
"Pickle bottle" boiler design, 72
Piermont (locomotive), 95
"Pig" type of locomotive, 157
Pitkin, Arthur J., 133, 137
Pittsburgh & West Virginia Railway, 199
"Planet" type of locomotive, *52,* 68
Plant System, *131*
"Plates," *10*
Pocahontas, 199
"Pocono" type of locomotive, 190
Poland, 67
Poor's Manual of the Railroads, 107
Poppet valves, 206
Post & Company, *86*
Potomac project, 18
Potter, Humphrey, 3-4
Prosperity Special, 163
Puffing Billy (locomotive), 11, *12,* 13, 63
Pumps, 126
    Duplex, *127*
    feedwater, 56
    reciprocating, 99
    steam, 99

"Quadruplex" locomotive, *144-45,* 147
Quick, John, 95
"Quintruplex" locomotive, *144-45,* 147

Railroad watches, *150*
Rails:
    "fish bellies," *38,* 40
    "plates," *10*
    Stevens's design for, 40-44
    "T" rails, *41*
Railway & Locomotive Historical Society, 90
Rainhill Contest, *15,* 25-31
Reaction turbine, *3*
Reciprocating engine, 5
Reciprocating pumps, 99
Reflectors, 83
Regent's Park, 7

Rensselaer & Saratoga Railroad, 84
Return-flue arrangement, 11-12, 14
Reuben Wells (locomotive), *117*
Rhode Island Works, *108,* 112
Richmond, 18
Richmond, Dean, 84
Robert Fulton (locomotive), 38
Robinson, William, 68-70
Rocket (locomotive), 14, *15,* 16, 38, *147*
Rogers, Ketchum & Grosvenor, 94
Rogers, Thomas, *94-95,* 101, *102,* 103, *104-5,* 112, *124*

Sail cars, *22,* 24
St. Etienne Railway, *14,* 18
St. Louis Exposition of 1904, 138
St. Petersburg & Moscow Railway, 67, 70
Sampson (locomotive), 64
Samuel D. Ingham (locomotive), 66
Sand dome, 88
Sander, locomotive, *86-88*
Sandusky (locomotive), *94-95*
Sanspareil (locomotive), 14, 16
"Santa Fe" type of locomotive, *131,* 136, 158, 178
Saratoga & Schenectady Railroad, 39
Schenectady & Troy Railroad, 71
Schmidt, Wilhelm, 153, 157
Schuylkill River, 59
Scott, Walter, *131*
Seabord Air Line Railroad, *131,* 199
Seguin, Marc, *12-14,* 18
Sellers, Charles, *63-64*
Sellers, Coleman, & Sons, 63
Sellers, George Escol, 62, *63,* 64
Sellers, William, & Company, 99
Semour, H. C., 98
"17-Mile Grade," 79, *80*
Sharp, Roberts & Company, *93*
Sharp, Stewart & Company, 99
Shay, Ephraim, 157, *158*
Shay, Matt H., 148
Simms, Clifford, 140
"Simple articulated" locomotive, 163, 169
"Simple Simon" type of locomotive, 163
Sinclair, Angus, 70, 82, *108,* 122
6-2-0, etc., *see under* Locomotive types
Six-wheeled guiding truck, 77
Six-wheeled switcher, 158
"Slim gauges," 107
Slippage, 11
Smithsonian Institution, 44
"Snake," *38*
Sommeillier, Germain, 122
South Carolina (locomotive), *33,* 36
South Carolina Railroad, 24, *34, 35*
    contract with Baldwin, 53-54
    night travel by, 32-33
    Phoenix and, 35

Southern Pacific Railroad, *114*, *120*, 162, 166, 178, 199
Spark-arresting mechanisms, 44, *45*, *159*
Stacks, 44, *45*
Starting torque, 206
Steam boats, 16, 17-18
Steam braking, 60, 127
Steam carriage, 8
Steam line joint, 56
Steam pump, 99
Steam turbine–electric, *203*, 206
Steam whistle, *94*
Stephens, William, 93
Stephenson, George, *12*, 13-14, *15*, 21, 24, 38, 53, 56, 63, 68, 71
Stephenson, Robert, 14, *15*, 38, 53, 56, 63, 68, 71
Stephenson, Robert, & Company, 110
Stephenson gear, *94*, *110*-11
Stevens (locomotive), 42, 44, 50, 53
Stevens, A. J., 119
Stevens, Col. John, 17-18, *19*, 21, 40
Stevens, Robert L., 40, *41*, 42-44, 48, *76*
Stillwell, Howard, 166
Stockton & Darlington Railway, 18, 88
Stoker, mechanical, 142-43
Stourbridge Lion (locomotive), *20*, 21, 24, 44
"Straight air brake," 124, *125*, 126
Straight smoke stack, *45*
Strickland, William, 18
Strong, George S., 120, *121*
Styling of locomotives, 82, *186-87*
   bells, 90, 93
   cabs, 98, 103
   headlights, 84-86
   sand domes, 87-88
Sun (periodical), *99*
Sunflower smokestack, 44, *45*
Superheater Company of New York, 153
Suspension systems, 39
Susquehanna River, railway between Philadelphia and, 18
Sutherland, Duke of, 107
Swiveling truck, 71
Syphon, thermic, *194*

"T" rails, *41*
"Tallowpot," 98
"Tandem compound" locomotive, 133, 136
Tank locomotive, 112
Ten-wheelers, *80*, *96*
Texas & Pacific Railroad, 169
"Texas" type of locomotive, 169, 175
Thermic syphon, *194*

"Three-cylinder compound" locomotive, 133, *135*
Timken Roller Bearing Company, 190
"Tokyo Express," 166
Tom Thumb (locomotive), *24-25*, 27
Tomales (locomotive), *109*
Tone:
   of bells, 90
   of whistles, 95
Torque, 206
Traction, 11, 59, 63, 78, 112
Traction increaser, 60, *62*
Tractive force, 71
Traveller (locomotive), 71
Treadmill locomotive, *23*
Trenton, railway between New Brunswick and, 18
Trenton Locomotive Works, 49
Trevithick, F., 76
Trevithick, Richard, 8-9, *10*, 11, 16
Tricycles:
   Cugnot's, *6*
   Murdoch's, *5*
"Triple valve," 124, 126, 128
"Triplex" locomotive, *144*, *145*, 147-49, 151
Trumpet smokestack, 44
Turkey, 67
Turner, Thomas, 93
Turntable pits, *174*
Twentieth Century Limited, *180-81*
2-2-0, etc., *see under* Locomotive types
Types of locomotives, *see* Locomotive types
Tyson, Henry, 79-80

Uncle Dick (locomotive), *119*
Underwood, Frederick D., 148
Union Pacific Railroad, *176-77*, 178, 190, 200-1
United States Railroad Administration, 158
Utica & Schenectady Railroad, 78

Valve gear, *46*, 48, *94*, *109-10*, *111*
Valves:
   cam-operated poppet, 206
   four-way, *6*
   intercepting, 141
   triple, 124, 126, 128
Van Sweringen, Mantis J., 169
Van Sweringen, Oris P., 169
Vanderbilt, "Commodore" Cornelius, 84
"Vanderbilt" type of tender, 169, *201*
Vapor jacks, 78
Vauclain, Andrew, *134*
Vauclain, Samuel M., 133, *134*, 137, 143, 147, 162-63

"Vauclain compound" locomotive, 133, 136
Vertical boilers, *29*, 31, 72
Virginia, 57
Virginia Central Railroad, 80
Virginian Railway, *144-45*, 151
Vulcan Iron Works, *153*

Wagon-top boilers, *94*, *102*, 103
Walschaerts, Egide, *109*, 111-12
War Production Board, *172-73*, 175
Warming shelf, 98
Washington, D.C., 18
Watches, *150*
Water bottom arangement, 42
Water-tube boilers, 18
Watt, James, 4, 5, 51, 53
Watt pumpers, 5
Webb, F. W., 133
Webb, Sim, *96*
Wells, Reuben, *117*
West Point (locomotive), *34*, 35
West Virginia, 57
Western Railroad, 70, 72
Westinghouse, George, 122, 124, *125*, 127-28
Whale oil, 83
Wheel-equalizing system, 66
Wheels, *163*
   bearer, 77
   flangeless, 72, *73*
   friction design for, 71
   gear, 11
Whistle signals, 97
Whistler, Maj. George Washington, 69-70, 72
Whistler, James Abbott McNeill, 70
Whistler, John, *69*
Whistles, 93, *94*, *95*, 96-97, 157
Whyte classification system, 64
Williams, William, 110
Winans, Ross, 70-74, *75*, 76-80, 112
Wolley, Leonides, 86
Wooton, Richens Lacy, *119*
Wootten, John E., 129, *136*, 153
World War II, 175
World's Columbian Exposition, *20*, 44
Worsdell, T. W., 133
Wylan Railway, *12*
"Wyoming" type of locomotive, 190

Yankee (locomotive), 70
"Yellowstone" type of locomotive, *191*, 199
York (locomotive), 27, *28*, 31

0-4-0, etc., *see under* Locomotive types
Zola, Emile, 206

A Union Pacific "Big Boy" was 604 tons and 19,000 cubic feet of steel and coal and water, poised upon 36 wheels spaced no wider apart than those of an automobile. That it could thunder safely over undulating and curved track at speeds in excess of 70 miles an hour was due in large measure to the efforts of two long-forgotten pioneers. As early as 1836, the basic system that held its wheels in equalized contact with the rails was patented by a Philadelphian named Joseph Harrison; and a French technical writer, Anatole Mallet, first thought to couple two driving units heel to toe below one boiler in 1874.